Ninety Days

Escape from Uganda

Rashmi Paun

To Carol and Robbie
With love
from
Rashmi.

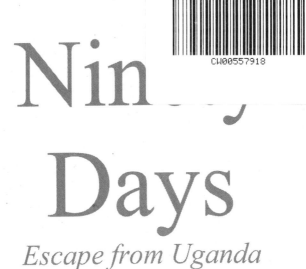

MOONLIGHT BOOKS

Ninety Days Escape from Uganda
FIRST EDITION : 2018
ISBN : 978-81-936313-9-3

Published by
MOONLIGHT BOOKS
20 Ekjot Apartment, Pitampura, Delhi-110034, India
Email : moonlightbooks2016@gmail.com
Website : www.moonlightbooks.in

Ninety Days is a work of historical fiction, set in 1972, when President Amin of Uganda ordered people of Asian origin to leave the country in ninety days.

Printed by Replika Press Pvt. Ltd., India

For my wonderful parents:
Kantaben and Jagjivanbhai Paun.

Acknowledgements

My wife Maggie, and our sons Ashim, Akash and Alay have been a source of constant encouragement, and given useful suggestions when writing this book.

I am grateful to my writing tutor Todd (Toekey) Kingsley-Jones for all his help and guidance.

Many thanks to Rich Voysey of Forge Branding Ltd for designing the cover.

Front cover image of Ugandan Asian refugees arriving at Stansted Airport UK - supplied by Magnum Photos.

Main Characters

Mitani Family

Devji (a Narrator)	A Lawyer
Savita	Devji's Wife
Lalita (a Narrator)	Devji's Sister
Ramesh (a Narrator)	Devji and Savita's Elder Son
Shashi (a Narrator)	Younger Son

Butt Family

Rehana (a Narrator)	A Lawyer
Zubeida	Rehana's Mother
Yusuf (a Narrator)	Rehana's Father

Mistry Family

Dhanji (a Narrator)	Devji's Friend
Kamala	Dhanji's Wife
Vinod	Kamala and Dhanji's Son

Patel Family

Kumar	Ramesh's Friend
Manjula	Kumar's Wife

In this account, Day Zero is the day Amin made his announcement on 4th August 1972.

Glossary and Notes

It is customary to add a suffix at the end of a name to show respect, or to address the person by his or her relationship to you.

Ba - Mother

Ben - Sister

Beti - Daughter

Bhabhi - Sister-in-Law (Brother's Wife)

Bhai - Brother

Chacha - Uncle

Kaka - Uncle (Father's Brother)

Masi - Aunt (Mother's Sister)

Motabhai - Elder Brother

Naniben - Little Sister

Prologue 1

Day Zero:
Friday 4th August 1972
Amin's Dream

"I had a dream last night," President Amin announced to the air cadets, a sea of khaki, sitting on the ground in a camp in eastern Uganda. The setting sun was behind him and an aura, long shafts of bright rays, seemed to radiate from his body; his large bulk a messiah-like silhouette against the light horizon.

"God spoke to me in my dream. He said, *Throw the Asians out of Uganda.* You see, I have often asked myself, *How come Asians run almost every business in Uganda?* I regularly visit Kampala town centre. Asians own most businesses there. When I go back to Kampala from here in Tororo, I will drive through Bugiri, Iganga and Jinja. And it is the same everywhere. It is like going into towns in India."

The president paused and surveyed the scene in front of him. The field behind the troops was a mosaic of green with patches of bright red earth. A massive mvule tree near the edge of the field cast a long shadow on the wood behind the field.

"Asians own most factories as well as shops. They are rich. They exploit us Ugandans. They are like leeches. And they sabotage our economy. They milk the cow but do not feed it to yield more milk. So I want every Asian out of Uganda in three months. In ninety days - OUT!"

There was loud applause and cheering while the president took out a big white handkerchief from his trouser pocket to wipe the fine film of perspiration from his face. When the applause faded, he continued, "I want every Asian out. Even if you are born here. Even if your parents and grandparents are born here. OUT!" As he shouted the word 'out', he jabbed the air in front of him as if admonishing a miscreant. "If you are a businessman. OUT! If you are a doctor, a teacher, a lawyer ... whatever. If you are an Asian, OUT! I am the President of Uganda for Life; Conqueror of the British Empire, King of Scotland, Lord of all the Beasts of the Earth and Fishes of the Sea and Field Marshal Al Hadji Doctor Idi Amin Dada, VC, DSO, MC, and I command you to leave the country in ninety days."

And that was Day Zero.

Prologue 2

1st November 1972
Devji: Escape from Uganda

A hornbill flies across my vision. Its yellow beak and bright plumage glow in the red rays of the setting sun. But it is too late to point it out to Savita and Lalita because just then, as I navigate round the bend, another roadblock suddenly looms up.

I slow down and Savita reaches under the seat. She takes out a large packet of bank notes wrapped in a paper bag. She looks at me and I nod my approval. The small packets have been adequate for the makeshift roadblocks set up by the low ranking army personnel. But this looks more official because the soldiers have erected several tents in a clearing in the Mbira forest by the side of the road. This is the third time in one hour that we are being stopped and once again I fervently hope that there will be no problems. I notice Savita murmuring with joined hands, *Please God, help us get through this safely.* I look in the rear-view mirror and notice that Lalita has slipped low on the seat, her forehead glowing in the red sunlight. Her eyes are shut tight and I am sure she is also praying.

I slow the car right down. There are two soldiers in the middle of the road with AK47s at their hips pointing at us. One of them motions us to stop in a space near the tent. He is a young man, slim and tall, and very likely still in his teens.

I get out of the car. The second soldier, who is short and built like a tank, approaches me with his gun pointing at my head. "I have a gift for your commanding officer," I say and hold out the packet.

He grabs it and tells me, "*Goja hapa* (Wait here)." He has a surprisingly high-pitched voice. Almost a whine. He orders me to stand with my arms on the roof of the car. I move to the passenger side so I can see him as I spread my arms on the dusty roof.

He goes to a green camouflage army tent pitched right back in the cleared foliage amongst the trees. I can see Savita looking at me anxiously and I smile reassuringly at her. I realise it is a wan smile for she still looks worried. Lalita has slunk as low as she can in the back seat.

I keep my hands on the car. The sun is warm on the back of my neck. There is the usual background of insect humming, punctuated by an occasional sharp birdcall. The soldier walks back with his commanding officer, a man of medium height with three parallel slashes of the Kakwa tribe on each cheek. He is in his khaki uniform but is not wearing a jacket. His hat, similar to the one Amin wears in all his pictures, sits askew on his head, giving him a jaunty look. The soldier shuffles a respectable step behind his superior.

"Where're you going to?" the officer says in English in his deep voice.

"To the airport." Of course he knows where we are going. The only journeys Asians undertake now are either to Kampala to get Visas from foreign Embassies, or to the airport to flee the country. But at sunset, the Embassies are closed; so the airport is the only place we could be going to.

"Your papers."

I bend to reach the papers on the dashboard with one hand, keeping my second arm still stretched out on the top of the car.

"Everyone, out of the car," he says without looking up as he flicks through the papers.

Savita and Lalita step out of the car and stand near me.

"So, you're Devji Mitani. She your wife?" he says pointing at Savita. I nod.

"And that your daughter?" he asks taking a long hard look at Lalita, who steadfastly stares at the ground.

"No, sir, she is my sister."

"Stay where you are," he orders, walking back to his tent.

Long minutes pass. The two soldiers come back from the tent. Without a word, they grab Lalita's arms and start frog-marching her towards the tent. She struggles to free herself and I lunge forward and try to pull her away from them. The nearest soldier lets go of her and swings his rifle at me. The butt strikes the side of my head and knocks me to the ground. I feel faint but I manage to grab the soldier's leg. He yanks his leg free of my grip and kicks me hard on my shoulder. The pain makes me groan but I grab his other leg. "Stop. I can give you more money," I barely recognise my own voice, which seems to come from far. The soldier lets go of Lalita and lifts his rifle ready to swing at me.

"*Wacha dugu yangu. Mimi na kuja pamoja wewe.*" ("Leave my brother alone. I am coming with you.") Lalita's voice is firm. She has mainly used Swahili to communicate with servants and is used to speaking in an imperious tone.

The soldier turns from me and takes Lalita by the arm again and the two soldiers continue to walk her to the tent.

As I lie on the ground, I listen to their footsteps crunching on the gravel. The sound fades towards the tent and then there is just the drone of the crickets. I feel tears of pain and hopelessness sting my eyes. "She is my little sister," I say, as I lose consciousness.

I have no idea how long I have been out. I become aware of a jolting movement. My head is spinning and a memory swirls in my head. I am transported back five years to India to the sparsely furnished living-room of my parents. My mother's kind and loving face stares at me, her greying hair piled in a loose bun on top of her head. I am trying to put her mind at rest. "Lalita is my dear little sister, *Ba*, and you know I will do all I can to ensure her happiness." My mother just smiles in response. She trusts me enough to let her darling daughter leave home to join me in Africa.

There is throbbing in my head and an acute pain in my shoulder. I try to think where I am and suddenly remember the events before I passed out. I open my eyes and find I am lying in the back of the car with my head in Lalita's lap. I try to sit up but am still a bit groggy and fall back. Savita is driving the car and it is dark outside.

"He has woken up," Lalita says as if I was just having a nap. Her voice is flat.

Savita is silent but gives me a quick glance over her shoulder.

"Are you ... are you ... ?" I stutter. I want to ask Lalita if she is all right when I know she is not. I cannot think of the right words.

"I am alive," she responds. "And so are you. Thank God."

I prop myself on my elbow and gently sit up. There is a bandage on my head, the long end of which dangles on my shoulder. I recognise it as the blue silken material from Savita's sari. I realise we are in a town because the orange glow flashes and fades as we drive past the lamp-posts.

"Are we in Entebbe?" I ask.

"No, in Kampala. We're going to Mulago first."

"Forget Mulago. There are better hospitals in UK. We can't afford to miss the flight. Just go to Entebbe."

Entebbe is about thirty kilometres from Kampala and we come across two more roadblocks. At each one they shine their torches in, notice my bloodstained bandage, Savita hands over a small packet, and they wave us on.

In the airport lounge we recognise several families. They gather round us to enquire what happened and if we need any help. We have not rehearsed our stories but we find ourselves saying the same thing: *Soldiers at the roadblock in Mbira forest attacked me. I passed out. Savita drove us to the airport.* No mention of Lalita's ordeal. Not now, nor ever, I expect, unless she needs to talk about it to heal her memories. But I doubt she will ever mention it. I watch her reactions. The *chandlo* on her forehead is a red smudge and draws one's attention away from her expressionless eyes. She is grim-faced but then so is everyone else until the plane takes off and there is a sudden release. It is like an interval at a music concert. Everyone suddenly starts talking. The envelope of voices is punctuated by some youngsters actually shouting out "yippee". There are smiles on faces. The old lady in the aisle next to me has her eyes shut tight; her wrinkled hands are folded as she thanks God.

We get a last glimpse of the land, which was our home, before the plane ascends above the fluffy clouds into the starry sky. I look at Lalita, who is sitting between Savita and me. Her eyes are closed and two big teardrops roll down her cheeks. I notice Savita is also looking at Lalita and she is crying too. We each hold a hand of Lalita. She gently presses our hands, opens her eyes and smiles at us through her tears.

I have not shed tears since when I was about five. My elder brother then told me to stop *crying like a girl*. But today I cried at the roadblock, and now again, for the second time in one day, tears well up in my eyes. I failed you, *Nani Ben* (little sister), when you needed me.

Part 1: Before the Announcement

Chapter 1
Two and a Half Years before Day Zero:
February 1970
Lalita: Karma

Karma! Whatever happens to you is pre-determined by your *karma*. At least that is what I believe. I know *Motabhai* (elder brother) holds a different view. "Since we have little control over external factors, unfortunate events are bound to occur," he says. "A belief in karma is a clever defence mechanism which makes it easier for us to accept any misfortunes in our lives."

"It is a brilliant theory," he once told me. "It also discourages people from acting in anti-social or inhuman ways because they are afraid that they will have to pay for their actions in future lives, if not in this life."

As always, Motabhai came up with a rational explanation because he is not particularly religious. And nor is *Bhabhi* (sister-in-law).

When I came to Uganda a couple of years ago, I was surprised that Bhabhi had only a tiny little shrine in a corner of the kitchen. And I have seen her praying there only on rare occasions, like on main festival days or if there is a death of someone close.

However, they both readily agreed when I asked them if I could make a larger shrine in the TV room. And that is where I am today. I have placed a lamp in front of the deities, have sung the *gayatri mantra* and just finished my morning prayers. The lamp is beginning to flicker. So I pour a little more *ghee* in the clay holder and the flame now casts a warm glow on the statuettes of the deities and pictures of the saints.

And I think about my karma. I must have done something wrong in my last life. Why else would I be widowed only a few months after my marriage? But then probably I was not all bad in that life. I must have also done some good deeds to have a loving family in my present life. Motabhai and Bhabhi treat me like a daughter and the boys act as if I were their elder sister rather than an aunt. But then I am only six years older than Ramesh. He is studying in the UK, but since I have been here he has been home a couple of times during holidays, and we get on splendidly. Shashi, my younger nephew, is an affectionate and amusing boy. I am extremely fond of both my nephews.

There is a movement in the corridor outside. I think it is either Motabhai going out to his dawn gathering with his friends, or it could be Shashi who has lately started going to the cricket field for a run.

I bow to the deities and scramble to my feet. Another day has started. It occurs to me that yes, I am happy. And yet ... and yet ... I feel a faint sense of dissatisfaction gnawing at the back of my mind. It is because I do not know exactly what I want from life.

Chapter 2
Two and a Half Years before Day Zero:
February 1970
Shashi: Jesus

Papa often tells us that one should always try and do the right thing. And not be too proud to admit it when you have made a mistake.

I have decided to confess to Papa and Ba (Mother) about something naughty I have done recently. And the lesson I have learnt from Lalita Auntie. I hope they will be in a more forgiving mood today, it being my fourteenth birthday.

Like most households we used to have a small shrine in our house. Ours was in the kitchen. It was really just a wooden box with a little statuette of Krishna in it. I had occasionally seen Ba light joss sticks and sit in front of it saying her prayers.

A couple of years ago, Lalita Auntie was widowed and came from India to live with us. One of the first things she did was to establish a shrine in the corner of our smaller living-room. It has the usual little statuettes: Krishna, playing the flute; Rama, Sita and Laxman standing with Hanuman at their feet; Buddha sitting in a lotus position; a slightly bigger figure of Ganesh with his pot-belly and elephant's head. Behind this array of deities is a silver framed image of Shiva with a snake wrapped round his neck and holding a trident next to him. There are also a couple of little pictures of saints - Jalaram Bapa and Sai Baba.

Auntie is the only person who regularly prays there. Early each morning, she sits on the floor, her legs folded in a lotus position, facing the shrine. She places a little lamp in front of the deities, lights a couple of joss sticks and meditates for a few minutes with her eyes closed and hands folded. She softly says a prayer and recites a few mantras. The complete *pooja* lasts barely fifteen minutes.

A few weeks ago, I happened to find a postcard depicting Jesus on the cross. His eyes were open and he looked at the viewer straight in the eye. When no one was around, I carefully stuck the image next to Shiva's picture in the shrine. Please don't get me wrong. I was not trying to hurt Lalita Auntie. In fact, I am very fond of her. I think she is great. It was really to tease her rather than hurt her feelings.

Next day, I woke up early and hung around just outside the room when she prayed. I wanted to see her reaction. But she did her usual *pooja*, and then sat there praying with her eyes closed for a few minutes. It was obvious that she had not noticed my contribution to her shrine. So, the following day I got up early again - but once again nothing happened. This went on for over a week. In the end I asked her, "Auntie, you pray every morning but do you even look at your shrine when you do that?"

"Why, what do you mean?"

"Have you seen what's in the shrine?"

"Ah," she said. "The picture. Did you put it there?"

"Yes," I confessed, ready for an angry outburst.

Instead, she said, "Oh, thank you."

Things were not going the way I had expected. I could only presume she did not recognise Jesus. Not surprising, considering she grew up in India, and is obviously not familiar with the image of Jesus on his cross. So I asked her, "Do you know whose picture it is?"

"Ishu," she used the Gujarati word for Jesus.

It was just conceivable that she thought that Jesus is one of the myriads of Hindu deities. So I informed her, "You realize he is a Christian God."

"I know," she said calmly. "I have read about him. He was a saintly person, helping the poor and needy, wasn't he?"

"Yes," I admitted.

"Then, why can't I worship him?"

I had felt nervous confessing my little act of naughtiness to Papa and Ba. I was sure they would be angry with me. Instead, they merely exchange a smile.

Chapter 3
One and a Half Years before Day Zero:
Saturday 6th March 1971
Shashi: A Mystery

Something is afoot. I can tell.

Just after five in the afternoon, when the day is less hot, I change into my white cricketing gear. I am in the hallway near the front door, and about to leave the house when the telephone rings. No one ever rings me but I answer it anyway as I am the one nearest to it. Most of the calls are for Papa and you hear, 'Is Devjibhai Mitani there?' Or more often 'Is *Wakil* (lawyer) *Sahib* there?'

"Devjibhai," the voice bellows. "Devjibhai, is that you?" The caller obviously does not use a phone regularly. You can tell because people who rarely talk on the phone seem to think that as they are far away they need to shout to be heard.

"One minute, I'll get him," I tell the caller but he does not hear me for he keeps repeating in his loud voice, "Is that you, Devjibhai?"

"I said I will just get him," I shout back and go to fetch Papa from the living-room. He is sitting in his chair, facing Ba and Lalita Auntie. Judging from their expressions and their hushed tones, it is obvious that they are discussing something serious. When I tell Papa that he is wanted on the phone, he springs to his feet - something I have not seen him do before.

I would have hung around to find out what it is all about if I were not already late for the game.

I sense tension in the air when I return, and my hunch is confirmed because at the end of dinner, Ba tells me that we are expecting visitors tomorrow. We have people dropping in all the time, and Ba never announces their visit formally like that. She then adds, "We will need both living-rooms, so tomorrow morning go and play at one of your friends' place."

Papa does not say anything and Lalita Auntie, who has remained quiet throughout the meal, stares at her empty plate. I shrug my shoulders and say, "OK."

I guess it is something to do with Lalita Auntie.

Chapter 4
One and a Half Years before Day Zero:
Sunday 7th March 1971
Lalita: The 'Interview'

I wake up with a start. It is a little earlier than normal. My first thought is *Oh, my God; it is the day of the interview*. I mutter a silent prayer: *Please God let him be the right man.*

I open the window and take a deep breath of cool fresh air laden with the delicious fragrance of frangipani. It is still dark outside and a low crescent moon hangs near the horizon. The chirping of crickets leads a cacophony of the humming and clicking of insects.

Within minutes, even as I stand there looking out of the window, the first light of the day spreads in the sky and the garden emerges from the dark in its green glory.

I want to wash my hair early in the morning, as it takes a long time to dry. So I go to the kitchen to switch on the immersion water heater, but find that it is already on. I wonder if it was left on all night. I have a bath straight away.

Later in my room, I bend forward with my wet hair forming a curtain in front of my face. I am vigorously rubbing it with my big white towel, when my bedroom door creaks open. I fling my hair back over my head in order to see who is at the door.

It is Bhabhi, and she is already dressed.

"Oh Bhabhi, whatever time did you get up?"

"Early."

"Ah, so it was you who switched on the hot water this morning."

Bhabhi smiles and holds out a neatly folded blue sari. "Look, I have brought this for you." She places the sari on my bed. "But first, let me help you," and she takes the towel from me.

I sit down on the floor with my arms round my knees and Bhabhi sits behind me, at first drying and then combing my hair with long strokes.

"I do hope you like him - Dhiren," Bhabhi says, not expecting an answer. She always gives long monologues when she combs my hair. "Respectable family. His own shop. Tall and fair-skinned. Lives on his own."

At one point, the comb encounters a thick tangle, and the pain makes me breathe in sharply through my teeth. Bhabhi slows down the vigorous combing momentarily, but soon resumes it with full force.

There is no break in her talking, though. "His first wife left him to go back to Dar-es-salaam. They say she just never settled down to living in a village. Nothing seems to be wrong with him. All the reports are good."

I was told all this yesterday but do not mind being reminded of it.

She finishes combing and bundles up my hair in a bunch on top of my head. "A woman's hair is an important part of her beauty. And look at your splendid mane. Such luxuriant black hair." She releases it and lets it cascade down my back. "He would have to be blind to turn down a beautiful girl like you."

*   *   *

The guests are expected at ten, but arrive half an hour late. Dhiren is accompanied by his parents, his sister, older brother and bhabhi. After exchanging initial pleasantries, they sit in the living-room. I wait in the kitchen and watch them through the gap in the half-open door.

Dhiren is tall and slim, except round his waist, where

his shirt is stretched a little tight. He has a thick head of hair, which is cut short. He looks nervous but then that is not surprising. His eyes seem to have a steely glint and his brother has a similar stern look. But their father has a round smiling face. I can only see the backs of the three women. They seem to be old-fashioned judging from their hairstyles, and the way they wear their saris in the Gujarati style rather than the fashionable Northern mode.

A few minutes later Bhabhi appears in the doorway and nods at me. I turn to pick up the tray with tea and snacks. But Bhabhi stops me and shuts the door. After closely examining me, she tidies up a loose strand of my hair, and crouches down in front of me to adjust the length of my sari. Then she gives me an encouraging smile, opens the door, and leads the way into the living-room.

I follow her with downcast eyes and place the tray on the circular table in the centre. I feel all eyes on me and freeze for a moment, not quite sure what to do next until Bhabhi says, "Lalita has made *masala chai* for all of us. It's OK, yes?" There are only assenting voices.

I pull out four quarter-shaped tables, which neatly fit under the circular table and place them in front of the guests. After serving them all tea, I hand out plates of snacks.

"*Chevdo* is home made by Lalita," Bhabhi points out to the guests.

"*Arre, wah,*" says Dhiren's father, waggling his head, "very tasty."

And again there is a chorus of assenting voices.

For a while, the older generation talks about their mutual friends and relations. It is obvious that while our side of the family are mostly professionals, Dhiren's are shopkeepers. But it does not matter because both our families belong to the *Lohana* community.

He seems to be listening intently to the conversation. Occasionally he makes a brief comment and he has a deep pleasant voice.

While the others talk, I stare at the floor most of the time but occasionally steal a glance at him. Once I catch him looking at me. As our eyes meet, we both quickly turn our gaze away.

After about a quarter of an hour, Dhiren's father addresses us. "I am sure you two want to speak to each other on your own." He smoothes down his white hair with his hand as he speaks. "It is not like in the old days. When we were your age, parents told you whom to marry and you did; in some cases, without even having set eyes on each other. But how times have changed! And one has to change to adapt to the new world. You are the ones who are going to spend your lives together and therefore should have the final say." He looks around proudly as he adds, "You see, I am quite *modern* in my outlook." He uses the English word *modern*, with its connotations of Western, liberal attitude.

My family have all along assumed that we would want to talk in private, and have kept the small living-room free for the purpose.

Motabhai nods at me. I stand up. Dhiren scrambles to his feet, but in his hurry he knocks over his bowl of snacks, which he has barely touched. I instinctively kneel on the floor to clear the mess and Dhiren bends down at the same time. We face each other at a close range and he smiles at me. The stern expression in his eyes softens, and smile lines near his mouth light up his face. I smile back.

"I will clear it up." Bhabhi says, and nudges me towards the smaller sitting room. Dhiren follows me.

We stand in front of two armchairs, which face each other. He waits for me to sit, and then gently lowers himself.

He looks around, taking in the furniture, the shrine in one corner and the television in the opposite corner of the room. "Nice to have a second living-room," he says.

"It's used mostly by my nephews."

"Do you play chess?" he asks, pointing at the board game on the table.

"Sometimes I have a game with my nephews. But I've learnt it only recently and I'm still not very good at it. How about you? Do you play?"

"No. Never tried it." There is a brief pause and then he adds, "I play volleyball. Or used to when I was in school."

"Oh, I never tried volleyball."

"Girls don't play volleyball," he gives a short laugh.

"I have heard that they do. In places like China."

"That's true. I've seen photos in papers showing them playing."

"Hm."

Neither of us seems to know what to say next. During the awkward silence I am conscious of excited shouts from children playing outside.

"But occasionally I do play badminton," finally I say desperately. "Why don't you anymore? Play volleyball, I mean."

"Now, with the shop, I don't have time." He runs his hand over his hair as if to smooth it.

"Does no-one else help?" I know many people who spend long hours in their shops, and I have always felt sorry for them.

"My brother and father run the main store in Kampala. I manage the smaller one with the help of two assistants."

"Is it also in Kampala?"

"No, it's only a few miles from Kampala, in Mengo. I live in the rooms behind the shop."

I have heard of Mengo but I have never been there. "How big is Mengo?"

He clears his throat. "Not big at all. And as for Asian families - only five of them. They all have shops. There are no other businesses around, unless you call a school a business. The African population lives on the farms around the town."

I wasn't told he lives in that small a village. I can picture a tiny cluster of buildings on its main street, constructed from corrugated iron sheets, with sheltered walkways built outside each shop; occasional cars driving through the town but the main traffic consisting of cyclists, almost exclusively men, with the carriers at the back having big bundles of plantains strapped on them, or else women perched on them.

He breaks my reverie with, "At the moment, Jayshree, you know, my sister, lives with me. She cooks and manages the house. But we are looking for a boy for her."

Ah, so he needs a housekeeper.

There is another uncomfortable silence before he asks me, "I understand you studied in India?"

"Yes. I grew up there and went to the University in Baroda. I only came here two years ago. How about you?"

"I was born in Kampala and went to school there. But after S.S.C., I joined our business," he informs me and then looks at his feet. His shoes are in the hallway and he is wearing bright blue socks.

"Hm."

I wait. He looks as if he is trying to decide how to ask a further question and I can half-guess what it is going to be.

"Were you ... I mean, did you marry straight after finishing your studies?"

"A year after I graduated. And he died five months after

we were married." I had rehearsed the answer numerous times in my head but could never quite get it right. Should I go into details? Tell him about how, when our marriage was arranged, no one had informed us that my husband suffered from TB? That when he coughed during the wedding ceremony, I thought that it was just an ordinary cough? And that a week after the wedding, when I saw him spit out blood, I actually fainted? Despite his deception in hiding his affliction, he was a nice, gentle and loving man. And I would feel disloyal complaining about him. So I do not elaborate.

"Must have been difficult for you."

"Yes," I say, grateful that he does not ask for any details. Now I ask him, "And what about your first marriage?"

"She was from Dar. Having grown up in a big city, she never adapted to living in a little village like Mengo. She went back after about a year." He smiles at me as he looks into my eyes. "How would you feel about living in a village?"

I do not know how I would adapt to a life with very limited communal activities. But I do not want to appear doubtful, so I smile back at him. "The place is less important than the people you share your life with. Are you happy living there?"

"I've got used to it now." He hesitates before adding, "One can find things to amuse oneself anywhere."

I notice that he has stretched out his legs and is rocking his feet from side to side. That is when I realise that I have been tapping my left knee with my right hand knuckle. It is a relief when I hear Bhabhi clear her throat outside the door. "Do you want more time?"

We both scramble to our feet.

Chapter 5
One and a Half Years before Day Zero:
Monday 8th March 1971
Lalita: Decision

I spoke to a stranger for less than half an hour. It was an awkward meeting as we were both highly nervous. And now I have to decide if I want to marry him, spend the rest of my life with him, love and cherish him and maybe bear his children.

I was afraid that Motabhai and Bhabhi might want an answer straight after the guests left. But they have not mentioned the interview all day. I do appreciate their sensitivity in not pressing me for my decision. I need time to think, to weigh the issues in my mind.

But I must be realistic. Motabhai and Bhabhi have always made me feel welcome in their home. They treat me like their daughter. But I must not be a burden to them for the rest of my life.

A few months ago, Motabhai and his friend Veljikaka from next door were in the living-room, when I happened to overhear their conversation.

"When I brought her to Uganda from India," Motabhai was saying, and he sounded agitated, which is extremely rare, "I promised my mother that I will treat her like my daughter, and do all I can to make her happy."

"It is obvious she is happy living with you. No-one could doubt that," Veljikaka assured him.

"I know. But what will happen after I am gone? She is young and deserves every chance to be happy with a family of her own. The society is unfair to women. Widowers have no problem finding a second wife but people object to a widow remarrying. It is an unfair custom. It is an unjust system. And I do not agree with it. I will fight it. I am terribly disappointed in you for supporting a cruel tradition like that. I would have thought — "

"You misunderstand me, Brother," Veljikaka interrupted him. "I, too, think it is an unjust tradition. All I said was that it will be difficult to find a suitable match because many men will not consider marrying a widow, no matter how young she is."

"I am sorry, Velji," Motabhai sounded contrite. "But I so very much want to see her happily settled."

"I know. I know." Veljikaka said soothingly to Motabhai.

There was silence for a while before Motabhai spoke, "The Bible has rules of behaviour. The Commandments, they call them. If I remember it right, one of them goes something like *Thou shalt not covet thy neighbour's wife*. Our society has gone to the ridiculous extreme by decreeing that *Thou shalt not covet thy neighbour's wife, ex-wife or even his widow*."

"In our case it is not the religion but the social traditions," Veljikaka pointed out.

"I agree and it is about time we moved away from middle-ages into twentieth century."

Just then I heard the front door open as Shashi came in with his friends. So I moved away from the corridor into the TV room.

Now as I sit in my room and recall the overheard conversation, I consider what to do. I have the misfortune of being born a woman. Life is so much more difficult for us. I know things are gradually changing, but it is still not common for a widow to re-marry. And if she does find someone, the chances are it will be a widower, usually with a young family, for the man needs a new wife to bring up the children. And it is even worse for a divorced woman. The man can re-marry fairly easily but if you are a divorced woman - forget it. No chance.

I stand up and look at my reflection in the mirror. I gather my hair into a loose pile on the top of my head and pout my lips. I ask myself, who would want a thirty-year-old widow like me? I should consider myself lucky to get someone like Dhiren. He has no children and is well off. Only his sister lives with him but that is to cook for him and to run the house. They are trying to arrange her marriage; so she will move away. He will have no relations living with him after he marries. That means there will be none of the stress involved in fitting into an extended joint family.

He is only thirty-two and is pleasant-looking - in fact he is handsome. And he has a lovely smile. It makes his eyes crinkle.

And yet it is those same eyes that make me wary of him. For when he does not smile there is a hard look in his eyes. It makes me uncomfortable. I tell myself that maybe I am imagining it. Yes, perhaps I am being harsh towards him. He was obviously nervous at our meeting. Also, it must have hurt him when his wife left him. Unhappiness is bound to stamp its mark on one's countenance. I wonder if I have a look of defensiveness on my face and if he is worried about that - and might turn me down because of it.

However, each time I think of him, it is his smile that I remember most clearly.

Today has been like a normal Monday. Motabhai went to work. Shashi went to school and Bhabhi and I did the usual housework. In the afternoon I read in my room. However, all day I wondered when they would ask me about my decision.

And I can't help worrying about Dhiren's response. What if he rejects me? I tell myself that whatever is written in my fate will happen.

In the evening after dinner, I go to my room and lie propped up by pillows on my bed, trying to read, but I cannot concentrate. There is a knock on my door and Bhabhi comes in. She places her hand on my shoulder and asks me if I am ready to talk. I just nod and follow her to the living-room, where Motabhai is in his favourite chair, waiting for us. Bhabhi occupies the sofa next to his chair and I sit facing them. Motabhai smiles at me.

"Have you given it serious thought?" His tone is gentle and caring.

I nod. I feel bashful and stare at the floor.

"Before asking you how you feel, let me tell you that we have heard from the other party," Motabhai informs me. "Their answer is 'yes'. They like you." He stops smiling and his expression becomes serious. "I also want to repeat what I have often said before. This is your home and we are not trying to get rid of you. So say yes only if you are sure. After all, you will be agreeing to a lifelong commitment."

"Yes," I murmur, my gaze still fixed on the floor. Then realising that I have probably mumbled it too softly, I repeat in a louder voice, "Yes. The answer is yes."

"Are you sure about it?"

"Yes, I am sure." I say. I feel a surge of joy as I imagine Dhiren smiling when my decision is conveyed to him.

Motabhai and Bhabhi are both beaming and stand up. I also rise to my feet. They embrace me and the three of us stand there for a while, me in the middle with Motabhai's arm round my shoulder and Bhabhi's round my waist. Bhabhi raises the end of her sari to wipe her tears and I find myself crying too.

"We will send a telegram today to confirm the engagement. This is a happy occasion," Motabhai says. "Savita, how about sweetening our mouths?"

Bhabhi reaches for a plate on a side table. She removes the covering silken cloth to reveal the contents, *penda*. We take it in turn to feed small pieces of the sweet to each other, and still with beaming faces, once again sit down to talk.

"Tell me," Motabhai wants to know, "did you discuss if you would live in the house behind the shop, or is he planning to build a separate house somewhere near it?"

"We did not talk about that."

"So what did you talk about?"

"Volleyball."

"Volleyball?"

"Yes, volleyball. And chess. And badminton." I cover my mouth with my hand as I struggle to control a sudden fit of giggles.

Chapter 6
One Year before Day Zero:
Wednesday 16th June 1971
Ramesh: The Rhythm of Life

Life has its own rhythm. You have to learn to attune to it.

Consider my case. I had imagined that after finishing my studies, I would take it easy - travel around Europe and the USA for a few months before returning to Uganda. And then I would carefully weigh up the pros and cons before deciding whether to work for an established firm or to start my own practice.

Instead, the day after I qualified, I had to catch a flight to Uganda to attend Lalita Auntie's wedding ceremony.

My best friend Kumar was on the plane with me. We have been close friends from early childhood. When in secondary school, we sat on the same desk for four years. Our friendship grew stronger when we shared a room as students in London, and we qualified at the same time. But he was in a hurry to get back home. His father died a few months ago and he is now the head of his family. On the plane, he mapped out his plans for the future. He had always dreamt of having his own legal practice.

"We have often talked of going into partnership," he reminded me. "Are you still willing?"

We were up there in the clouds, in reality and metaphorically, and I said, "Sure, I am, my friend."

I arrived home on Friday, Lalita Auntie's wedding was on Sunday, and on Tuesday afternoon Kumar was sitting in our living-room, clutching in his hand a folder with the relevant papers to start our legal practice. He had it all worked out.

"Sign here and here and here. We register tomorrow, and we are in business. Mitani and Patel, the Law firm."

"No," I said firmly. "Not Mitani and Patel. We will call it Patel and Mitani. You have made all the effort, and I insist your name goes first."

After a brief argument he gracefully accepted my suggestion.

We shook hands upon it, and I said, "We can now start looking for suitable premises."

An enigmatic smile hovered upon his face. I know that look.

"What is it?" I asked. "No, don't tell me. You've found an office already."

"Only provisionally."

Today, it is Wednesday, six days after we left London. And here we are, Kumar and I, partners in a law firm, looking at an office, hoping to rent it for our firm. The premises are in Lubas Road, near the *Lido Cinema*. It is perfect - five rooms on the first floor, the biggest of which could be the reception area for clients where the secretary would sit. We would have a room each and the other two rooms could be used if we decide to expand our practice and take on more partners. The rent is very reasonable.

Kumar stands by the window and looks at the almost deserted street as he addresses me, "Now all we need to find is a secretary."

"I am surprised at you," I say to his back. "You've found everything else."

He turns round and faces me. "I wouldn't appoint anyone without you agreeing to it first."

"Well, I have someone in mind."

"Who?"

"Kintu."

"Who is Kintu?" He looks puzzled at first. Then a smile develops on his face. "You mean Kintu! Kintu Mukasa? Our school-mate?"

I nod. I got in touch with Kintu only yesterday. He has a job in a law firm in Kampala but is not very happy with it. Also, he would like to move back to Jinja.

"Can he start tomorrow?" Kumar wants to know.

Kintu can join us a month later. So we decide to set up the office the following week with a temporary secretary.

And so that is the end of my plans for travelling and then gradually easing into a job. Instead big changes have taken place in my personal life - from a student to a partner in a law firm - all in the span of a week.

I started by saying 'Life has its own rhythm'. At the moment Life seems to be dominated by Rock 'n' Roll rather than Gregorian Chants.

Chapter 7
One Year before Day Zero:
July 1971
Shashi: Twisted Logic

Our house feels all different. I do not mean the building itself or the garden at the back. That has not changed. It is how I feel living in it. And it is obviously because two major changes have taken place.

One, Lalita Auntie has gone away to her own home after her marriage. And two, Ramesh has returned home after five years studying in England.

Auntie's absence has left a gap in our life. No more do I smell the incense sticks burning in the shrine in the corner of the small living-room in the mornings. Ba and Auntie were like close friends and I miss the sound of their voices and laughter from the kitchen. And Auntie used to pop into my room most afternoons for a chat, and to ask me how things were at school. Of course, I am happy for her but miss her at the same time.

And as for Ramesh being at home, it feels like he has filled a different gap in our lives, which we did not know even existed. Now that sounds crazy! Isn't a gap there due to something not existing?

So if 'a gap' did not exist it means that 'something that did not exist' did not exist. This is crazy. I'll talk to Ramesh about it. It's the sort of logical twist he enjoys.

Chapter 8
One Year before Day Zero:
15 July 1971
Lalita: Married Life

I am a married woman now. And have been for thirty-four days.

We got engaged a week after Dhiren came to see me but we decided to wait about three months before getting married so that my nephew, Ramesh, who was due to return from UK, could attend our wedding ceremony. Neither Dhiren nor I wanted a big reception and so we invited only the family and close friends. It was a small affair with only about two hundred guests.

Since then I have been living in Mengo and feel quite at home here. Dhiren's sister has moved back to her parents in Kampala, and it is just the two of us in the house. There are five Asian households as neighbours and we are like a family.

As I have been at my marital home for over a month, I am due to visit my family according to our custom. And today Motabhai has come to Mengo to drive me back to Jinja.

Dhiren and I have shown Motabhai how we plan to extend at the back of the house.

"We will have two more bedrooms and an extra bathroom," Dhiren proudly proclaims. "So next time you come here, you must spend a few days with us."

"So useful to have more rooms. Not just for guests but for the family if ..." Motabhai leaves the sentence unfinished, but I blush. It is too early to start planning children.

Now the two men are sitting at the dining table in the living-room. As I serve them their meal, Motabhai exclaims,

"Oh, *Naniben* (Little Sister), you shouldn't have gone to so much trouble."

"It's no trouble," I say. I have cooked *puran-puri*. Actually, it is quite a bit more effort than making plain *rotli*, but Motabhai loves the delicacy.

"I just realised that I still call you *Naniben*," Motabhai remarks. "You are a married woman now and not little anymore."

"To you, I will always be Naniben."

He smiles, acknowledging I am right; after all he is twenty-two years older than me.

I serve them their meal and come back to the kitchen. I make more puran-puri by stuffing the dough with sweetened lentils and roll it and bake, before applying a generous spreading of *ghee* (clarified butter) on it.

Then I take the freshly cooked puran-puri to the dining table, and just as I am about to give one to Motabhai, he covers the plate with his hands. "I will have rice now."

"You can't move on to rice already. You have eaten hardly any puran-puri," I insist.

"I couldn't eat any more. I had two."

"Just one more, for my sake." I try to slip the ghee-sodden delicacy onto the side of his dish but Motabhai pushes my hand away.

"I'm not a guest here. You don't need to force more food on me."

Dhiren lends me support. "You mustn't count how many you eat. Have just one more."

In the end, after more tussle, Motabhai accepts half of one as a compromise. "I will grow big and fat."

"Your sister has cooked them especially for you," Dhiren says, as he helps himself to rice.

"Someone ought to do research on the relationship between obesity and the number of meals one has with one's sister. I wonder how many calories there are in a single one of these," Motabhai says as he chews a mouthful with relish.

"You will burn off those calories when you go for your evening walk," Dhiren suggests.

"I'll also feel sleepy on our journey home."

"I will talk to you to keep you awake," I promise.

I keep my promise. I chat away as we drive home in the afternoon heat.

"Imagine. Just five Asian families in the village. I know it is nice to have a bigger choice of neighbours but they are all very friendly. And a lively bunch, so we have lots of laughs."

We pass many small farm holdings, with crops of cassava low on the ground. They are interspersed with paw-paw trees, looking like miniature palm-trees, or with *mtoke*, displaying its large rectangular-shaped leaves, and bunches of green bananas dangling on the plants. In the bright tropical afternoon, the lush green vegetation contrasts sharply with the orange-red soil. I notice a woman digging with a spade, her baby tied securely on her back.

"I do admire these African women," I comment. "Even when they are doing heavy work, they manage to have their babies with them rather than leave them unattended."

I tell Motabhai about my friends, "Most of the women in our group are older than me. Their children are grown up; a couple of the kids are still teenagers but they stay with their grandparents in Kampala to be near the school. As Dhiren's sister has gone back to Kampala to live with her parents, Gulzar is the only woman my sort of age. She is expecting, and is three months gone."

We pass by little village stores and a cafe, where an excited crowd is watching two men playing a game of *Bao*.

"Most days we meet and chat or play cards," I continue. "If there are only four of us, we usually play *satiyu*. Occasionally, we play *teen patti*."

"Did I hear you right? *Teen patti*?"

"Yes, but we don't gamble, Motabhai. We play with bottle tops. Each one is allowed a hundred tops. The men folk sometimes play for real on Saturdays. And we keep Sundays free to go to Kampala for weddings and social functions."

"What else do you do to pass your time?" Motabhai wants to know. "Don't you help in the shop?"

"I would gladly do that but Dhiren says he does not need any help. He is quite emphatic about it. He has two assistants there, anyway."

Near Lugazi, Motabhai slows the car right down as we are stuck behind a large lorry laden with a giant mound of sugar canes, nearly fifteen feet high. On the side of the road are the fresh green fields of cane, carpeting the gently rolling landscape. The lorry turns into a side road and Motabhai speeds up again. Now the road goes through the dense Mbira forest with huge tropical trees casting giant shadows across the road.

"I have also been reading a lot," I continue. "In fact, I've finished reading almost all the books I borrowed from our house. Yes, even *War and Peace*. I will change them over this time, if I may."

"Ah, so that explains why one of your bags is so heavy. When putting it into the boot of the car, I wondered what you had in that bag. ... Oh, look. Look."

I have been too busy talking and miss whatever he was trying to point out to me.

"What was it?" I ask him.

"A hornbill. A big one."

"Oh, I would have loved to see it. I've never seen one before." I scrutinise the dense wall of trees by the side of the road, before continuing my chatter. "And I have taken up sewing again. You should have seen the frock I sewed for Florence, our maid Mary's daughter. She is four and ever so cute and has just started going to the local village school. I went to see the school and the head says they may be able to give me a part-time teaching job. If not, I will go and work as a volunteer there. I am waiting to hear from the Head."

"How does Dhiren feel about it?"

"I haven't told him yet. I am sure he will be pleased that I am going to do something useful. So I am saving it as a surprise for him."

Motabhai smiles at me and I know he is glad to see me happy.

When we arrive home, Bhabhi rushes out to greet me. We embrace each other and then head straight for the smaller living-room to chat.

"You know I was a little worried that you might find it difficult to adjust to living in a tiny little village." Bhabhi confesses. "But I am so glad you seem to be happy."

"Oh, I am," I assure her.

"And it seems Dhiren treats you well."

"Yes, he does. He makes me happy," I say and then blush.

Chapter 9
Nine Months before Day Zero:
November 1971
Shashi: My Gang

Papa loves telling me stories. Legends and myths and also our family history. One of his stories that made a huge impression upon my mind is about King Harishchandra, also known as the *Satyawadi* (One who always tells the truth) Raja, a king who never lied in his life and always followed the moral path - a bit like Yudhistir from the epic Mahabharata. In order to keep his word, Harishchandra gave up his kingdom, and he and his family became slaves. However, his kingdom was restored to him because these trying events in his life were engineered by Gods, who were testing his integrity. Papa says that like the King, you should always follow the righteous path, even if the price to pay is your kingdom, or even your life.

A few days ago, while browsing through Papa's books in our library, I saw a book called "The Two Cultures" by C.P. Snow. *Great*, I thought. *A novel about people like me, who are exposed to cultures from the East and the West*. Instead, it turned out to be a non-fictional account of the different traditions in Science and Arts. It was boring. But I still think a story portraying the lifestyles of youngsters in the West and contrasting it with those living in a traditional, conservative society like ours would be fascinating.

I mentioned this to Ramesh. "You're right," he said. "Perhaps you should write one. Mind you, you get a comparison of cultures as you see as many Hollywood films as Bollywood ones."

He described some of the Western films about the young

people, which were produced before I started going to see movies in English. He mentioned *The Young Ones* starring Cliff Richard, of which I know the title song. And then there was a dramatic film about young lovers called *West Side Story*. He told me its plot in brief. It is a modern day version of Romeo and Juliet. And then we talked about how in our culture we had groups of friends but no formal gangs.

He then commented on how gangs in UK have changed over the years. I learnt that in the 50s there were the *Teddy Boys*. In the 60s, based on the styles of the clothes they wore, there were two different types, the *Mods* and the *Rockers*, who even had pitched battles.

Later, I told my friends what I learnt from Ramesh and we decided to form a gang, too. We discussed the important feature of a gang - its name.

"How about *Jinja Sixteens*?" Vinod suggested.

"Hm. I am not sure." I had another name in mind.

"We live in Jinja and we are sixteen years old," he elaborated.

"We're not stupid. We can guess what it means. But we will all soon be seventeen," I pointed out. "We would have to change the name to *Jinja Seventeens* and then to *Jinja Eighteens* and so on."

"And one day we would be called *Jinja Twenty-Eights*," Nilu offered.

"And eventually *Jinja Eighty-Sevens*," Anver joined in the ridicule of Vinod's idea.

"Alright, maybe it's not quite suitable," Vinod agreed.

"We should not blindly follow the West," I said in a serious tone. "We do not want to glorify violence or leather clothes. Let us be totally different. Let us call our gang *The Satyawadi Team*. (The team that always follows the truthful path.)"

My suggestion was met with enthusiasm by all except

Vinod, who grudgingly accepted it.

I was thrilled that at last I belonged to a gang and could not resist boasting to Ramesh, "We have just formed a gang now. Like boys in UK do." I informed him proudly.

"Really? By the way, it is *the UK* not just *UK*."

I sighed inwardly as I wondered if older brothers all over the world acted in this annoyingly superior way. "But it's great you have formed a gang," he went on. "What do you call yourselves?"

"The *Satyawadi* Team."

"Whose idea was that?"

"Mine," I told him rather defiantly because I could see that he looked amused.

"Interesting," he said. "Why that name?"

"Because our members vow to always follow the righteous path," I was not trying to sound pompous, though it came across like that.

"Hm. I see, so it is a bit like a religious sect."

I was horrified at the thought. "Certainly not. We are not a gang of *Masi Ba*."

"You don't have to be an auntie to be religious. And why proclaim to the world you are *Satyawadi*?" He had an extra serious expression on his face now, which I had seen before and I could tell he was trying not to laugh.

"Are you practising your cross-examining skills?" I retaliated because, even before he went to UK, people used to say he should study law due to his habit of interrogating everyone.

"Oh, no. I am just interested. The name intrigues me. It conjures up images of a Brotherhood of Monks rather than a gang of boys. But don't get me wrong. I like it. So tell me what rules do the members have to follow?"

"Never tell a lie." That is the only oath we had taken.

"That's really admirable. And what else?"

There was nothing else. I looked around the room for an inspiration. Like many other families, we had The Morality Monkeys; three little monkey figurines, carved in white sandstone, sitting on the mantelpiece staring me straight in the eye.

"Speak no evil, hear no evil, and see no evil. Like the Monkeys there," I said, pointing.

"Ah. Sounds as good as any religion. But how do you decide what is evil?"

"Well." I was put on the spot and had to improvise."We speak no evil - that means we tell the truth, do not swear or criticise someone behind their back."

"Great."

I felt encouraged to carry on. "We hear no evil - we cover up our ears if someone swears or makes nasty remarks about others."

"Wow!" he said. "And what sights do you avoid looking at?"

"Anything evil." I realised I didn't immediately have an example of this and panicked a little.

"Like what?"

"Like, like, dirty scenes in movies," I blurted out.

"What do you call dirty scenes?"

"Kissing."

"I know Hindi movies censor kissing but you see many English films. Most of them have kissing."

"From now on we are not going to those movies unless they are worth seeing for their other qualities."

My friends and I had only formed the gang a few days ago, so we were still in the process of evolving our structure. We had not discussed any of these details. So as a moral person I realised I was stretching the truth.

Ramesh was smiling. "And when there is kissing in those films?"

"We will cover up our eyes."

"I see," is all he said.

Afterwards, I told myself that there was nothing wrong with me formulating the rules for our gang, as I am the *de facto* leader anyway.

Later I revealed the laws to my gang. They listened in silence and no one objected. Even if they intended to break the rules, they were not going to admit to being immoral, watching men and women slobbering over one another. Ugh!

More than a week has passed since I spoke to Ramesh about my gang. Today Ramesh took me to see a Hindi movie with some of his friends. After the interval, the trailer of an American film showed a couple kissing. Ramesh had obviously told his friends about my Gang's Rules. Why else would all six of them lean right forward and peer at me to see if I covered my eyes. I had no option. I did.

When the scene was over, they all shouted, "OK. Now you can look." And laughed loudly. Everyone in the cinema turned round to find out what was the cause of all that mirth. Luckily, it was too dark for them to see me blush.

Chapter 10
Eight Months before Day Zero:
December 1971
Shashi: An Encounter

Healthy bodies, healthy minds. We have often been told that at school and at home. So, a number of times in the past, some of my friends and I have taken up running in the morning. We do it for a few weeks. Then for some reason or other it lapses. Some months pass by and we get enthused yet again and the cycle continues.

Now we have resolved to go for a run at least three times a week. We walk through the quiet pre-dawn streets to the Jinja Recreation Club's cricket ground. The air is still cool and the birds are just waking up and welcoming the spreading light with their melodious calls.

Nilu says his father told him that running barefoot on dew-covered grass is beneficial to one's eyesight. "So we won't need glasses until we are very old," he assures us.

The sky is just brightening as we get to the field and the dew droplets glisten like tiny diamonds on blades of grass. We take off our sandals and step gingerly onto the cool lawn. Anver starts off and we follow him. Just before we get to the other end of the field, he stops abruptly and spreads his arms out wide, so we halt next to him. Before we have a chance to ask him the reason for stopping, we notice it ourselves. A couple of hippos are standing still on the Gymnasium side of the ground. Their beady eyes regard us for a few seconds before they turn around and lumber away towards the exit. They then break into a trot and disappear out of sight. Hippos normally remain in on near the river and only twice before I have seen them actually in the town.

We are excited and start speaking all at once. "Wow, did you see the one in the front?"

"Wasn't he big!"

Vinod has ambitions to be a songwriter and so I suggest to him a title for his next song- *There is a new hippo in town.*

Chapter 11
Eight Months before Day Zero:
December 1971
Shashi: Papa's Gang

Papa regularly goes for a walk by the river at around dawn. He and a group of friends sit in the Coronation Park. There are about a dozen regular ones, but if there is some exciting news, as many as thirty to forty of them turn up. They exchange gossip, discuss important events of the day, and then rush home, get ready and go out to work. In the past, Papa has mentioned occasionally seeing hippos in the park. So, I told him about my encounter with one.

"That must have been really exciting," he said. And then he reminded me not to approach the hippos too close as they can be dangerous.

I then had a long chat with Papa. He said he was glad that we had started going for a run in the mornings. "If you regularly exercise from a young age, you stay mobile even when you are old."

So I told him my theory. "One can map out human life by its mobility. First you learn to walk. Then to run. Later, you can't run, so you only walk. And then you lose even the ability to walk. Back to where you started. The cycle completes."

Papa laughed and then added, "That could be one of the reasons why they call old age a second childhood."

"But we still respect the old, Papa."

"That's right. Wisdom comes with experience."

"Is that why they call you *The Sages*?" I asked him.

"Me? No one calls me that." Papa and his friends do not seem to realise that many people in town refer to them as *The Sages*.

"Not you. Your gang," I informed him.

Papa was highly amused. "I can't wait to tell my friends that they are members of," he laughed and shook his fist, "a gang!"

Chapter 12
Eight Months before Day Zero:
December 1971
Lalita: Marital Breakdown

"I belong to a gang now," Motabhai told me when he rang me this morning. He was truly amused by Shashi referring to *The Sages* as a "gang".

One needs friends in life. Motabhai meets his 'gang', Bhabhi has a large circle of friends and they call on each other most afternoons. Shashi hangs around with his gang and Ramesh goes to the Amber Club after work. I have friends here and I get along fine with them. But there are only six Asian women in our town. Most are much older than me and have busy family lives. They often have guests or they are away visiting their children or grandchildren. Only Guli is my age and she is not always free. Besides now that she is pregnant, she often rests in the afternoon.

I like to read but I can't spend all day glued to a book. For some time now I have been feeling bored and wishing I could do something useful that would give focus to my life.

And now my wish has come true.

This afternoon I paid another visit to our local school. Mr. Okello, the head teacher, was in the playground talking to a group of kids. He waved to me as he saw me arrive and led me to his office.

"Good news," he said. "I have heard from the Education Department and your application has been approved. You can start work here as a teacher from the 1st of January." He shook my hand vigorously. "Looking forward to having you as a member of our team."

Pity Mr. Okello doesn't call his team a gang. Then I could tell Motabhai that I am joining a gang as well! I am so excited at the prospect.

*   *   *

"No." Dhiren says. There is finality in his voice and a hard glint in his eyes that I had noticed the first time we met.

I am taken aback at his vehement response. "B... but ... why not?" I stutter.

"I have already told you, the answer is NO." He looks down at his plate, covers a *batetawada* with tamarind sauce and stuffs it into his mouth.

"Is it because I arranged it all secretly? I wanted it to be a surprise for you."

His face is impassive. He finishes chewing his last mouthful before answering. "No, that has nothing to do with it."

"Then I don't understand why not. I will be teaching only three mornings a week. And they are offering me a higher scale, despite my lack of teaching experience."

"I couldn't care less what scale they offer you," he shouts. "It's still a piffling amount of money. And even if the pay was good, we don't need it. The shop provides us with plenty."

He is visibly angry now. The look in his eyes frightens me. Timidly, I ask in a subdued tone, "Can you tell me why you are so set against it? You don't let me help in the shop and I can't just hang around here all day doing nothing."

"You have friends. You can visit them and chat and play cards. And do whatever else you do with them." He has stopped eating now even though there is food on his plate.

"With this job, I would feel I was doing something useful."

"You have housework to do."

"That takes very little time with Mary helping in the house."

"Then find some other activity. Do more sewing or take up embroidery, or whatever." He pushes his plate away from him and stands up. "I am not hungry anymore," and he stomps out of the room.

He ignores me all evening, and when we go to bed, he turns away from me to face the wall.

This morning his tone is conciliatory, "Look, I am sorry but do not argue."

It is obvious what he means: *just do what you are told.*

By mid-morning, I have got the lunch ready, apart from rolling the *rotli*, which I always make fresh after he comes in from the shop. I sit down to read the novel I am halfway through, but find it hard to concentrate. I stand by the window and look out. Nothing very interesting happens on Mengo streets. A couple of women are standing on the pavement near the shop, talking to each other. Each has a baby tied with a colourful cloth on her back. One of the babies is asleep and the other one is looking around. Then the women move on. The street is totally deserted until a cyclist goes by, pedalling at a careful pace as he is carrying a small chair tied on the back of his bicycle with a thin rope. The sun is strong and the sharp elongated shadow of the man on the bicycle with the chair at the back looks like an exotic creature gliding along the footpath. And then the street is empty once again.

I pace around the room for a while and then sit down with a sigh. My hand rests on the book beside me. I notice I am tapping on the book without realising it.

This is ridiculous, I tell myself. *If I can't go out to work I will do something useful in the shop.* I spring to my feet and march into the shop.

It is Saturday, half day, when the business is usually very brisk. There are two groups of customers. Dhiren is busy showing new dress material to a man accompanied by three women. One of his assistants, Ndidi, is also busy. She is dealing with a middle-aged woman and her children. The other assistant, Patrick, just finishes serving a young lady and is unoccupied at the moment. He is leaning against the counter. I go over and chat to him.

Dhiren hears my voice and turns around. He raises his eyebrows at me and flicks his head in the direction of the door into the house through which I have just come. I pretend not to have understood his gesture and continue talking to Patrick.

A few minutes later, the customers leave and Dhiren joins us. He tells Patrick to go and tidy up the rolls of material that he has unfurled at the other end of the shop. Then he grabs my arm and leads me firmly back into the house. He pulls me into our living-room and pushes me down on to the sofa.

"What are you up to?" he demands angrily.

I am afraid but I manage to maintain a calm tone when I answer, "Nothing. What do you mean?"

"What were you doing in the shop?"

"I came to help in case -"

"I told you! I don't need your help there."

"OK, today you weren't that busy but I have noticed customers waiting to be served in the past."

"How many times do I have to tell you- I don't need your help in the shop! You look after what needs doing in the house." His face is flushed with anger and his eyes have that frightening glitter.

I swallow nervously. "I'm sorry, but I don't understand why you do not want me to be involved."

"What's the matter with you? Are you stupid? Don't you understand plain language? NO. I said NO, I do not want you working in the shop or in a school, or anywhere else for that matter. There are to be no more arguments about it." He straightens up, glaring at me, and marches out. I sit in silence, unhappy and numb, until I hear the shop door slam behind him. Then I burst into tears.

When he returns a couple of hours later for lunch, I cook fresh rotli for him and he eats mostly in silence. Saturday being Mary's day-off, I take some time washing dishes and clearing the kitchen. I imagine he has gone to the bedroom. So far, every Saturday afternoon he has persuaded me to join him for siesta and has been extra affectionate as we enjoy intimate relations.

Today I have no desire to join him. So I go to the living-room only to find him in there. He is lying back on the sofa, with his eyes closed and legs stretched out on the floor. In his right hand, he clutches a square-shaped bottle. A smell of alcohol assails my nose. An empty box lies on the floor by his feet. It has an image of a European man in a hat, holding a stick as he strides forward and there are two words in big black writing, *Johnny Walker*.

I watch him take a long swig from the bottle before he opens his eyes and notices me standing by the door.

"What? What is it now?" His expression is hostile.

"I didn't know you drank."

"So? Now you know. I can drink if I feel like it." His voice is already slurred.

I am too shocked to move or say anything further.

"Don't stand there looking so disapproving." He has difficulty saying disapproving in his half-inebriated state. He picks up the empty box and throws it at me. He is obviously too drunk to aim straight and it misses me and bounces off the wall.

"Just leave me alone."

I run back to the bedroom and throw myself down on the bed. Trembling, I curl myself up and bury my face in the pillow to stifle my sobs.

*   *   *

Dhiren is now drinking frequently. And when he is drunk he becomes aggressive. I try to avoid him then.

Increasingly I seek refuge in prayers as I spend more time by the little shrine I have made in the kitchen. I ask God, *Am I still paying for sins from my past lives or are you testing me?*

One day Dhiren tries to talk about the situation in a conciliatory tone. "Look, I'm sorry but I like to drink occasionally," he tells me. "But I won't have you being judgemental."

"Other people drink. I could put up with that, but you become so aggressive when you are in that state."

"I didn't drink for months but you have driven me back to it."

"I? I've driven you to drink?" I have no idea what he is talking about.

"Yes, you." He picks up the bottle on the floor by his sofa, reaches for a glass by his side and pours whisky into it.

"How?"

He gulps a mouthful from his glass. "Because you make me angry. With your goody goody ways and demanding to go out to work."

"But I haven't mentioned work recently," I protest.

"And you better not. I know why you are so keen to go out to work."

"If you know my motives, why do you oppose it?"

He wipes his mouth with the back of his hand. "Ha. You take me for a fool? Your motives! Wanting to do something useful! You can't fool me with that rubbish."

"It's not rubbish. Why do you think I want to work?"

I can see his jaw muscles moving and he looks angry. "So that you can meet new men. I've heard you talking in that coquettish voice to Patrick. And wanting to go to work in a school, when we don't need the money! Ha. It's so you can meet those young teachers there. Go on, admit it."

"Admit it?" I suddenly snap. "You're mad," I scream at him. Then, as he makes a move towards me, I run out of the room.

*   *   *

He has barely spoken to me for a couple of days but this evening he tried to be intimate with me. I rebuffed his advances. He responded by slapping me hard. He then forced me onto the bed. I feared even greater violence if I resisted, so I let him have his way. Afterwards, I felt emotionally and physically numb.

He is now drinking every night and though he isn't usually violent, the threat is always there. If I have to go into the shop briefly for some reason, I greet Patrick but am careful not to get into conversation with him. And when I speak to Motabhai or Bhabhi on the phone, I try to sound my normal cheerful self. And I also put on pretence of happiness with my friends in the village.

*   *   *

Yesterday morning I had just finished cooking lunch and had sat down to read a novel when there was a knock on the door. It was Gulzar's husband, Salim, from the house across.

"Could you do us a favour?" he asked. "Guli has pains in

53

her stomach. Very likely it's nothing serious, but to be on the safe side I am taking her to the doctor in Kampala. We have some washing out on the clothesline. Could you please take it in if it rains?"

"Of course I'll keep an eye on it," I assured him.

In the evening, Dhiren was morose at dinner and then went into the living-room and closed the door. I retired to the bedroom and lay down on the bed with my book. I heard a movement and looked up. He was standing in the doorway, his left hand clutching the frame to support him.

"So, now you have started entertaining men at home while I am working. No point pretending to be surprised. I saw Salim come out of the house. You think I don't notice these things because I am busy in the shop. But I notice everything."

He advanced towards me, walking unsteadily. I stood up and tried to dodge round him and escape but he managed to grab my arm.

"You shameless slut. I will teach you a lesson you won't forget," he shouted and started hitting me around the head. Desperately I wrenched myself free and fled into the spare bedroom and locked the door. He followed and kicked at the door, swearing and shouting.

After a couple of minutes he gave up and I heard him stagger back to the living-room.

This morning he knocked on my still locked door and asked if I had made his breakfast yet. He sounded sober and I felt it was safe to come out. I said nothing to him and waited for him to go to the shop.

As soon as he left, I rang Motabhai's home. Savitabhabhi answered.

"Please come and get me," I pleaded tearfully. "Otherwise I will kill myself."

Chapter 13
Six Months before Day Zero:
February 1972
Lalita: Bye, Dhiren

Having made the phone call, I now feel calmer. I pack my
suitcase and then push it under the bed, out of sight, in case
Dhiren comes back before Motabhai arrives.

Mary has finished sweeping the floor. I call her, shake her
by the hand and give her a few pieces of cloth that I had
got from our shop. I tell her, "I am sorry but I will not have
time to sew any more dresses for your beautiful little Agnes.
I will miss seeing you, Mary." She looks quizzically at me but
thankfully asks no questions. However, she presses my hand
warmly. I think she knows what is happening.

I go to the living-room and switch on the radio. The station
is blaring out Hindi film songs. I switch it off. I decide that
I will act as if nothing has changed, until it is actually time
to leave. I put rice on the boil and make dough for rotli. I
decide to cook *undhiu*, Dhiren's favourite curry. I send Mary
to the street market to buy some aubergines and fresh peas.
I have the flour dumplings steamed and ready by the time
Mary comes back with the shopping. So I assemble undhiu
and put it on the stove to cook on a low heat. Soon the spicy
aroma of the dish permeates the kitchen. Every now and
again, I go to the window to see if Motabhai has arrived.

Just after eleven, his car pulls up outside the house. There
is someone else with him. When they emerge from the car, I
can see that it is Ramesh. I desperately hope Dhiren hasn't
noticed the car arrive as it passed the shop in front.

I rush to the door and let them in. I have managed to keep
calm all morning but now I feel tears behind my eyes. "At last

you are here." I burst out. "Let us go. Right now."

Motabhai puts his arm round my shoulder. "All right, Naniben," he says. "If that is what you want. But are you sure we could not talk to Dhiren and try and iron out your problems?"

I can just imagine Dhiren turning on his charm while they are here and then reverting to his real self. I panic at the thought and burst into tears. "No, no. I can't bear the thought of staying here a minute longer. Please, Motabhai. Take me away now. Right now."

"Of course, Naniben, if that's what you want," Motabhai comforts me. "Where are your things?"

I hurry to the bedroom and pull my case out from under the bed. Ramesh carries it to the car.

"Have you told Dhiren that you are leaving or should I go and inform him?" Motabhai asks me.

Just then the door leading to the shop bursts open and Dhiren storms in. He stops short, taking in the scene, his legs apart and his arms akimbo. I can't help noticing that there is a biscuit crumb near his mouth. An angry flush starts to spread across his face.

He hisses, "What's going on here?"

"I am leaving," I say.

He takes a step towards me. "You're not going anywhere," he growls.

"I am," I say defiantly. I'm not scared of him now.

"Are you deaf? Didn't you hear what I said?" He takes another step towards me, with a murderous look of rage on his face. "You're my wife and you will not set foot out of this house without my permission."

"She isn't happy here." Motabhai says calmly, placing himself protectively in front of me. "I'm taking her home."

"You keep out of it," Dhiren now rounds on him. "This is a private matter between husband and wife." His eyes take on the merciless glint I have seen many times lately.

"I'm taking her home, Dhiren," Motabhai repeats in a firmer voice, and he grasps my arm. "Let's go Naniben."

"You stay where you are," Dhiren screams.

Clenching his fists, he moves to head us off as we start towards the open doorway. But he stops as Ramesh rushes through it and grabs my other arm. Dhiren is taken by surprise as he did not realise Ramesh is here, too.

"You stay where you are," Ramesh warns him, and he and Motabhai escort me safely out of the house, leaving Dhiren seething behind us. We hurry out to the car.

Dhiren stands on the threshold of the house and glowers at us. His face is flushed. As we climb into the car, Dhiren screams and shouts at me. "I am warning you, this is your last chance. Don't you dare leave! I forbid you. You go now and that will be the end. You'll never be able to set foot back into this house. I command you. Come back now. Now. This minute." His shouts get louder as he gets angrier.

I make no reply. Motabhai remains silent. And Ramesh puts the car in gear, and presses down on the accelerator.

Chapter 14
About Five Months before Day Zero:
March 1972
Shashi: Me, a Teacher

Poor Lalita Auntie. She is back home and is once again in her old room. I felt really sorry for her when she came back to live with us, as she looked so unhappy. Nobody has discussed openly what happened to her, but I have gathered that her husband was foul to her. For a while, her eyes were red and swollen each morning, as if she had been crying in her room at night. But now, thank goodness, she is beginning to look happy again, and more like her old cheerful self.

And she has started making enquiries about jobs in schools. Meanwhile, she is keeping herself busy running classes for children at our home. Every afternoon, eight to ten kids from our neighbourhood arrive clutching their slates and pens. I don't think she does it for money because I heard her telling one of the mothers, "Don't worry about paying, Sudhaben. Just send your Chetna to the class."

The children sit on the floor in the dining room and I often hear them reciting their times tables. They do so with gusto as if they were singing the latest pop-song. At other times, they sit quietly learning to read and write.

This afternoon it was really hot, I was thirsty and went to the kitchen for a glass of water. As I passed the dining room, I decided to go in and check on what the kids were learning today. They were sitting cross-legged on the floor. I noticed that little Chetna was bent forward, a look of concentration on her face, the tip of her tongue sticking out of one side of her mouth, as she wrote down the word to describe the picture in the book in front of her. I saw she had written 'dameda' instead of 'tameta' (tomatoes). An easy mistake to make, because in Gujarati the letter 'd' (S) is a mirror image of 't' (S pointing in the opposite direction). So, I sat down next to her and helped her write it correctly. She wrote it out twice more and then smiled at me. It made me feel good. I looked up and realised Lalita Auntie was watching me. As she caught my eye, she, too, gave me a wide smile and nodded. It made me feel even better and I realised for the first time that teaching can actually be fun.

Chapter 15
Five Months before Day Zero:
March 1972
Shashi: Dances

Some fruit bats rest upside down in the little awning outside my window. After dinner, Ramesh comes to my room and notices me watching the bats. He sits on the bed and in silence we observe them.

They are big animals, almost the size of crows. Their wings are neatly folded in front of the lower part of their faces, as if they are covering their faces out of modesty. Their little furry ears twitch, their large dark eyes dart in different directions. They suddenly get agitated and flap their angular, leathery wings like a boat furling shiny black sails. Then they emit their high-pitched squeals and take off.

"Fascinating creatures!" Ramesh remarks as the bats show off their flying skills prior to melting away into the dark.

"Yeah," I agree. I often watch them and they are almost like friends to me. But I cannot understand why Ramesh is impressed by them. After six years in London, the world's most swinging city, he is back in this sleepy little town in Uganda, and has to get his thrills by watching these ordinary bats. So I tell him, "You must think life is boring here."

I know when he is seriously considering a question because he always runs his fingers through his long hair as he weighs the arguments in his mind.

"You think this is a boring place? Recently you must have read in the papers about what they call the Bloody Sunday in the UK. About ten thousand people gathered in a place called Londonderry in Northern Ireland for a civil rights march. The British Army stopped them from marching, which led to riots. The Army used water cannons and rubber bullets and eventually live bullets. Thirteen people were killed. The papers thought it was the most newsworthy item at the time. Weeks later it is still one of the top news stories in the UK. They are still trying to analyse what went wrong. Whereas here, in the couple of years since Amin has come to power, many more people are killed each day than those killed on the Bloody Sunday in the UK. Thousands of Amin's opponents have been jailed and tortured. Surely, you agree that military coups score higher in the drama table? No, this is not a boring place, but I wish it was."

"This is different. We are not directly affected by the regime."

"That's because we mind our own business and we choose not to let other things disturb our comfortable lifestyle." Ramesh shakes his head. "But for how long can we bury our heads in the sand?"

"So what can we do? Even the African population is not rising against the tyranny."

"You're right. There is little we can do, *Chhote Bhaiya*." He uses the Hindi expression for 'Little Brother', which he picked up from a Bollywood movie many years ago and now uses it fondly on some occasions. "If we openly opposed the regime in any way, Amin would treat us like Hitler treated the Jews." I think he is about to say more but he stops himself.

I shrug. "We have learnt to live with the threat hanging over us. So we don't feel the danger. Mind you, I can do without excitement of that type."

"What sort of excitement do you want?"

"I don't know. Parties for example? Discos?"

Ramesh smiles. "We have plenty of parties."

"We don't."

"We do. What about last Saturday?"

"Where?" I think he is making it up. I don't remember going to a party.

"I saw you standing near the entrance talking to that pretty girl. Now, what's her name? Smita, that's it," he says with a smile.

"That wasn't a party. It was a wedding."

"So?" He says, spreading his hands out sideways. "In my book, when a group of people gather together to have fun, it's a party."

"You know what I mean." I decide he is just being annoying for the sake of it. "Our so-called parties are always full of older people."

"That's because we believe in mixing generations."

"But in UK they have their wedding parties as well." I am not going to give up that easily.

"Sure they do. But tell me how many weddings did you attend last year?"

We don't attend all the weddings we get invited to, but maybe a couple of them per month and maybe a few more in the high season. I didn't know what he was driving at but I tried to guess anyway. "Twenty? Thirty?"

"Well, in England if you attend three weddings in a year you will go round saying how this has been a busy year for weddings." I must be showing my disbelief, for he repeats, "Yes, three."

Now that came as a revelation to me. "How come?"

Ramesh explains that the weddings are much smaller there. On an average about a hundred or a hundred and fifty guests compared to six or seven hundred guests that we have. At Harikaka's son Dhiru's wedding they had two thousand guests. Almost the whole town turned up.

Ramesh then goes on to create a theory about it. "You see, I reckon you can tell how closely knit a society is from the size of the wedding. Or alternatively, you could say that the English value their privacy more than we do. They like to celebrate a joyous event only with people they know really well."

After a short pause I say, "Our weddings are fine for socialising. But I was thinking more about parties where there is dancing."

"We have the *Navratri* dances," he says, grinning.

I know he is trying to wind me up, but I keep calm. "You know it is not the same thing. Those are folk dances performed on just nine nights of the year. For a religious festival. And in the temple grounds at that."

"Ah, now I see your objection. You want a western style dance where you can hold a girl in your arms and maybe dance with her cheek-to-cheek."

"I am not interested in girls," I almost shout. "I just think those dances are more fun than five hundred people dancing in unison round a religious shrine."

As I storm out of my room, he calls out, "Be more honest with yourself. As for me, I certainly prefer a dance where I can hold the girl in my arms."

Later on before going to bed, I go and tell Ramesh that I am sorry for getting upset. "I realise one has to be totally honest with oneself if ..." I do not finish the sentence with *if one wants to be a great writer* because that will sound rather vain.

He puts his arm round my shoulder and says, "No offence taken. And anyway, it was my fault. I shouldn't have been teasing you about it. But you see, when I was your age we never had dances like that. And even now, only girls from more liberated westernised families attend. And come to think of it, I did see you dancing with Smita at the Christmas dance." He just can't help teasing me.

I do not mind it at all and I laugh as I remind him, "Oh we were only jigging and not dancing in each other's arms. Besides, her big brother Chiman was sitting nearby watching her."

Chapter 16
Five Months before Day Zero:
March 72
Ramesh: John Ngala

It has been a long and tiring day. When my last client leaves, I stand up, stretch my arms, breathe in deeply and yawn. I shake my head as if to clear it of thoughts about work.

I go to the reception room to tell Kintu, "We'll lock up. You may as well go home."

"Thanks." Kintu's teeth gleam as he smiles.

I then go into Kumar's office and flop down in the chair facing him, where his clients normally sit.

"Phew," I sigh. "Another hard day."

"Yes," Kumar agrees. "I guess we'll have to turn some clients away in future. Unless we take on more partners."

"We often talk about it," I remind Kumar. "We just don't get round to it. This time let's not put it off. Besides we have to comply with the Government policy anyway."

We have already received a circular from the Ministry informing us that we should appoint an African partner as part of the Government's Africanisation Policy. A deadline has not been specified but we are urged to proceed as soon as possible.

"And, while we are at it, let us also appoint a woman colleague." We have discussed the suitability of a woman when we have sensitive cases involving domestic disputes. So we agree to appoint two new partners, an African and a woman, or preferably two African women. We are aware that there are very few lawyers in the country and expect very few applications.

"I will place an ad in the day after tomorrow's paper and we will interview the candidates as soon as we receive the applications. How about that?" Kumar believes in wasting no time once he has made a decision.

"Yeah, why not," I agree. "But you will have to interview them on your own. Remember I am off next week?" I am going away for two weeks to attend a cousin's wedding in Mumbai.

"Oh, damn." He is not happy. "We'll have to put it off until you get back."

"Why wait? You can decide," I suggest.

"I would rather you were here."

"I trust your judgement. Besides, if there are any problems, I could blame you."

"Ha!" Kumar gives his short laugh. "That's what I'm afraid of."

*   *   *

Four Months before Day Zero: April 1972

By the time I return from Mumbai, Kumar has already appointed Rehana Butt, who has studied law in the UK and has excellent references. She cannot start work till July, for personal reasons. Today we have arranged to interview our first African candidate.

After my lunch break at home, I decide to return to the office by car because massive dark clouds have gathered in the sky above the town. I park the car a mere two minutes' walk away but the heavens open in a heavy tropical downpour. I get drenched walking the short distance to the office. Kumar is sitting in the reception area talking to Kintu, who is behind his desk.

"Have you just had a bath?" Kintu teases.

"And not bothered to dry yourself?" Kumar joins in.

I respond by spraying them with droplets of water as I vigorously shake my head at them. Long hair is not just for looks - it can be very useful in situations like this.

"Stop!" They shout in unison, laughing at the same time.

Kintu goes into the inner room and returns with a couple of small white towels.

Just then, a young African man rushes into the office foyer. His hair, which is long by African standards, is completely soaked, and he has water running down his face. "Hello, I am John Ngala," he says, drying his face with a small handkerchief. "I have come for the interview. I assume you are Patel and Mitani's Law Firm."

"No, we are more like Patel and Mitani's Hairdressing Salon," I quip, offering him a towel.

"Hairdressing was a major part of my Law course in the Makerere University," John says with a wide smile as he accepts the towel.

We take to him straight away. We do not interview any other candidates.

Chapter 17
Two Months before Day Zero:
June 1972
Ramesh: In Love

I love the idea of falling in love at first sight - it is the standard fare in Bollywood movies; it is what happens in many books I have read.

But I know I have to be realistic. And so I have already embarked upon the traditional path. There have been several approaches made from suitable girls' families. My parents gather information from their extensive social network to determine the suitability of the girl - her family background, character, education and looks. They then short-list the most eligible ones for me to meet.

So far I have taken part in typical interviews with four girls. In each case, I have visited the family, accompanied by my parents and Lalita Auntie; I have exchanged pleasantries with the parents of the girl; I've been introduced to her and then left alone in a room with her to check if she is the right life-partner. How can I decide in half an hour or so? I found them all attractive but then I find most girls attractive. I can imagine marrying any one of them but none of them has struck me as my dream girl. When I met them my heart did not go aflutter, my throat did not feel dry and for days after the interview I did not lie awake in my bed, tossing and turning in my bed, thinking of them.

Just after lunch today, Lalita Auntie comes to my room. I am reading the *Uganda Argus* before going back to work.

"I have news to cheer you up, so stop looking so glum," she teases me.

"Well?"

"We have found this girl for you, beautiful as a crystal doll, sweet as honey and well-educated. She is called Kirti."

I smile. "You call that good news? If she is as good as you say, then she is bound to reject me and I will be crestfallen."

Auntie playfully slaps me on the head. "Don't talk like that. Any girl will be lucky to get you." She then adds, "Kirti is from Mombasa but is coming to Kampala next weekend for a wedding. We have arranged for you to see her on Saturday. So cancel any appointments you may have then."

Later in the afternoon, just as I finish rescheduling my meeting with Wilson Ssengoya from Saturday to Monday, Kumar puts his head round the door. "Hey, come to my office for a few minutes."

I remember to pick up my jacket because, despite the afternoon heat, Kumar's office is cold, as the air conditioning is always turned on too high. A woman is sitting in the room, with her back to the door, leaning forward on the table looking at a document.

When she turns round, my heart skips a beat. She is young, fair-skinned and has a heavenly sparkle in her large, dark, almond-shaped eyes; her long black hair roughly twisted, falls over her left shoulder. She smiles at me and a small adorable dimple forms in her right cheek.

"This is Ramesh Mitani," Kumar introduces me. "And this is Rehana Butt. She is the new partner joining us."

"Pleased to meet you," I say, extending my hand. "I was away when you were interviewed for the job. Mind you, I have heard a lot about you from Kumar. Only positive things, I assure you. But, I thought you were starting on 1st July."

"Rehana rang earlier this morning to ask if she could start a fortnight earlier than planned, just to familiarise herself with the business," Kumar says with his characteristic short laugh. "I told her she was more than welcome."

I sit down and face Rehana. She is dressed in a western style - a light grey skirt and a cream coloured blouse. Kumar paces the room with his slight limp. When Kumar was seven he caught polio. He had to undergo a series of operations to restore function to his right leg, but it remains a little shorter than his left leg.

As he limps back and forth, he explains the main features of our work to Rehana, before turning to me. "Look, I know you are busy, but I also know you do not have any appointments this afternoon. So would you terribly mind showing Rehana some of our office practices and our idiosyncrasies? But don't put her off too much." He gives another one of his short laughs.

Rehana and I spend all afternoon talking. We talk not just about work but also about our lives and our likes and dislikes. We tell each other about our experiences in England.

And now it is after midnight and I am tossing and turning in bed, wide awake, thinking about her.

*   *   *

I can't wait to get to the office so that I can see Rehana. I find she looks even more beautiful in a traditional sky blue *salwar* and *kamiz*. Her eyes hold a different glow, a mixture of excitement and anxiety.

We talk a little more between my appointments. And after work, I drive her to the pier. It is the time of the day when the afternoon's prickly heat mellows into pleasant warmth. People then promenade on the lakeshore road and gather near the pier. They buy roasted peanuts, popcorn or *mogo* (cassava) chips from the vendors as they chat to their friends. But mainly they come to watch the spectacular sunsets, the demise of the day reflected in the lake surface.

As I stop the car overlooking the lake, she sighs, "Oh, it is so beautiful here."

"This is what I like about Jinja - the huge lake. It is almost like the sea."

Her face is glowing in the sun. "It is amazing to think that the river cascading out of the lake is the same Nile as the wide majestic river far away in Egypt."

"I have only seen pictures of it in Egypt," I say. "I was hoping to stop in Cairo on the way home for holidays, but it never worked out."

"I find Egypt fascinating. You know. The cradle of civilization and all that." As she talks, she continues to stare at the water, which is turning almost orange now as the sun sets. "After I finished my studies, I made a point of stopping in Cairo before I returned to Jinja."

"I didn't know you had been to Egypt," I say, while thinking, *Oh, she is so beautiful.*

"There's a lot you don't know about me." She smiles. "Remember? We only met yesterday."

"I find it difficult to believe."

"It feels like we have known each other for ever," she admits and immediately blushes.

I suddenly find myself telling her that she is beautiful. Her blush spreads further like the sunset that we are witnessing. I feel myself melting with a delicious and acute ache as she lowers her eyes, making her long black eyelashes even more noticeable.

And I can't stop myself. It all just comes out in a rush, like a river bursting its banks. I tell her I love her and that I have loved her from the moment I set eyes on her. She looks at me, her eyes soft with a tender glow, and declares that she fell in love with me at first sight, too. She reaches out her hand and I press it warmly with both of mine. But before I can say anything, a few people walk past the car, and she quickly pulls her hand back.

We now sit in silence, as if the enormity of our mutual confession has robbed us of speech, while the world grows even more beautiful around us. Several gaggles of geese fly in v-formations to their roosts. The edges of the woolly mass of clouds turn scarlet as the sky metamorphoses from pink to deep red. The sun is now nuzzling the horizon. We watch it disappearing, rapidly melting the tropical twilight into night. And we sit spellbound by the serenity of nature and the joy in our hearts.

The promenaders leave. The noise of their chatting and gossiping fades and is replaced by the twitter of the birds and then by the background drone of crickets accompanied by the high-pitched squeals of bats.

Finally, in the darkness, Rehana and I turn to each other and exchange our first kiss. Having grown up in a puritanical society, neither of us has kissed before. There is an initial crash of our noses but soon we master it - partly in my case anyway, helped by having seen many romantic Hollywood movies.

After I get home, I tell Auntie to inform my parents that I will not go to Kampala to see the girl they have lined up for me.

"But I thought you moved your Saturday appointment with a client to Monday," Auntie says. She stops braiding her hair and looks at me quizzically.

"I had - I mean I have. But I have decided not to go and meet the girl."

"That's not like you, changing your mind after agreeing to go." Her eyes narrow thoughtfully. "You'll let me know if you have someone else on your mind, won't you?"

"It's a bit difficult," I say, debating in my head whether to tell her.

"Go on, you can tell me."

I make a snap decision. "Actually, I have met someone."

"Oh, how wonderful," Auntie says with genuine pleasure and then adds playfully, "And how long were you going to keep it from me, eh? You are getting secretive as you grow older. We must tell your parents about the girl. They must share in the happiness."

"No. No. Not yet." I feel the situation is getting out of my control.

"Why not? Just because it is not arranged? You know how *modern* our family is?"

"They may still raise objections."

"Ah, a girl from a different community? That won't stop them welcoming her. Your parents have always maintained that they're not in favour of all this caste and community nonsense. You know that."

After a pause I say, "It's a bit more complicated than that."

Auntie has finished braiding her hair and swings her head to the side and flips one of the long pigtails back. "It's complicated only if you make it complicated. At this stage it is simple. A boy meets a girl. They fall in love. They marry. Then comes the difficult part. If they are lucky, they live happily ever after. Otherwise, they separate. Like me."

"Look, Auntie, I'm sorry. I did not want to raise any painful memories for you."

Auntie smiles. "Don't be silly. It's all in the past now. The memories are not painful anymore. In fact, I am fine now. But tell me, who is this mysterious girl?"

"Only if you promise to keep it a secret. I must be the one to break the news to my parents."

"OK, I promise." Auntie places her palm on her heart

solemnly. "Well?"

"Rehana," I say and wait to see her reaction. Auntie's smile freezes and then gradually fades.

"Rehana?"

I nod.

"A Muslim girl?"

"Yes."

"That changes things a bit," Auntie says in a flat voice. She moves one of her pigtails to the front and fiddles with the ribbon at its end.

Chapter 18
A Month before Day Zero:
July 1972
Ramesh: True Love

I can feel it deep inside my being. It is true love, and not an infatuation or a passing fancy. I have never felt such an intense longing in my life. I cannot concentrate on anything. My whole being is suffused with a sweet ache.

I have lost my appetite. Today, for lunch, when I do not finish even a single *rotli*, Ba asks me if I am not feeling well.

"No, I'm just not very hungry today," I tell her, and then to reassure her, I add, "I am fine, Ba, really." My parents have always emphasised the importance of speaking the truth. And I am telling the truth. I am not just fine, I am in heaven.

The image of Rehana hovers in my mind all the time - Rehana smiling shyly, lowering her eyelids bashfully and managing to look flirtatious at the same time, her smooth fair cheeks rapidly colouring light pink when she blushes, that delightful dimple forming in her right cheek when she smiles. But the image which causes the greatest pleasure, and therefore the greatest ache, is the one of her closing her large, dark, almond-shaped eyes and sighing after she kisses me. I keep reliving this and can feel her arms encircling me again, her hands on the back of my head as she presses her lips against mine. She smells faintly of jasmine. I feel dizzy with happiness as I remember the feeling of her moist lips, her tongue darting in my mouth. I find myself sighing and then realise from the expression on Ba's face that she has noticed me sighing. But she makes no comment.

Some of my married friends tell me that love does not matter at first. In their experience, it grows after the engagement or after the marriage. During the engagement period, the couples are allowed to meet each other openly. However, usually they are from different towns, in which case they exchange long letters, and love blossoms as they declare their feelings for each other.

Out of all my close friends, Kumar is the only one who has married a girl from Jinja and knew her beforehand. Kumar wasted no time in settling down after we came back from the UK. Within a fortnight he announced that he was getting engaged to Manjula.

Manjula was in school with us but she was a couple of years our junior. I knew that Kumar fancied her. A few years later, she came to London to do a secretarial course, which took only a few months to complete. Kumar saw her couple of times during her stay there, but never mentioned her after she left.

So it came as a surprise when just a month after we started our practice, he asked me to accompany him to a simple engagement ceremony. "They will be discussing *paithan* (dowry) there," he said with a smile.

"*Paithan*? You're asking for a *paithan*?" I found it difficult to believe. "I have had to put up with many a discourse from you about how it is a socially harmful custom that is responsible for many problems in our society."

Kumar laughed. "That is why I want you to be present there, so you can listen to one more speech from me condemning the evil tradition. It is alright for you *Lohanas*. You do not have a custom of dowries. Amongst us *Patels*, it is not as common as it used to be, but it still exists. We need to change and I am doing my little bit to nudge the society in the right direction."

After the engagement ceremony, Kumar asked if he could say a few words. And not being a man of few words, he gave a fairly lengthy speech denouncing the custom of dowry. As the tradition is no longer as prevalent as it used to be, several of the adults sat there nodding their heads in agreement. But even if they disagreed, they would not interrupt the speech given by the man of the day. He was chuffed when he received loud applause.

Afterwards he agreed to Manjula getting presents from her family as long as it was not a negotiated dowry. I felt proud when Kumar introduced me to the gathering saying, "This is Ramesh, my closest friend. And he agrees with me about the evils of the dowry system."

Two weeks later, Kumar and Manjula were married. And now their baby Nimisha is two months old.

Chapter 19
Three Weeks before Day Zero:
July 1972
Ramesh: John and Patrick Ngala

It has been a busy day and we have no more appointments with clients. Rehana has left to go home. I have tidied up my files and am just about ready to leave when Kumar walks into my room.

"Can you spare a couple of minutes before you leave? I wanted your opinion on a dispute over the Will."

"If it does not take too long," I say. I have just under half an hour to go home, change and then pick up Rehana near the Odeon Cinema.

Before Kumar can answer me, John Ngala knocks on the door before coming in. A shadow of worry clouds his normally bright expression.

It is obviously a serious matter that occupies his mind. So I say, "What's the matter? Here, sit down and tell us."

"Oh, nothing. Nothing really," comes the unconvincing reply. He sits in the chair facing me. His concerned face shines in the sunlight streaking through the window. He shields his eyes with his hand.

"It's obvious you're bothered," Kumar says. "Well?"

John hesitates. "... I'm not sure. Not sure I should involve you in my problems."

"Let us judge that for ourselves. We'll tell you if we want to keep out of it."

"The trouble is you would automatically be involved if I tell you."

Kumar and I nod agreement at each other before Kumar addresses John. "I presume, what you mean is sharing a piece of information, and keeping it confidential, makes us part of a conspiracy, if I may use the word, without really knowing the actual nature of the case. Under the circumstances, I would like to stress that despite our relatively short period of acquaintance, we do not think of you just as a colleague but we harbour true feelings of friendship towards you. Also --"

I cut in. "Look man, just tell us what the problem is. We would like to help, if we can."

"Thank you my friends," John says. "But I am having second thoughts about involving you in my affairs. I would never forgive myself if I exposed you to danger."

John leans forward, resting his hands on the table in front of him. Kumar reaches out and puts his hand on top of John's left hand, and says, "Correct me if I am wrong, but I can guess it is something to do with Amin. Having openly expressed our opposition to the military regime, we have already incriminated ourselves in the eyes of our dictator and thus placed ourselves in considerable peril. So any information that you divulge to us is not likely to expose us to any more danger than we have already placed ourselves in by revealing our political colours and the opprobrium we feel towards the military rule. We may not express our opposition to tyranny from the top of a roof, but our position is unequivocal and -"

I again interrupt. "I want to assure you that we would like to help you as friends." I pause and turn to look at Kumar, who nods. "But even more to the point, we want to do something for Uganda and its people. We have been against Amin's regime from the very beginning because he was not democratically elected. We could never support a dictator who grabbed power in a military coup."

John stands up and paces up and down the room indecisively. Kumar and I wait patiently for him to make up his mind. Finally, he flops down in the chair next to Kumar and clears his throat. "You are aware that President Obote is in Tanzania trying to raise support to oust Amin. Well, I'm involved in that organisation. Many of Obote's supporters are from Northern tribes and need help to go south to Tanzania to join the Freedom Force."

"We can certainly give some financial help."

"Thank you for the offer. Any help will be appreciated. But we also want to spread the message to our fellow citizens."

"I can assure you that as far as the Asians are concerned, a majority would welcome Obote back, even though he wasn't all that friendly to them," Kumar says. "But they would support him because he was democratically elected. However, we are peace-loving people and mind our own business. You know that on the whole, if possible, we keep out of politics." Kumar points out.

"I know. I would not want you to try and drum up support for our cause openly. Far too dangerous!"

"I thought you had a more specific problem," I say.

"Yes. You are right." John places his elbows on the table and strikes his palm with his fist. "Sometimes we are betrayed. And you know what Amin is like." He makes a slicing gesture across his throat." He pauses and stares at the window. There are a couple of large dark clouds in an otherwise blue sky. We wait for him to regain his composure. After a brief pause, he turns his head to look at us. He clears his throat. "This time it is also personal. My younger brother Patrick is on the run. He needs to lie low for a few weeks, while we get his papers sorted. If the army finds him, within a few hours his body will be floating down the Nile."

"Where is he now?"

"With a sympathiser. Not an ideal place because it is a

small house and there are kids there, whose friends are in and out all the time."

"He can hide in our house," Kumar says. "We have a guest room."

"It won't work. An African in an Asian household will stand out. No. Even if he doesn't go outside, your servants will notice him."

"Can we ask Kintu to help?" I wonder aloud. "Let's ask him. He is a good man."

"No, no." John shakes his head violently. "We can't be absolutely certain of him. Kintu is from the Baganda tribe. And you know too well that Obote made many enemies amongst them when he removed powers from their king, Kabaka Mutesa."

"So, what do you suggest?" I ask him.

"I don't know." He shrugs. "I was hoping one of you might have a holiday home or something where Patrick could lie low for a few weeks. When the heat is off, he could make his way down to Mwanza."

We sit in silence. We can hear Kintu in his room talking on the phone, although the words are not quite distinct.

Kumar stands up now and limps to and fro across the office, frowning. His limp is more noticeable when he is agitated. He stops abruptly and says in an excited voice, "I've got it. My uncle has bought a house on Oboja Road near the law courts. It's rather old and has a corrugated iron roof. They're hoping to knock it down and replace it with a modern bungalow. They're waiting for planning permission. Meanwhile, it's empty."

John's eyes light up. "That sounds like an ideal hiding hole. It is a quiet location."

"Yes, but you know Oboja Road," I point out. "Hardly a

soul there most of the day. Then at about 6 p.m. half the town walks down the road to get to the pier to watch the sunset."

"He will just have to stay indoors during that time." Kumar says. "And I would advise him to use the room at the back so that no lights can be seen from the street after nightfall."

We agree that it sounds like the best solution under the circumstances.

"But we'll have to get him there secretly," John cautions. "No-one else apart from us three should know about it."

We arrange the details. Kumar will get the keys from his uncle without raising any suspicions. John will bring Patrick to the house after it gets dark at 8 p.m.

"It sounds perfect." John says as he gets up to go.

"Not quite," Kumar smiles. "I forgot to mention that the house is supposed to be haunted."

"I would choose a ghost over Amin Dada any day," John tells him seriously.

*　　　　　*　　　　　*

I telephone home to tell Ba that I will be late today, and go straight to meet Rehana. She is standing on the footpath just past the Odeon with her friend Jyoti, who greets me before walking away.

Jyoti provides a cover for Rehana. She calls on Rehana in the evenings and they leave together. Rehana's parents assume that the two friends are going for a walk by the lake, as they have regularly done for years. But now Jyoti accompanies Rehana up to the Odeon, where I pick up Rehana in my car and we then go and park in a remote spot, away from prying eyes. Most people walk by the lake shore near the pier. So we go and stop in the car park by the Owen Falls dam.

Today the car park is totally empty, except for a couple of cranes, which flutter their large wings noisily before flying to another corner of the space. Rehana and I exchange a long kiss before we hear another car pull in to a space not far from us. We then sit there, holding hands and talk.

I tell Rehana about John's problem and that we have only a short time together today, as Kumar and I have arranged to meet John later in the evening. Rehana squeezes my left hand with both of hers, then raises it to her lips and kisses it. She then holds my hand against her cheek as she says, "I am glad you are helping John. But please do not take any foolish chances." And kisses my hand again.

*   *   *

I tell my parents that I am going out to meet Kumar, which is true. It is dark when Kumar and I arrive at his uncle's house on Oboja Road. We open the door noiselessly and slip in. I go to the window to see if John is coming. The nearest streetlamp is about twenty metres away and a tree casts a giant shadow over the building. Behind the house there are more trees whose leaves rustle loudly in the blustery wind. A colony of fruit bats that live in their branches are flying around outside the house. I draw the curtains and we wait in silence.

Just after 8 p.m. there is a soft knock at the back door. Kumar unlatches the bolt and the two brothers walk in without a word. John carefully secures the door before he introduces his brother.

Patrick has the same lean features and long hair, just like John. And when he smiles, his eyes twinkle in an uncannily similar manner to John's. The only distinguishing feature is a mark from a healed wound under his left ear.

"Gosh," I exclaim as I shake hands with him.

Kumar gapes at Patrick. "Incredible. You didn't tell us,

83

John, that you were twins."

"We are not. I'm nearly two years older than him." John stands back to back with his brother, and straightens up, before announcing, "Also, I'm taller. See." He is barely an inch taller but is obviously proud of the fact.

While Kumar explains a few things about the house to Patrick, I try not to stare at the jagged pink scar under Patrick's ear. I suspect the wound wasn't caused by an accident.

As we are about to leave, Patrick asks if he can break the lock on the back door.

"You don't need to." Kumar is puzzled. "I have brought a set of spare keys for you."

"No, it is better if I break the lock." Patrick has obviously thought it through. "It would look as if I broke into the house. If the army happen to find me here, they wouldn't suspect you of aiding me."

He produces a large screwdriver and a hammer from his bag and knocks the lock out. He then chisels the wood around the lock so that it looks as if the door has been forced open from outside. Finally, he stands back so we can admire his handiwork.

"Very professional," Kumar says. "You'd make a good burglar."

"I am one." Patrick grins at him. "I've just broken into your house, under your very nose; but you don't know I have. Do you?"

We all laugh.

*　　　　　*　　　　　*

I have spent the night worrying about John's and Patrick's situation. And so obviously has Kumar. We both arrive at the office earlier than normal, but at the same time. We share our similar concern and reach the same conclusion.

We ask Kintu to tell John, when he arrives, to wait in my office, and drive to the bank. We come back with a little bag full of bank notes. Before we ask, Kintu informs us, "John is not in yet. That is not like him."

We look at each other. It is worrying. We go to my office, and sit in silence, waiting. Kumar drums his fingers on the table. Fortunately, we do not have to wait long. We hear John come in through the front door and greet Kintu in his cheerful voice. A moment later, John appears in the doorway.

"What's the matter, my friends?" he asks. "You look very serious."

I get up and close the door behind him and then come straight to the point. "We're worried about you and Patrick. We're worried about how closely you and your brother resemble each other."

"But I am taller, remember?"

"Being taller by an inch or so obviously means a lot to you," I say. "But do you think the army would care to check such a minor detail? We're afraid for your safety, not just Patrick's. Either they'll mistake you for Patrick or they'll arrest you anyway, simply because you are his brother."

It is obvious from the look on John's face that the possibility has not crossed his mind. But he needs no convincing. "Gosh, you are right, my friends," he says in a solemn voice.

"You better get away from here. Soon as you can. Today, if possible. You were planning to go to Tanzania eventually anyway."

"And take Patrick with you," Kumar says and hands him the bag of bank notes. "This is all we can raise at short notice but there's plenty to get both of you out of the country. The rest can go towards the cause."

"We're not trying to get rid of you," I assure him. "We've loved working with you and you are not just a colleague any more. You are a good friend. We'll miss you. But we'd rather miss you than see you dead."

"I know. I'll miss you too." He gazes at us and then shakes his head. "What can I say? Except, thank you so much, my dear friends." He puts an arm round each of our shoulders. "But Patrick can't go for a few weeks. Apart from needing his papers, he has to sort out a few things in the organisation."

"Okay!" I nod. "We'll give him more money when he's ready to go. Meanwhile, you should leave. Now. Here put this on." I reach in my drawer and pull out a cream-coloured baseball cap. "Any disguise is better than none."

I drive him to his house, where he packs a little case with a few belongings and we head for the bus station. A couple of hours later, he is on a bus on his way to Kisumu in Kenya. From there he plans to go by ferry to Mwanza, where the liberation army is being formed.

I return to the office enveloped in gloom. Kumar is sitting slumped in a chair in his office. I join him. We sit in silence for a while.

Then Kumar turns towards me and asks in a quiet voice, "Do you think we will ever see him again?"

I remain silent.

Chapter 20
Seven Days before Day Zero:
28th July 1972
Shashi's Journal: Last Day at School

I have often made a resolution that I will write my journal regularly - and regularly failed. Here is yet another attempt.

Last day of the term! Hurrah! Then no more school for a month. I know we have our 'O' Level exams in December but I can revise at home, especially in the afternoons, when it is too hot to venture outside.

As it is the last day, we have only the first four half hour lessons and then a break, followed by a cricket match between the staff and the students.

The first lesson is Gujarati with Mr Joshi and there is no chance of distracting him from serious work. He comes in with a book open in his hands. We stand up and say in unison, "Good Morning, Sir."

"*Beso.*" He uses Gujarati even when all he wants to say is 'sit down'. He avoids using English except if he is quoting from an English text, like today.

He holds up the book in his hand with the cover facing us. It is a thick hardbound edition of Kipling's work. The author's name is embossed on the front in large black writing.

"How many of you have heard of the writer? And can you name a book by him?"

A few hands go up, mine included. He looks at the front bench where the girls sit and asks Smita.

She scrambles to her feet and says, "Kim."

"Good." Mr. Joshi smiles. His black moustache curls up when he does that. "Kipling also wrote poetry. I am going to read just the first two lines from one of his well-known verses.

I am sure some of you know it." He puts the book down on the table. The book is only a visual prop for he knows many poems and long passages from books by heart. He walks to the window and stands with his back to it. The sun is behind him and his black carefully greased hair glistens in its rays. He clears his throat and in almost a singsong voice recites, "East is East and West is West. Who knows the next line?"

I put my hand up along with three others in the class. He looks at me and nods.

"Uganda is best," I say. The class roars with laughter. He is smiling, too. I quickly add in my defence, "I know it is *Home is best* but Uganda is our home."

"In Kipling's poem the next line is *And never the twain shall meet,*" he says. "What you referred to is a common saying, which goes, *East is East and West is West but home is best.* That is the line I was leading to anyway. It is our theme of the lesson today," he pauses and paces to and fro. "Home. And why is home best? Because of the memories associated with the carefree days of our lives when we are growing up. Many of these memories are precious, not because of the location but more due to the people associated with them."

He then asks if we remember any of the poems by the poet Kalapi. He has a pleasant voice and clear diction: *Queen's Gujarati,* one could say. He has us spellbound as he recites several poems in a singsong way, including the only one that I know well.

> *Jyan jyan thare najar mari*
> *Tyan tyan bhari yaadi tari*
> (Wherever rests my gaze
> There dwell memories of you)

"So," he says, "Your holiday assignment is to write about your home. Snippets that you would recall fondly when you

88

are old and narrate to your grandchildren. It does not have to be anything fancy but little things that form the mosaic of your life. Scratch beneath the surface of your mundane life to reveal hidden gems. Or let your imagination soar to create a fictional situation. Come on, give me an example."

A couple of hesitant hands go up. "Yes, Vinod."

"Playing marbles in the back alley with my friends," Vinod says, hoping to raise a laugh.

"Good," says Mr Joshi.

And then several more pupils volunteer their suggestions.

"Walking by the lake in the evenings."

"Spraying people with coloured dyes for the *holi* festival."

"My dog Poppy."

"Hundreds of people dancing in unison for the Navratri festival."

And so on. Mr Joshi responds to each of them with a smile and a nod or a compliment: 'That's good'. Or 'Yes, very good.'

Just before the bell goes, he says, "I would like you to write your essay using as pure Gujarati as possible, but don't go overboard like *Bhadram Bhadram*. You remember the story, don't you?"

We laugh at the memory of it. It is about a man who decides to use only unadulterated Gujarati and avoids the use of imported English words. So, he invents words. *Roshan pichkari* (light spray) for a torch; a radio becomes *akashwani* (speech from the sky); a train engine is translated as an *agnirath* (a fire chariot) and so on. It however becomes ridiculous, for example, when he starts calling a railway station an *agnirathviramsthansthala* (the place where the fire chariot stops for a rest).

Mr Joshi overruns on time slightly so that when he leaves, Mr. Nkole, who teaches us Physical Geography, is waiting outside the classroom. He is the only African teacher we have.

As it is the last day of the term, we do not fancy doing any written work. So, as soon as Mr. Nkole tells us to sit down, one of the boys puts his hand up and asks, "Sir, for the exam, the syllabus has not changed, has it?"

Mr Nkole looks a bit like Louis Armstrong and is endearingly jolly with an infectious laugh. But he does not find the syllabus funny. The very word gets Mr. Nkole going. "Yes, it is the same syllabus, I am afraid. A whole section with questions about Australia. And in Physical Geography do I teach you about the magnificent Rift Valley that runs through East Africa?" The question is rhetorical, and he pauses, waiting for a response. We shake our heads. He is pleased that we agree with him. "No! Many of you are not even aware that there is a branch of the Rift Valley that actually runs through Eastern Uganda. Instead, they ask us about where would you see Oxbow Lakes and I have to teach you to say 'near Alfriston in Sussex'. For heaven's sake! Alfriston! In Sussex! I ask you! How many of you are ever likely to go to this 'famous' place, Alfriston? It is because we still haven't updated the syllabus. And so we still teach you the same stuff pupils learnt in colonial times. The books we use are published in the UK and some of them have not even a single mention of Uganda."

Once started on his hobby horse, he continues talking for most of the lesson. So we get away with doing very little written work.

Our next lesson is History with Mr Nayyar. He is a slight man from South India but has a powerful voice. He sometimes talks loudly for part of the sentence and then suddenly drops his voice. The trick always works in capturing the class's attention. He tells us about the French

Revolution. I use the word tells and not teaches deliberately because he says afterwards, "By the way, this is not in your syllabus, so don't worry if you cannot remember the details. But I hope it gives you a wider picture."

He often does that, especially when he describes the injustice of colonialism and then tells us, "History is written by the victors and therefore is not always a true account. But remember that you are going to sit a Cambridge O Level exam and not a Kampala or a Calcutta O level. So when you answer a question in the exam, write the official version. How the colonies benefited from having leeches, oops, I mean the colonial powers ruling over them. And so on. But at the same time, have your mind open to the alternative version that I have just presented to you."

The last lesson is Physics with Mr. Awasthi. He arrives a few minutes late, holding his brown leather briefcase in his right hand. There is white chalk dust all over his case and over his jacket. He walks in and dumps the case on the table and waves his left arm up and down indicating we can sit down, but in doing so, he notices that he has put only his left arm in the jacket sleeve. The rest of the jacket flops behind him. With one impatient movement he pulls the jacket off and places it on the table on top of the blackboard rubber. We grin in amusement to see his jacket pick up even more chalk dust. He looks at the class and smiles his gentle smile.

Vinod asks a question that we all know is bound to get Mr. Awasthi going. "Sir, you told us that the sun is much bigger than it appears to our eyes. Is it as big as the whole continent of Africa?"

Mr. Awasthi raises his eyes heavenwards and sighs. "Let me try and impress upon your minds for one last time about how insignificant we are on a cosmic scale. The sun is not just bigger than Africa. It is larger than the whole world. And not just a bit bigger. You can fit a million earths inside the sun. You may then imagine that the sun is the biggest object in the universe. But not at all. It is only a medium-sized star. There are stars, Red Giants we call them, which can be hundreds of times larger than our sun."

Now that Sir's imagination is fired, we just sit back and enjoy the lesson without having to write anything down. "And our group of stars, The Milky Way, contains billions of stars. And there are billions of these galaxies."

At the end of the lesson, I tell Mr Awasthi that I find it all fascinating. He is very pleased. "It was worth it if I could fire the imagination of one lively mind," he says patting me on my back with his chalk dust-covered hands. "We human beings take our little kingdoms so seriously that it helps to have a wider perspective. When we realise that we are just a speck of dust on a cosmic scale, it creates a little humility and detachment from material possessions."

I enjoy almost all the subjects but some more than others. That means I am not sure what I will study when I go to UK. I doubt if I could do a course that includes Astrophysics and Gujarati Poetry.

After the lessons are over we watch the cricket match for a short while. I am disappointed not to be picked for the pupils' team. So I do not stay to the end of the game. When we leave for home, the teachers have lost five wickets for only forty-eight runs.

Chapter 21
Seven Days before Day Zero:
28th July
Ramesh: A Chat at the Amber Club

I manoeuvre my car into a tight parking space at the Amber Club. As I walk into the newly refurbished building, I notice some of my friends sitting round a table in the dappled shadow of the mango tree. I can hear their laughter and voices. I wave to them but go straight to the changing-room and a few minutes later emerge in my swimming trunks.

I pause by the edge of the pool before plunging into it. I savour the refreshing coolness of the water and swim several lengths without a pause. After a quick shower I join my friends for a drink.

Charles De'Souza greets me, "Long time, no see, Ramesh,"

"Been quite busy," I give my usual excuse.

"Now, let me guess. Could it be due to business meetings out of office hours with a colleague?" Dinesh pauses for effect before continuing. "A particularly good-looking female colleague? Just possibly?"

There is raucous laughter amidst the group.

I smile but make no comment. My love for Rehana is the most important concern in my life. She is in my dreams and in my thoughts from the moment I wake up to the time I go to bed. But I have not openly discussed our relationship with even my closest friends, except Kumar. Both Rehana and I are waiting for suitable opportunities to broach the subject with our parents before we announce it to the world.

Just then a waiter appears and we stop our discussion.

The waiter repeats the order, "Two Nile Lagers, two Tuskers and three Cokes."

"Also a Scotch on the rocks," Nikhil says as he pulls up a chair and joins us.

"Yes, Sir," and the waiter leaves.

"Just before you guys came we were talking about the laws which discriminate against Asians in the country." Dinesh explains to me. "Two of my uncles have recently moved to Jinja because their trading licences in Kaliro were not renewed. The Africans wouldn't buy their businesses because they know that my uncles would have to just abandon the shops. Why pay when you can have them for nothing?"

"I know of quite a few similar cases," Shiraz pipes up. "How can the government justify this law? We are now restricted to trading only in a handful of big towns, even though we are Ugandans. And why is that? Simply because we are not black. Amin criticises the apartheid system in South Africa but this is equally racist. What do you think, Ramesh? Tell us from a lawyer's point of view."

"It's perfectly justified under the law." I say in a matter-of fact voice.

There is a chorus of protests. "What? How can it possibly be?"

"It's simple. Amin's word is now the law. So," I spread my arms out to emphasise my point, "anything he decrees is the law of the land."

"This is the price we pay for having a dictator," Dinesh says in an animated voice. "I know that some of our people were actually pleased when Obote was overthrown. The mind boggles at the thought that they actually welcomed a ruthless dictator."

"You lot with your Western liberal attitudes forget that this is Uganda and not the UK," Nikhil asserts aggressively.

"Besides, a lot of the anti-Asian legislation was introduced by Obote. Amin is only following in his footsteps."

"I know Obote was also hostile towards the Asians. But not to the same extent, and he acted within the law. So there were restrictions on what he could do under the constitution," I point out. "But above all he was a lawfully elected leader. How could anyone in his or her right mind support a man who grabbed power in a military coup? A democratically elected government may make mistakes but at least they have the mandate of the people. Whereas under this regime, there is no point discussing if something is legal or not. The regime itself is illegal."

Nikhil thumps the table. "You lot criticise Amin but do you know him? I mean really know him. I bet none of you have ever met him socially. Go on. Have any of you?" He glares challengingly at all of us and then continues triumphantly, "No, I thought not. Well, I have. I have been to his palace on several occasions. He is not the monster you paint him to be. He is a normal man, like you and me. A family man. He plays with his kids, has a sense of humour and laughs readily."

"Hitler was nice to kids, they say," I retort, but then notice the waiter returning with drinks, and so change the subject by asking, "Are there any parties this week?"

Nikhil insists on drinks being charged to his account and then responds to my question. "I am planning a really groo... oovy party next week." He inclines his head towards the bar. Perched on stools sit two young black women in high-heeled shoes. Their body-hugging frocks are cut low to reveal generous cleavages. The hems of their dresses have crept halfway up their thighs. Nikhil points at them. "I have spoken to those girls and told them that they can bring their friends, too. They charge a reasonable amount. Pretty cheap, in fact.

I am thinking of holding the party at my hotel in Kampala so you need not worry about your families finding out about it. I can book rooms in the hotel for all. Just let me know how many of you can come."

We all decline the invitation. Only a couple of us bother to give an excuse.

"Oh, well, let me know if you change your mind." Nikhil shrugs and gets up. He walks up to the bar, sits on a stool between the girls and drapes his arms round their gleaming, bare shoulders.

*   *   *

In the evening, I eat dinner quietly before retiring to my room. I lie on my bed propped up by a pillow. I am thinking about the conversation with Nikhil when there is a gentle knock on the door. Shashi walks in.

"What's bothering you?" he asks. Nothing escapes his notice.

"What makes you think I am bothered?"

"It's not often I see you in a vacant or pensive mood,"

I smile, recognising the line from the Wordsworth poem, *Daffodils*, and respond, "I am thinking about daffodils."

Shashi laughs. I then tell him about Nikhil's opinion of Amin.

"You know what I do if I am worked up about something?" Shashi asks.

"I know. You write about it."

"You should try that. Best medicine, I assure you, and very fulfilling, too."

"Thank you, Wise Uncle. I think I will try. Why not?" I say and sit down at my desk, remove the dust cover from my typewriter and put a paper in it. Shashi goes back to his room.

A couple of hours later I enter Shashi's room, clutching a wad of papers. "I didn't think you would be asleep. Reading in bed, as I expected. Interested in listening to a bed-time story?"

Shashi grins and moves to make room for me to sit on his bed.

My Story: A Nice Man

Hannah woke up in the morning to the melodious calls of blackbirds. She felt light-hearted and realised with joy that her blinding headache had disappeared. As she got dressed, she hummed an old folk song from her childhood.

Just as she sat down for breakfast she heard the sound of a car pulling up outside her door. She knew from the engine's roar that it was Rudi's car. She put down her fork and knife neatly crossed on her plate, dabbed her lips with the blue flowery napkin, placed her hands primly on her lap and waited. As always, he knocked twice softly, followed by one short hard knock.

"Come in, Rudi," she called.

Rudi, handsome Rudi, in his smart officer's uniform, his khaki hat under his arm, stood silhouetted in the doorway against the morning sun.

As Hannah stood up, he rushed forward and hugged her. "Oh Mother, you're up and dressed and you look well. I'm so happy."

"Shouldn't you be at your office now?" She half chided him.

He bent down so she could kiss him on his cheek.

"I'm sorry I couldn't come yesterday. We had a very late meeting - it went on to midnight. So I'm stopping on my way to work."

"Well, you need not worry about me anymore. I am feeling fine now."

Just then Lucas, Rudi's chauffeur, appeared at the door, greeted Hannah, and placed a large box on the counter in the kitchen. He made a sharp about-turn and went out to the car to fetch the second box.

Hannah held Rudi's right hand in both of hers and raised it to her lips to kiss it. She felt tears gather behind her eyes. Her heart could break with mother's love. "Bless you, son. My pride and joy. I don't know what I would do without you. You are not just good to your own mother but to all the neighbours in the block, too," she added, referring to the second box that Lucas carried into the kitchen. "They all think I am so lucky to have a loving, caring son like you." She sniffled and picked up the blue napkin from the table to dab her eyes.

"Don't start being sentimental about it, mother. You know I'd do anything for you. And you have taught me from when I was this little," - he held his hand at knee level above the floor - "to love thy neighbour. These are hard times and it is our duty to help our fellow citizens. But I must rush now. Have a lot to attend to at the office today." He turned round at the door just as he was leaving. "I forgot to mention. There are some picture books for Marie's grandchildren. Give my love to all."

Hannah watched him walk briskly to his car. Lucas shut the passenger door after him, touched his cap at Hannah and climbed into the driver's seat.

In the car, Rudi asked Lucas about his father. Lucas dropped his usual formal tone and thanked Rudi profusely for his concern and conveyed his father's thanks for the food supplies Rudi had sent for him the previous week.

At the office, the doorman, Tim, rushed to open the door for Rudi. Tim felt greater loyalty towards Rudi than towards any of the other officers because Rudi had gone out of his way to find a hospital bed for his injured wife.

Rudi's secretary, Ingrid, stood up and greeted him with a big smile. It was no secret in the office that she was head over heels in love with her boss. She felt a deep ache inside her as she looked at his cleanly shaved slim face with a tiny black mole on his sharp jaw. She had to restrain the urge to caress the tiny wrinkles at the corner of his mouth as he smiled at her. She was sure that Rudi was aware of her feelings but she also knew that he would never do anything improper, as he was a happily married man, devoted to his wife and children.

"Could you please ask Michael to come and see me now?" he asked Ingrid with a gentle smile.

Like everyone else, who came in contact with Rudi, Michael was absolutely devoted to his boss. Having grown up in a household with dogs he was very fond of the creatures. He was with Rudi once when they saw a dog, which had been run over by a passing truck. Rudi had asked Lucas to stop the car in order to attend to the whining creature.

It was Michael's job to bring over a summary of the previous day's reports from all different camps to Rudi.

"Hmm." Rudi ruminated as he glanced at the summary. "I see yesterday's figure was only 4,365. Too low. Could you please send a memo to the camp commanders? Ask them to increase their efforts. I think 5,000 is the minimum we should aim for."

"Yes, Commandant Hoss," Michael replied.

"Otherwise, we will not be able to achieve the *Final Solution* by next year," Rudi observed. He then stood erect and stretched out his arm in front of him before adding, "Heil Hitler."

Chapter 22
5 Days before Day Zero:
Sunday 30th July 1972
Shashi: The Dark Side of Jinja

After reading Ramesh's story, I feel inspired to tackle my holiday assignment today - an essay about our hometown. But I am not sure of the approach I want to take.

It would be easy to describe the positive aspects of Jinja. We are fortunate to be living in such a lovely place. The equator passes barely fifty miles from us but our climate is equitable because Uganda is on a plateau, about four thousand feet above the sea level. So it is always pleasantly warm, neither too hot nor too cold. Green vegetation just springs up wherever there is space.

Many of my class mates will describe the beauty of the town, lying on the shore of Lake Victoria with its cavernous expanse of water and how the mighty Nile is born in Jinja and sets off on its journey all the way to Egypt.

There will be essays describing how by about six o'clock, almost all the businesses shut down, and in the balmy evenings Main Street swarms with people going for their evening stroll, some of them going only as far as the Post Office, but the majority continuing to walk round the DC ground, down Oboja Road to the Lake in order to witness the spectacular sunsets. They chat to friends on the way or sit by the Pier, the social hub of the town at dusk.

Some of my friends will write about the friendly community spirit with people of all religions living in harmony, and about the festivals when the whole community gathers and the town is like one big family. We all think it is the best town in this corner of the solar system.

After some deliberation, I think I might concentrate on the people of Jinja in my essay. I will be going to UK in a few months' time for further education, and for inspiration I ponder what images of the people I will carry in my head.

I close my eyes and various pictures of communal activities spring to my mind: large gatherings at weddings; people walking by the lake shore at sunset; crowds letting off fireworks on Main Street for Diwali; hundreds of people dancing in the temple for the Navratri festival; cheering fans at cricket matches at the Jinja Recreation Club ground; boys running around the town spraying each other with colour dyes when it is the Holi festival; mothers weeping as their darling daughters leave their family homes after weddings.

Several images of individuals stand out as well: little Chetna from our street, with her thumb in her mouth and her long blue blanket trailing behind her, half walking and half running as she tries to keep up with her mother, who walks fast in long strides; and talking of rapid strides, Mr. Aggarwal, our Maths Teacher, who walks round the lake on his own, because, we think, none of his friends can keep up with his brisk pace; the peanut vendor we all know as *Mlefu* (tall), because he is about six feet six inches tall, who is always outside the school during recess times and knows many of us by name, and who gives us peanuts on credit, and trusts us as he keeps no account (and I hasten to add that we always scrupulously pay him back); my friend Chitu knocking down mangoes from trees with accurate shots of stones; and another friend John De'Souza, who calls Papa *Guru*, because when he was collecting for RSPCA, Papa asked him if he was a vegetarian; when he said he wasn't, Papa queried his suitability for collecting for a charity which was trying to stop cruelty to animals; that made him think about it and he gave up eating meat (at least for a few months until his mother refused to cook separate meals for him); or his lovely sister Maria, who always gives me shy smiles but never says anything; and talking of lovely girls, Smita, who, well, she is lovely and in my class; and finally her brother, Chiman, whom we saw in the Coronation Park, a few days after his marriage, pushing his wife on the swing (meant for youngsters); and she laughing with such unrestrained delight that my friends and I, who were going to use the swings, felt as if we were intruding and instead ended up going to the other end of the park so as not to curb their exuberance.

I could easily conjure up any of these images or I could describe some of our neighbours and friends of the family, and I can think of many positive things to say about them. But I will record all that in my diary some time in future. I will not base my essay on them.

As far as the essay is concerned, I decide I will focus on a different angle. The dark side of Jinja.

A substantial majority of people live by the rules of a civilized society. There are a few men who drink, and I think possibly two or three of them, who drink heavily. There have been rare occurrences when they have been known to beat their wives in a drunken stupor. But the neighbours usually intervene and such cases are rare. Our society certainly frowns heavily upon such behaviour.

There is, however, a blot on our paradise. Money. Or to be more precise, Worship of Money. I know some people might accuse me of having been *corrupted* by Ramesh's socialist influence. Maybe so. But I do have my own mind and can think for myself. And I can see that our society values anyone who has been successful at making money. They show him enormous respect even if he is not a nice person, but then they may criticise him behind his back.

The Subedar family are a good example of this. I will describe them in my essay, though, of course, I will change their name.

Nikhil Subedar is an obnoxious young man, arrogant and unpleasant. He drives around in his black convertible Mercedes and has no time for you if you are not rich. He mixes only with fellow UK-returns. None of the other UK-returns act so superiorly. They usually wear their hair long and dress in the latest styles but are not arrogant with it. They are like Ramesh. Or Kumar. Nice guys. But not Nikhil. He is polite to me when I come across him, but then he knows that I am from a reasonably well-off family. Most of my friends think he is horrid.

A couple of times I have seen him with heavily made-up African girls in his car. They somehow do not look like your average black women. I once told Ramesh about it and he said that Nikhil had casually mentioned that this type of girls are cheap here and easy to find. Nikhil wanted to arrange a secret party with some of these girls. In a small town like Jinja, it would not be a secret for long. So he proposed to use his family's hotel in Kampala for the purpose, but none of his friends showed any interest.

The head of the Subedar family is Nikhil's father, Laljibhai. People try to avoid him. They say that just seeing his face first thing in the morning would ruin the rest of your day, possibly to such an extent that you may not even get your meal that day. And yet when they meet Laljibhai they are all smiley-smiley and welcoming. They go: *'Hello Sir, How are you?'* And *'Do sit down'* and *'Can I get you a drink, Laljibhai?'* The hypocrisy annoys me no end.

Laljibhai's wealth stems from a few cotton ginneries and even more importantly from his properties. I have heard that he probably owns about a hundred houses in the town. There are several stories circulating about Laljibhai as a ruthless landlord.

I have met him at a few social functions and he has always been civil to me. So, when I first heard the stories about him, I dismissed them as idle gossip until I actually witnessed one incident.

A few months ago, I was playing chess with Vinod in their family living-room. The doorbell rang and, as it was Vinod's move, I got up to answer the door.

It was Laljibhai at the door.

He marched past me into the hallway.

"Call Velji. I want a word with him."

I was shocked. You always address another adult with a suffix of *Bhai* (brother) or *Ben* (sister). Or as *Kaka* (uncle) or *Masi* (aunt) if they are older.

"Veljikaka is not here," I informed him. "I will get Maltimasi."

"Right," he said and marched into the living-room. He was dressed as usual in a grey striped three-piece suit with a silver shiny tie and a gold tiepin. A gold chain hung from a belt loop and ended in his trouser pocket. I have often wondered what is at the end of the chain. A key to his safe? A watch? A statuette of Jalaram bapa?

Maltimasi heard Laljibhai's voice and emerged straight away. She was flustered and repeatedly wiped her hands with the hand towel she carried with her.

"Do sit down, Laljibhai," she said.

I noticed that Vinod had moved his knight to check my King and threatened the Queen at the same time. I had completely overlooked that knight lurking behind his bishop. And now my chances were as good as finished.

Maltimasi turned round and called in the direction of the kitchen "Arre, o Sunita. We have a guest."

But Sunita, was already on her way, for she appeared a second later with a glass of water balanced on a circular tray. Laljibhai waved her away. "I just had some water. Where is Velji?"

Maltimasi looked at him anxiously. "He is at work. Another half an hour before he gets in."

"Tell him to come and see me. Today."

I noticed Maltimasi hesitating before saying, "Is it about the rent?"

"I do not discuss business matters with womenfolk. Just send him to me."

Maltimasi persevered. "We are poor folk but we always pay off our debts. He is still waiting to be paid for the last job. And we have had so many unexpected expenses this month. Sunita's not been well and the doctor's bills –"

Laljibhai who had been sitting there expressionless with his back totally straight and his hand stroking the material of the sofa, interrupted her, "All that is of no interest to me. The rent was due on the first and today it is the seventh. I have been patient. Tell Velji I must get the payment by tomorrow." As he stood up, he brushed against the chess board and knocked a few pieces off. He strode towards the door and turned round, one hand holding the door open. "I notice you have new sofas. You have money for sofas but not for your rent. Paying your rent is more important than wasting your money on furniture. Sell them, if you need to."

"We didn't buy them. We got them free from –" Maltimasi started to explain, but he cut her off.

"It's of no interest to me," he said and strode out.

I wanted to shout after him that Maltimasi was telling the

truth. These were our old sofas, which we gave to Vinod's family when we got new ones.

Maltimasi sank down on the sofa and sobbed. Vinod and Sunita sat on either side of her and put their arms round her to comfort her.

I felt like an intruder and went home. The chess game was ruined anyway.

I was dying to tell Papa and Ba about the incident but they were away in Kampala for a wedding. I told them soon after they got back around mid-morning the next day. Papa got up immediately and went to Veljikaka's house. I followed under the pretext of wanting to see Vinod.

Vinod looked sad and we sat in his room but we could hear snatches of conversation in the living-room.

Veljikaka spoke in a flat voice instead of his usual lively mode. "He is sending round bailiffs next week unless --"

"Why haven't you spoken to me about it?" Papa chided him. "That is false pride. We have known each other since our childhood days. Aren't I like your brother? ... Listen to me. It's not just you. You have the responsibility of your mother, wife and children. Don't worry about paying me back. Do it when and if you can ... I want you to go this afternoon and pay him off. No, not tomorrow. Today! So that tonight you and your family can sleep without any worries. And in future don't be too proud. It is foolish."

Two months later, I was at my cousin Nirmala's wedding. I noticed a few friends at the other end of the hall and just as I made my way towards them, I heard the unmistakable, high-pitched imperious tone of Laljibhai. I realised that he was talking to Ramesh. So I stopped to listen.

"This modern fashion of casual looking clothes that you youngsters wear is tasteless and makes you look like hippies, like members of the lower classes," Laljibhai said to Ramesh, who was dressed in a blue silken tunic and cream coloured trousers, while Laljibhai was in his usual three-piece grey suit with the gold chain trailing into his pocket.

Then he stood erect, drawing himself up to his full height of five feet and five inches, the top of his head just reaching up to Ramesh's shoulders, his brown pate shiny and his dark eyes contemptuous of others. "I have been to England many times and let me tell you: not everyone dresses like you. When Nikhil was there he always wore a suit and a tie, and so did all his friends. He even wore a bowler hat when he went to work in the City for a while. And look at you. You don't even wear a tie."

"But Kaka, what's so special about a tie?" I admired Ramesh for keeping cool in face of such imperious behaviour, still addressing the proud man as *uncle*, and answering with an easy smile. "You know how ties became popular in the west?"

"How?"

"A French prince had a sore throat and his physician put a bandage round it. The prince had to go to the court and thought the plain cloth wrapped round his neck made him look dowdy. So, he tied a colourful cloth over the bandage to mask it and added a flourishing touch by letting the ends of the cloth hang loose.

Next day all the courtiers appeared at the court with fabrics of various colours and patterns tied round their necks.

'Have you all caught a sore throat from me?' the Prince wanted to know but then realised that the courtiers had mistaken his colourful bandage as a fashion statement."

"You just made that story up," Laljibhai said dismissively.

"And it is not just the clothes. Look at your hair. You UK-returns keep your hair so long. Have you ever examined yourself in a mirror? You look like the Beatles. It is disgusting."

"And what have you got against long hair, Kaka?" Ramesh shook his wavy tresses and smiled. Ramesh should have replied *you are jealous because you are practically bald*.

"Having your hair so long shows you have forgotten our culture. You are blindly copying the West." Laljibhai said triumphantly and pushed his thumbs into his waistcoat pockets.

I wanted to say, *You stand here in this tropical heat wearing a three-piece Western suit, and accuse my brother of forgetting our culture. You have a nerve.*

I thought Ramesh would show some irritation but he was totally cool and composed. He smiled broadly, "But Kaka, Krishna is shown with shoulder-length hair in all his images. Lord Rama is also always portrayed with long hair. We have just one picture of my grandfather and his hair is as long as mine. I am sure your father and ancestors wore their hair long, too. And look at our priest in the temple. He has shoulder-length hair. Much longer than mine. Shall I tell you how the short hair style became popular?"

By now a group of listeners had gathered around, mostly young men but there were also some older men, including Papa. Laljibhai was shifting on his feet as if he wanted to walk away but a couple of older men said, "Yes, do tell us."

Ramesh was obviously now enjoying the encounter and he held Laljibhai's gaze. "Well, during the First World War the soldiers spent a long time in trenches. It was difficult to keep their hair clean. To stop getting lice, they started cutting their hair short. Since serving in the war was like a badge of honour, even civilians started copying them. And so it became the fashion. I suppose you were only a child during the First War."

Laljibhai looked around and then waved to someone - I am sure it was an imaginary friend. He thrust his thumbs in the pockets of his waistcoat and excused himself. He then pushed past the small crowd surrounding him.

Ramesh just turned round and started talking to his friends nonchalantly. If I were him, I would have shouted *yippee* and jumped for joy. I nearly did anyway.

Chapter 23
5 Days before Day Zero:
Sunday 30th July
Lalita: A Calamity

I am always the first one to get up in the house, as I like to finish my prayers and meditation before anyone else is up.

Today it is Sunday, but I get up at my usual time of about six in the morning. No-one else is up. I switch on the hot water and go back and lie down on my bed, reading. The water is fairly hot in about half an hour and I have a bath. When I am ready, I go to pray at the shrine in the smaller living-room.

After my prayers, I go to the kitchen, and find Savitabhabhi is already there. Despite it being Sunday, she is out of bed early, as we are going to help cook for a large wedding. We prepare breakfast for the family and leave it covered up in the kitchen before heading for the community hall.

Bhabhi drives slowly and carefully, not being a regular driver.

"I like these old traditions," she says.

"What traditions?"

"You know. People going to help prepare a communal feast for weddings, especially medium or large ones with a thousand or more guests. Pity the tradition is not so common anymore."

I can think of an explanation. "Well, maybe that is because when you come to help, you still need to go back home again to change for the reception. And if you live far, it's difficult without a car."

"What a wise sister-in-law I have!" Bhabhi teases me. "However, I still think it's nice when the members of the community co-operate. It helps create a closely-knit society."

"And a community spirit," I agree.

"And I'll tell you what binds the society. Gossip. Pure gossip. When information is shared, people feel closer."

"I see you are here just for the gossip." It is my turn to tease Bhabhi now.

There are plenty of parking spaces in the car park. A couple of men are tying garlands of mango-leaves across the doors of the hall, the age-old custom of welcoming wedding guests.

As we approach the hall, we hear loud voices and hearty laughter. A group of women, most of whom are Bhabhi's friends, and who I also know, are sitting round a wooden table outside the entrance to the hall, enjoying the warmth of the early morning sun. They greet us and shift a little to make room for us. Bhabhi reaches into a bag she is carrying, produces our rolling pins, and we join the others in the communal task of rolling *puri*.

One of the women plucks some dough from the large mound in front of her, and moulds it into round balls, *goynas*, which she then places into a large stainless steel bowl in the centre of the table. The rest of us reach into the bowl, pick up a *goyna* and roll it into a *puri*, effortlessly producing perfectly round shapes, honed by years of practice. We place the *puris* in large flat trays in front of us. When a tray is nearly full, it is replaced by an empty one by Ali, an elderly African man, who has been an assistant to the chef, Karsanji*maraj*, for many years, He takes the rolled puri to the chef who deep-fries them in the huge frying pans.

"Have you heard Jayaben's good news, yet?" Kantaben, whose purple sari glows in the sun, asks Bhabhi.

"No. What have you been hiding from me Jayaben?" Bhabhi reaches and puts another rolled puri in the tray.

Jayaben beams. "Well, we are planning a *filling the lap* ceremony for my daughter-in-law, Usha."

"Really? That's great news. When? And why have you kept it a secret from us?"

"Oh, it's just three months now."

"That's all right, then." Bhabhi nods in understanding, for it is the accepted practice that a pregnancy is not announced until after the third month.

"With God's blessing everything should be all right now," Jayaben says smiling.

"And you will be a *Dadima* (grandmother)," Bhabhi tells her.

"I can hardly wait now. It's all due to God's grace." Jayaben dabs her eyes with the corner of her sari.

Some of the other women, who already have grandchildren, now join in. One of them tells Bhabhi, "You better find a bride for your Ramesh soon. Then you can look forward to being a granny, too." She then retracts it quickly by adding, "But of course it's all in God's hands. We mere mortals cannot plan these things."

"I pray to God," Bhabhi says, folding her hands together in a praying gesture. "But today's generation is so fussy. Especially *UK-returns*. You know, we have shown our Ramesh a few girls. Beautiful, well-educated girls. He said he would think about it. And now he even refuses to go and see any other girl. I tell him, *You have to decide quickly. The best girls will be snapped up by other families*. You know Bhimjibhai's son Mukesh recently got engaged to a girl from Mombasa. Well, she was originally supposed to see my Ramesh. But, I don't know what came over him at the last minute. He refused to go to Kampala, where we had arranged the interview for him. Ask Lalita here if you don't believe me. Tell them what he told you?"

I sit there with my gaze lowered and make no comment.

"Go on," Bhabhi insists. "Tell them what he told you."

I say in a quiet voice, "He says he is not ready to see girls at the moment."

There is a hush. I sense awkwardness amongst some of the women. A couple of them exchange meaningful glances and in the end Kantaben addresses Bhabhi in a heavy voice, "Listen Savitaben. You're like my sister, so I'm telling you this. Ramesh is seeing some Muslim girl. They are discreet, but you cannot hide the truth for long. The whole town will soon be talking about it."

It is as if Bhabhi has been struck by a thunderbolt. She almost reels from the news but quickly recovers. "What kind of a tale are you telling me?" she responds.

"We have seen them in a car together." A couple of other women corroborate the statement.

Wanting to save her son's reputation, Bhabhi offers an explanation, "Ah, I believe that could be this new woman lawyer who has joined their practice."

"It is. She's our neighbour Yusufbhai's daughter Rehana," Kamlaben says.

Bhabhi is shocked at the news but tries not to show it in her voice. "Ramesh probably just gives her a lift to work."

"I am afraid it doesn't look like just a business relationship," one of the other women says. "They've been seen together a few times in the evenings after work. Near the lake."

"It can't be." Bhabhi tries to sound confident but her voice lacks conviction. She turns towards me. "Do you know anything about this?"

I have dreaded this moment. I have urged Ramesh to

inform his parents about his relationship with Rehana, but he has prevaricated. Last time I spoke to him about it, I told him that I will not tell a lie if I am asked the question outright, like now. But I certainly do not want to announce it in front of all these other women. So I keep my eyes down and finish rolling the last of the *puris*. I am saved from answering the question because just then some of the women at the other end of the table get up, and go to the taps to wash their hands before heading home to change for the wedding reception.

Bhabhi and I do not exchange a single word as we drive home.

"I am going to get dressed now," I say as soon as we arrive home. I get out of the car and head for my room.

A few minutes later as I head for the bathroom, I notice that Bhabhi is in the small living-room sitting in front of the shrine. I have seen her pray only on rare occasions.

I go to my room and sit at my dressing table, with my elbows on the table, and rest my face on both my hands. I look blankly in the mirror. A few minutes later there is a gentle knock on my door and Bhabhi enters the room. She looks troubled but determined.

I pick up my comb and start to run it through my hair. Bhabhi stands behind me and catches my eye in the mirror. She holds out her hand and I place the comb in her hand. She starts combing my hair.

In her agitated state of mind, she combs my hair with short sharp strokes. She only becomes aware of it because at one point, when it is painful, I take a sharp intake of breath.

Bhabhi hands the comb back to me. She sighs and meets my eyes in the mirror.

"It's true, isn't it? What Kantaben said. And you knew it." She holds my gaze. "Why didn't you tell me?"

I turn around, hold both of Bhabhi's hands and say to her,

"I promised not to say anything until Ramesh had spoken to you. I can't tell you how I have dreaded this day. I did urge him to speak to you and Motabhai but he keeps putting it off."

"Didn't you point out the error of his ways? As an aunt and a friend?" she chides me.

"I tried to, but ..."

"Yes, yes I know he is a headstrong boy. He is going to be the death of me."

"You must not say that." I lean forward and hug Bhabhi.

We sit there for a few brief moments before Bhabhi breaks the silence. "Well, we must all talk to him. Point out the error of his ways. He's out now but tonight his father will speak to him, and we will also add our weight to it. He is bound to see that it just cannot happen. And I hope the poor girl's reputation is not ruined forever. I never thought this could happen in our family. How can I face the society?"

I make no reply.

*　　　　　　　*　　　　　　　*

It is just after midday now and we are at the wedding. Bhabhi and I are sitting on chairs facing the *mandap*. Many women are sitting on mats spread out on the floor in front of us. We do not join them in singing the nuptial songs. I glance at Bhabhi every now and again, but she sits there staring in front of her most of the time. She is enveloped in a thick gloom.

It is an average sized reception with about seven hundred guests but we do not mingle with any of them.

After the ceremony and before the lunch is served, Kantaben joins us. She holds Bhabhi's right hand in both of hers and gently presses it. "Look, I am sorry, but as a friend I thought it was my duty to tell you. Much better you hear it from me than from someone else."

"Yes, I agree." Bhabhi says. Her voice is almost cracking as she tries to fight back tears. "I just can't believe it. How could he do that to us?"

"He is a good boy. He will do what you and Devjibhai tell him," Kantaben tries to comfort her. "It's his youth. They see these love stories in cinemas and get carried away. Their folly needs to be pointed out to them by respected adults to guide them back on to the right track."

"Ramesh is such a headstrong boy, I just hope ..." Bhabhi leaves the sentence trailing.

Kantaben continues to soothe her with more hope. "You remember what happened to Vajiben's Chandu. *Either I marry this girl or I will remain a bachelor all my life*, he told his parents. Vajiben told him, *"We are Vaniyas, and she is a Vanza girl. How could you even consider marrying her?"* Her *father is a good builder, in fact, one of the best in town, but they are a different community*. And look at them. In the end, Chandu listened to the voice of reason. You surely remember the incident?"

Bhabhi nods. I am sure she remembers the mini-scandal. "I know he is the one who runs his father's jewellery shop near the bus station. Didn't he marry that girl from Nairobi?"

"Yes, that's the one," Kantaben confirms. "They now have two children. And the girl he wanted to marry is well settled in a family from her own community in Kampala. I am sure your Ramesh will also follow the right path in the end."

Bhabhi still looks worried. "At least Chandu wanted to marry a Hindu girl. But Ramesh has to be difficult. It is because of *your brother* - you know what he is like." Bhabhi follows the old tradition of referring to one's husband as *your brother* or *he*, and not mention his name in front of others.

I know that when they applied for British passports and the official asked her husband's name, she did actually say it. She later told me that she voiced it in an almost inaudible whisper. She felt so embarrassed that she blushed as if she had been seen kissing or caressing her husband in public.

"*Your brother*," Bhabhi continues, "often says all human beings are equal and that we should dissolve the barriers of castes and communities. I am sure all that talk has given my boy these lofty ideas. I have often told him 'don't voice this sort of views in front of the boys'. And he says, 'Why not? We should instil right values in our boys.' And now look what has happened. His irresponsible talk has come home to roost."

Just then some other friends join us, and the talk turns to other topics. Bhabhi says little. She sits looking around at the milling crowd, people standing or sitting around in groups, and then moving on to join other groups. The air is filled with cheerful voices of people greeting each other and talking in excited voices. There is a lot of laughter and jolly camaraderie. I can see some of my friends near the stage, but I do not go and join them as I feel Bhabhi needs my support today.

Bhabhi is now staring at the group of young men and women near the stage. "Look," she says, "Ramesh is there. I may be biased, but who can deny he is dashingly handsome." I look at my slim and fair-skinned nephew, and reply, "I fully agree." Bhabhi then refers to a couple of girls in the group, looking pretty and elegant in their colourful saris and all their wedding party finery. She says, "Why can't he choose one of them?"

Just then Kantaben rejoins us and follows Bhabhi's gaze and her thoughts. "Your Ramesh could get any girl he wants, so handsome," she says.

Bhabhi sighs, "Whatever God wills."

Suddenly Kantaben grabs her elbow and says in a whisper, "Look who has come in. Rehana." Friends from other communities are often invited to the large wedding gatherings, so it is not surprising to see her here.

"Which one?" Bhabhi asks for confirmation.

"The pretty one in the blue Punjabi dress."

Neither Bhabhi nor I have seen Rehana before. She is a striking-looking girl and I can't help saying, "She is gorgeous."

Bhabhi says rather grudgingly, "Yes, she is beautiful." Then she adds, "But there are many beautiful girls in our community, too. Why does Ramesh have to look outside the community?"

Chapter 24
Five Days before Day Zero:
Sunday 30th July
Devji: Social Changes

While waiting for Ramesh, I have been thinking: *This is life. Ups and downs. Smooth sailing and rough seas. But one has to maintain one's equilibrium.* I renew my resolution to deal with this calamity in a calm manner, not to lose my temper or demand my own way, as I have heard happens in many families. I also realise that secretly I have been cherishing a hope - a delusion perhaps? - that he might just say that it is only a rumour or that he has changed his mind.

I have half rehearsed an argument in my mind, one that would uphold the broad-minded upbringing we have given to the boys, and at the same time indicate the folly of such an extreme action.

Ramesh walks into the living-room and sits on the sofa facing me. He looks tense but composed.

Without any preliminaries I ask him if it is true that he is hoping to marry a Muslim girl. He nods and all my good resolutions suddenly vanish. I say in a loud stern voice, "This is madness. You just cannot do that."

He makes no reply. He is focussing on the wooden giraffe figure behind me and is avoiding my eye. It brings back memories of him as a child stubbornly refusing to budge when he had set his mind on something. My outburst seems to have disturbed Savita more than him. She gently presses my hand. It has the desired effect.

More calmly, I say, "Look, Ramesh. We are worried. Deeply worried that you do not realise the serious nature of the step you are proposing to take. We are your parents and cannot just sit back and let you go down the disastrous path of marrying this girl."

"She is called Rehana," he points out.

"Never mind her name. If you marry her, you will ruin your life. Our society will never accept it."

He raises his chin defiantly. "It is my life. They have no right to dictate how I live it."

I can visualise the scene after he leaves. Savita will turn to me and blame me. "I have always told you that you are spoiling the boys. Always encouraging them to talk freely. And to think freely. And now look what has happened. They have become too *azaad*. (Unrestrained.) We have lost our son."

I try to reason with him. "Listen, you are not in the UK any more. We do not live in an individualistic Western society with its nuclear families. I can't help feeling that you do not realise the gravity of the course of action you intend to follow. You would be a pariah in your own society and the girl in hers."

"I - we are aware of that. The chances of us being accepted will be further diminished if our own families do not stand by us."

"But how can we willingly let you embark upon a relationship that is bound to fail?" I ask him.

"Why do you assume that?"

"For a marriage to be successful, it is important for both people to have similar backgrounds, values and aspirations."

"Rehana is from a middle-class background and -"

"You know very well what I mean. She is Muslim."

He looks me full in the eye. "You have always taught us that all human beings are equal." His tone is measured as if he has been preparing his case in his mind. "Did you mean they are only equal as long as they are Hindu? And what you have been advocating all along under the banner of universal brotherhood - has it been about uniting all the Hindus but not others?"

It suddenly dawns upon me that I am arguing a case against my lawyer son. And I have often remarked that he has learnt many of his techniques working with me and observing me in court.

"No certainly not. Each community has different values and views on how life should be lived. And the couple must share their ideals and aspirations."

"And it is not as if there are no conflicts amongst couples who are from the same community." I notice his tact in not raising the failed marriage of Lalita. "Rehana and I have similar views on most world issues."

Love is blind, they say. He cannot possibly have thought this through. Wisdom, or some of it, comes with experience. "Oh, of course that is important. You may share your socialist ideals. But conflicts are more likely to arise from relatively mundane issues. Everyday concerns like food, for example. Would she not want to eat meat when she lives with us? And would she not expect to cook it in our kitchen? And feed it to children, when you have them?"

"She has become a vegetarian now. And we have agreed that we will bring up our children as vegetarians."

I notice Savita dab her eyes with the end of her sari.

I look at Ramesh and although we are arguing, I cannot help but feel proud of him. He has grown up into this fine-looking young man, wavy black hair, wide dark eyes, thoughtful and playful at the same time, a ready smile on his handsome face, and so mature. And calmly arguing his case in a logical intelligent way. Is this not what I had wished him to be all the time?

I become aware of Savita as she reaches to the side table for her handkerchief, presumably to wipe her tears. I look at her and realise that she shares the same mixture of feelings of pride and frustration. And love and concern.

I feel my opposition to the marriage has now dissolved into a gut feeling only. I know there is not any rationally justifiable opposition that I can attempt. I try a more amenable track.

"Look, Ramesh, I can see that you have carefully considered this relationship but even if we accept it, our society will not. And whether we like it or not, we have to live in society." I look towards Savita for her support and she nods almost imperceptibly.

"Society, as you have always said, needs to unite people not divide them."

"But the step you intend to take - it is too revolutionary and our people are just not ready for it."

"And how does society change?" he leans forward and holds my gaze.

"What do you mean?" I can see what he is leading towards but I do not want to be the one to say it.

"I mean what is the mechanism of its change? It changes because someone challenges the taboos. When several people break the convention it suddenly becomes acceptable to society, which is just a fluid structure. It has great inertia but it is not set in stone."

"But why should it be you who challenges it?" I say it and almost bite my tongue.

"Oh, Papa, I have no illusions. I am doing it for my happiness and if my action nudges society towards being more tolerant, that is a bonus." And then he adds in a soft voice, "Surely, you can see that I would be miserable if I do not marry Rehana. And in that case I can't imagine you or Ba being happy."

"Look, even if your mother and I accept it, I am not sure about our extended family." My reasons now sound increasingly feeble.

"They will follow your lead, I am sure."

"Have you thought about the future? What about the children?" I glance at Savita and know that I am voicing our joint feelings. "Would they be brought up as Muslim or Hindu?"

Ramesh now looks more relaxed, he realises that he has overcome most of our objections. "Surely, you are not worried about that, when you are not religious yourself."

"I am not talking about all the Muslims but there are some who are over-zealous about their religion." I know this stems from ingrained prejudices but I state it anyway.

"Rehana is like me - not very religious."

"How will she bring up the children? Will they go to a mosque? Or will she take them to a temple?"

"Like you took me to the temple? Since when has going to a temple become an important issue to you?"

"Well, you know that many Hindus say their prayers at home. So would you bring them up as Hindus or Muslims?" I persist.

"Neither. We intend to bring them up as good kind human beings, who are broad-minded and tolerant."

I feel there are no more objections I could raise against the proposed marriage.

"I am still a bit apprehensive about the step you are proposing to take. All I can add is, do not rush into anything. Think twice before you commit yourself."

I look at Savita, who now speaks up. "Even if you have accepted his decision, how am I going to show my face to the world? I would be too ashamed to set foot outside the house."

"There is nothing to be ashamed about, Ba. I would have taken an unusual step but not a disgraceful one."

I lend my support to Ramesh. "The society is changing all the time. Think of how different our customs are now as compared to when we were young in India. In those days the boy and the girl sometimes did not even see their prospective partners before marriage."

"I know," Savita says. "But this is a big leap, a Hindu - Muslim marriage."

Ramesh and I try to convince Savita that the greatest obstruction will be if the society perceives Ramesh's action as a defiance of his parent's wishes. If they see us accepting his decision then there will be few objections, even if they do not exactly approve of it. It does not require much convincing. The thought of her son's happiness is paramount in her mind.

"I saw her at the wedding," she says with a smile. "What a beautiful girl. Like a *fillum* star."

Chapter 25
Four Days before Day Zero:
31st July 1972
Shashi: Religion

I go to the living-room to watch television. Papa is sitting in his favourite chair reading a letter. He pushes his reading glasses up on his forehead and turns to me. That is Papa's *Let's have a talk* mode. So instead of switching on the TV, I take the seat by the window.

"I am sure you are aware of what's happening. About Ramesh, I mean," he says. He assumes the answer is yes from my expression. "What do you think?"

"I don't know." I am not sure why he is asking me, so I am non-committal.

He looks me in the eye. "You know he is thinking of marrying a Muslim girl, don't you?"

I nod.

"I just wondered how you feel about it?"

"It's not for me to approve. Or disapprove."

"Oh, I agree," he nods. "I do not want you to misunderstand my initial opposition to it. That certainly was not just because she is not Hindu. We do not discriminate against anyone on the grounds of race or religion."

"Yes, you have often told us that."

"Britain ruled India by using a Divide and Rule principle. So, when I was a student, I often went on independence marches with a banner saying "Hindu Muslim *Bhai Bhai*" (brothers). I truly believe that we are brothers." Yet another one of Papa's favourite stories "It wasn't just a slogan. We just worship God in different ways. That's all. So my opposition had nothing to do with her religion."

"If it wasn't religion then what was it?" I am still trying to understand what his main objection to the match was.

"It was because different faiths have different customs and attitudes. And that could lead to conflicts later."

"But Rehana has become a vegetarian."

Papa smiles. He guesses that not only do I know that there has been an argument about Ramesh wanting to marry a Muslim girl, but that I have eavesdropped on it.

"Yes. That shows great commitment." He pauses and seems to be considering how to phrase what he is going to say next. "You must know that I never try to impose my belief or lack of it onto others. Conflict often arises because many people believe that theirs is the only true religion. And that their Holy Book is the Word of God. That makes anyone following a different religion an apostate."

"Isn't it common to all religions?" I ask.

There is a long pause. I look out of the window and notice dark clouds on the horizon, and wonder if we will have one of those spectacular tropical storms. I love watching their ferocious play.

Papa clears his throat. "I agree," he says. "But there is a relatively small number of fanatics amongst Hindus. Hindus accept other religions more easily. Even in the *Gita*, Krishna refers to yoga, which simply means one's union with the divine. He says that there are many ways of achieving that union and describes *Jnana, Karma* and *Bhakti* yoga. The paths of knowledge, action and devotion. No path is superior. One follows the path that suits one's temperament. Which is why there are so many branches of Hinduism. We think of Buddhism as just another offshoot of the religion, although some Buddhists may disagree. And the same applies to Jainism. Also, there is yet another branch of Hindu school of thought called Sankhya, which is actually atheist in its beliefs." He then adds with a smile, "So, it appears what I am saying is that only Hinduism tells us that it does not matter how one meets one's spiritual needs or how one worships the Creator - or Nature for that matter. In other words, all religions are the same. Hinduism teaches us that no religion is superior to others, which, one could say, makes Hinduism superior."

We both laugh at the paradox. Just then Ba walks into the room. "What's so funny?" she says.

"Religion," Papa replies. And then tells Ba what he told me.

"Ha," she says. "It is like being proud of one's modesty."

Part 2: Day of the Announcement

Chapter 26
Day Zero:
4th August 1972
Rehana: Women's Lot

"It's harder for us women," I sigh. "Much harder." I am sitting in a car with Ramesh in the small parking space overlooking the Owen Falls dam. The young river Nile, barely a couple of miles old, furiously dives through the open sluices in the dam with a deep roar, whilst the bulk of it goes through the turbines to produce most of Uganda's electric power. I watch a group of large storks that is scurrying around searching for food in the grass field near the car park. Another involuntary sigh escapes my lips.

Ramesh takes my hands in his and gently presses them. "I know, my love. I can't bear to think of you facing your family alone. If only I could talk to them."

"I wish you could, but it will only make the situation worse. I must talk to them when I get home, before they hear from others." I am filled with dread at the prospect of revealing my relationship with Ramesh to my parents. But I have steeled myself to facing the task tonight. "I know that Abba will go absolutely mad. Amma will oppose it but can be reasoned with, a bit like your parents."

"I know I have been lucky. My parents have been so very understanding."

Ramesh also dreaded the task and was ever so relieved when his parents accepted his decision with relative ease.

"Yes, they have been great." I agree. "But I can't help wondering if your parents would have agreed so easily, had it been their *daughter* wanting to marry a man from a different religion. It's OK for a man. He can break traditions and get away with it. But if a woman does, it is as if the very foundation of the civilization is being threatened. What is it that makes men see red if a woman challenges conventions?"

Ramesh comes out with an explanation straight away, as if he has been thinking about it too. "Could it be that the women are more self-sacrificing and therefore not expected to challenge the conventions? They are also more likely to adapt to the new community without causing waves."

"Or is it because women are almost treated as the chattel or property of the men?"

"I am willing to be your property anytime." Ramesh declares with mock solemnity.

I smile. "Ha. I will remind you of that one day."

*   *   *

In the evening, after supper Amma and I tidy up the kitchen, leaving the rest of the clearing for our servant, Musa. Just as we finish, I say, "Amma, I need to talk to you and Abba."

Amma carefully hangs the towel with which she is drying her hands, takes a deep breath as she turns to face me and says in a resigned voice, "It is about a boy, isn't it?"

She knows it already, I tell myself. I nod.

"It's the young man, the lawyer, you work with, isn't it?" She needs no answer. "I've been worried sick ever since someone told me. I've been telling myself that maybe it's just a rumour. When I heard it, you had already stopped eating meat, and I thought perhaps it was just a coincidence. I didn't want to look at the evidence in the face. A Hindu boy." She takes a deep breath. "Look, you know very well that it is just not possible. And what about Hussein? Have you forgotten that we have promised your hand in marriage to him?"

"Amma, please try to understand. I love Ramesh and I can't

131

imagine my life without him." I make no attempt to wipe the tears that now trickle down my cheeks. The last time Amma saw me cry was at the airport, when I had just come back from England. But those were tears of happiness when Amma and I had cried together in a joy-felt embrace.

I can see Amma is trying to hold back her own tears as she carries on. "The best thing is to resign from your job and go away for a while to get this boy out of your mind. I will explain to Abba that you need to travel a bit before you settle down. Go and visit relations in Kenya, Zanzibar, Mumbai, Karachi, anywhere. Even London. Or how about Canada? You said you wanted to visit Shokat Uncle in Toronto." Amma pleads. "Just forget this boy. You know how it will upset your Abba. He will not allow it. My daughter, please do this favour for me."

"Amma, I would rather die." I sob. "Oh, Amma, please help me. I feel so miserable."

Amma strokes my hair and then hugs me. We stand embracing in the middle of the kitchen when Abba walks in, pauses and says, "What's the matter with you two?"

Amma motions to Abba to follow us as she leads me to the living-room. I am dry-eyed by now. I sit next to Amma, facing Abba. After a brief hesitation, Amma breaks the news gently to Abba or at least as gently as one could with information like this.

Abba sits in silence staring into space for a while. Almost as if he has not heard what Amma just said. He then shakes his head in disbelief. "A Hindu boy?"

I nod.

"You wicked girl! Have you no sense?" Abba shouts as he stands up, his palm up to his shoulder level ready to strike me. But Amma springs to her feet and blocks his path.

"No, *Mere Jaan!* Stop!" Amma's voice is firm and commanding. I have never heard her use that tone with Abba or to address him as *Mere Jaan* (My Soul) before. I guess she uses it in private. She holds up her forefinger and shakes her head almost imperceptibly. It is obvious that after years of marriage Abba knows how to interpret these small signals. And the slight gestures speak volumes. He restrains himself.

"I will not permit it." He sits down with his elbows on his knees and hands on his head. When he looks up, anguish and anger intermingle in his eyes. "We should have never sent you to a university in UK or given you all this freedom. You have taken advantage of it. I can see I was wrong. Uncle Mehboob told me years ago that we should have gone ahead with your marriage to Hussein. But I foolishly supported you. *We do not live in the middle ages anymore*, I told him. *Rehana is a bright girl. Let her develop her talents. And they are both young. They can marry after she gets her degree.* And when you came back and said you wanted to work for a while to familiarise yourself with the local law, once again I supported you and asked Mehboob to wait. And now you are paying us back with a poison chalice. Did we feed you and bring you up, not realising that it is a snake we are rearing? Did we teach you about our culture and religion for you to cast it all aside when it does not suit you? I should have known something was up when you suddenly stopped eating meat. Oh, I have been blind. So blind."

I go and kneel next to Abba, take his right hand in both of mine and hold it against my cheek. "Abba, can't you see, nothing has changed. I am still your daughter. And I am so thankful that you gave me the opportunity to study and to get qualifications. Wanting to marry a man I love is not a sin. Please, Abba, give us your blessings." I had never imagined I

133

would one day have the courage to talk to Abba so openly about a relationship with a man.

Abba makes no attempt to withdraw his hand but his tone does not soften, "Aren't you ashamed, talking about love to your own father? This is not England. You yourself do not find someone to love and marry. You are too young to judge characters. It is the elders in your family who make those decisions. They have the experience and they are only thinking of your happiness and your future. You will marry Hussein and there will be no more of this nonsense. I just hope the news of your entanglement does not reach Hussein, for then it will be he who will decide to call it off, and who could blame him for it?"

"Abba, it is not Hussein I wish to marry."

"But you two get on so well. I remember it so clearly how Mehboob and I watched you two in this very room. You had set up a little camp together in that corner and were playing ever so happily together when Mehboob looked at me and said, *'Brother, you know what?'* And I had said *'I know exactly what you are thinking. They are meant for each other.'* And we had agreed there and then that you two would marry."

"We were only kids and playing together like kids do." I cannot remember the occasion but I remember another time when I wanted Hussein to play at being ill, so I could pretend to be his mother and offer him medicine. Instead, he wanted me to be an enemy soldier whom he would defeat in a battle, and take as a prisoner.

Abba elaborates further. "Hussein is a fine boy, handsome, with an Economics degree from a British university and a good job. You should count yourself lucky. And anyway what's wrong with him?"

"Nothing. It's just that I think of him more as a brother - he is my first cousin after all."

Abba's anger has not subsided. He says in a firm tone, as if trying to muster all the authority of the head of the family into it, "You are such a headstrong girl, I feel that reasoning with you is getting us nowhere. Besides, one does not argue about such things. This matter is not open to discussion. We have given our word. And we will keep it. I will simply not permit you to proceed with your foolishness. I will ring Mehboob right away and set the date for your marriage. Or perhaps not right away. It's Friday and he'll be in the mosque. It will have to be tomorrow." And he stands up and goes out into the hall, shoves his feet into his shoes by the door and walks out of the house. The door slams loudly behind him.

Chapter 27
Day Zero:
4th August
Devji: Idols and Ideals

I am lost in thought as I sit in the temple grounds by the statue of Gandhi. The evening sun reflects off the marble statue of a loin-clothed frail figure striding forward purposefully. His stance evokes his stand against the British colonial masters and reminds you to tread the righteous path. I barely notice the large flock of swifts as they dart around the statue, missing it narrowly, their shrill squeaks dominating the other dusk songs of the birds.

"Why aren't you inside the temple, praying?" Velji teases me, putting an extra emphasis on the word *inside*, as he eases into the chair next to mine. Most seats are already taken and some people are sitting on the lawn. We are at a public meeting organised by the Temple Committee.

The first speaker is Karsanji Maraj, the caterer, who also lives on our street and is one of *The Sages*. He walks to the front of the gathering purposefully, his slight limp barely noticeable to the crowd. He twirls the ends of his black moustache up before he addresses the crowd. "We have *Krishna, Rama, Ganesh* and *Hanuman*. We have a *Shiva lingam*, which admittedly is popular with female worshippers. But there are no Goddesses. About time we addressed the issue." He goes on to propose building a shrine dedicated to the Goddess *Amba*.

Velji leads the opposite camp. "Jalaram Bapa is the most revered saint in our community. It is shameful that we have no shrine to worship him in Jinja."

Several people then speak - the support being almost

equally divided between the two shrines. The arguments get quite heated, each side convinced of the merits of their case. People express their personal preference rather than offering any new ideas. While the argument drags on, we can see a stream of regular worshippers going into the temple along the path at the edge of the ground. We can hear the bells being rung and the *aarti* being sung, and the faithful leaving the temple clutching their packets of *prasad* of nuts and *shiro*. The meeting continues while the number of people coming out of the temple dwindles and the bells stop tolling.

The organisers have arranged the meeting in the evening, expecting a short discussion. Instead the brief tropical twilight slips unnoticed into the night and the floodlights are switched on in the grounds.

I put my hand up, catch the Chairman's eye and am called forward to speak. Velji smiles at me, confident that I will support him.

"Who amongst us could doubt that Jalaram Bapa was amongst the gentlest and noblest human being? He was kind to all, his fellow beings and even to animals. His life is a shining example to us all." Velji and several of his supporters chorus, "Hear, hear."

"However, I cannot help wondering if Jalaram Bapa, known for his humility, really would want his statue in a temple? And as for having a shrine to Mother Amba, all our ancient scriptures are full of the importance of celebrating the two aspects of Creation. Male and Female. *Shiva* and *Shakti*. We must not overlook the feminine aspect of the creation, especially considering the fact that the majority of the worshippers are women."

Karsanji's camp make jubilant noises and Velji and his friends sit in stunned silence. *Et tu Brutus*, Velji would say if he had read Shakespeare.

I continue. "There are said to be three hundred and thirty million gods. The number no doubt arose because that was the estimated number of stars in the heavens and the Sanskrit word for God -Devta- also means fire, a star in other words. We all take the number with a pinch of salt. We know that there is only one God. *Ishwar* is what we call him. We worship different aspects of creation. And all these gods simply represent those different aspects. The statues only help us concentrate on the God. We are really nature worshippers at heart. We hold rivers and mountains sacred. Their beauty evokes in us awe and wonder of the creation. We even worship trees and many animals. We see God in all His creation. So we respect all life forms. Now my point is this. I take it that we all agree there is only one God and that when we pray we can pray to whichever aspect of His divinity we want to. So, why do we need yet another shrine and more statues? And if we must, why not put up a statue of Jesus? He was a good man, a saint."

Some people have started trying to interrupt me when they realise the drift of my speech. I speed up what I have to say. "I wish to make a proposal before I sit down." It is becoming difficult now to make myself heard. I look at the chairman, Mr Bhatt. I know that he is a fair-minded person. He raises his hand, like a traffic police signalling stop, and the objecting voices quieten down.

"Let us hear Devjibhai's proposal first. Please give him a fair hearing." Mr Bhatt appeals and then adds with a smile, "He probably does want a statue of Jesus." There is a ripple of laughter.

"Actually I do not want any statues. Can we not spend the money on some social project? The money we have raised, and we should be proud of raising a substantial sum like that, is to serve the people. We have three temples in the town, not counting the adjoining shrines. We are well provided for places of worship. But we have many young people who do not receive higher education. I propose that we set up an educational trust fund with the money we have raised and use the interest to provide scholarships to the bright and deserving young. I also propose that we open up the programme to youngsters of any religion and of any race. We have prospered in our adopted nation. Let us show our thanks by also helping our African brothers and sisters."

A sea of hands goes up. Many people who have been passive listeners up till now suddenly feel the urge to make their point of view known. There are a few who criticise me. Someone even points out that he has never seen me in the temple, and asks if I really understand what the devout need. But the majority of the speakers, mostly young men and women, support me.

"Please understand," an earnest looking young man in steel-rimmed glasses reasons, "I fully support the idea of helping those who need it most, irrespective of religion or race. But I feel we do not have the mandate from the donors. The money has been raised from the Hindu community and they were not informed beforehand that it would be spent in helping other communities."

Indira, my friend Yashbhai Kotecha's daughter, gives a rousing speech in which she asks the old to wake up to the modern world. "Praying is very well but it won't get us jobs. Qualifications will. How many gods do you need to worship in order to make you kind and considerate? And if you need another model of a saintly person whom you can worship, follow Devjikaka's advice and occasionally go and say your prayers to Jesus Christ." she says, pointing in the direction of the Catholic church, situated less than five minutes' walk away, its steeple, a dark silhouette in the night sky, visible from the temple.

Mr Bhatt then stands up, adjusts his thick-rimmed glasses on the tip of his nose and says in his trained lawyer's voice, "I believe we have considered all the relevant points now. Unless someone has a totally different proposal, we shall vote upon the main choice - a shrine or a scholarship?" Suddenly the supporters of the shrine seem to have vanished. Even their previously most vocal supporters now vote for the scholarship fund. There is a second vote in which it is decided that the scholarship will be open to all, with part of the fund reserved for African students.

I do not wait for Velji, who is busy talking to some other people and set off home with Indira. We walk along the Bell Avenue, past the large bungalows and well-manicured gardens of some of Jinja's rich folk. At one point I stop and take a deep breath.

"Are you alright, Uncle?"

"Oh, I am fine." I smile, touched by Indira's concern. Again I inhale deeply and sigh. "Oh! The fragrance of *langi-langi*. After dusk I cannot walk by these gardens without stopping to appreciate its divine smell."

"Do you think, Uncle, that amongst those millions of Gods that we have accumulated, there is a God solely responsible for *langi-langi* fragrance?" Indira swings her pigtails back over her shoulders as she laughs, an open laugh that shows her perfectly formed white teeth. A lovely girl, Indira.

We turn left on Gabula Road and an aroma of cooking food wafts to our nostrils from some open doors. Indira bids me farewell at her house, "See you, Uncle."

I respond, "See you, *Beti*." I ponder, as I walk on to our

house, about how the young are becoming westernised. She used the phrase *see you, uncle* in English and it sounded natural coming from her. I realise that I had replied in a mixture of languages, *see you* in English and *Beti* in Gujarati, instead of *daughter*. I smiled at the realisation that this was a perfect example of progressive Westernisation in our society.

As I enter our door, I pass Savita on her way to the kitchen. "What are you smiling about?" she asks, and without waiting for an answer continues, "You are definitely not going to the Thakkar's party tonight, are you?"

"No, no, I am not in the mood for a party tonight," I say and go into the living-room and sit down with the *Uganda Argus*, which I have not read today. I can hear Savita in the kitchen singing, accompanying the Hindi song playing on the radio.

A little later, Velji bursts into our house, furious, hurt and perplexed. He sits on the sofa facing me, leaning forward. "You are lucky I thought of our friendship and did not denounce you to the town as a *nastik*," he informs me. "I was sorely tempted."

"Look, I am not exactly an atheist. I am more of what they call an agnostic." I use the English words - *agnostic* and *atheist*.

"What's the difference?" he demands.

I explain as well as I can.

Velji is still upset. "Having two different words in English fudges the issue. You doubt God's existence in either case. When you say you have an open mind, it implies that there are questions you have which need to be satisfactorily answered before you believe. That is no Faith. Faith implies believing without questioning. A conviction. And *nastik* means one who has no faith. That makes you a *nastik*." Velji spluttered.

"Come to think of it, agnostic sounds like the Sanskrit word *'agnani'* (one without knowledge.)"

"You are calling me ignorant, aren't you?" I tell him. "OK I am ignorant of the knowledge of God. OK I am a *nastik*. But it is only a label. I believe in helping fellow human beings. Spend money on them rather than on yet more statues."

We may have gone on arguing. But Savita comes in with freshly squeezed orange juice and snacks on a tray, places it on the coffee table between us, and says with a sweet, yet half teasing, smile, "You two still talk to each other like you probably did when you were in school together."

Velji calms down as we eat and leaves a few minutes later.

Chapter 28
Day Zero:
4th August
Ramesh: Religion

After dinner I go to my room and lie on my bed thinking about Rehana. She may be breaking the news of our relationship to her parents at this very moment. I am sorry I cannot be there with her to face the difficult task.

There is a knock on the door.

"Come in," I shout and Shashi enters the room.

"Hi," he says.

"Hi," I respond.

He sits on the edge of the bed and fiddles with his watchstrap. It is obvious he wishes to talk about something and I can guess what it is.

"Go on. Let's hear it. What is it?"

He hesitates at first and then gushes, "Papa told me about you wanting to marry a girl from a different community. A Muslim girl. I know it does not really matter to you what I think. But I just wanted to tell you that you can count on my support."

I sit up and rest my arm on his shoulder and say, "Thank you. It means a lot to me."

He grasps my wrist. "Papa and I had a discussion about religion and then, just before dinner, I overheard Papa and Veljikaka arguing about it. Papa was telling Kaka that he is not so much an atheist as an agna...agnastic?"

"The word is 'agnostic'," I smile at him and relax back on the pillow.

"That's it," he says. "I think I'm an agnostic, too. How about you?"

"Same here," I say. "It is a safe option, keeping your mind open. If religion makes you follow a righteous path, then fine, be religious. But then there are people like Papa, who do not need God to make them virtuous. One does not have to be religious to be a kind human being."

"How would you feel if tomorrow someone proved beyond any doubt that God exists?" Shashi wants to know.

"I would be very pleased. It is a comforting thought - a Higher Being looking after us all. But I guess that it will never be proved beyond all doubt. Belief in God will always be a matter of faith."

Shashi sits in silence as he ponders over it.

Then I make up a theory - a school boyish theory - and Shashi likes it. I tell him that it is possible that the human race will never know if God definitely exists. If someone did discover the truth, the shock of so tremendous a revelation would kill him or her. Probably that is what happens when one is about to die. You find out for sure whether God exists or not. In either case, the shocking revelation kills us. And nobody lives to tell others about this most important discovery.

Shashi chuckles. "There has to be a God to inspire you with such wisdom," he says as he gets up to go to his room.

"May God bless you," I call out after him.

Chapter 29
Day Zero:
4th August
Shashi: Discernment

Another day of the vacation gone. Today I try to follow my revision schedule, but then give up. I tell myself that I made the plan to help me, not to control me.

After about four hours of revision this afternoon, I seem to have done so little. It never seems enough.

I revise a bit of biology. Read about parts of a flower: pistil and stamen and filaments and so on. Quickly get bored with it and move on to Geography. The physical features of Australia. Boring! What I want to know is why do we have to study Australia of all the places?

One day I did raise it with Miss Sandhu and she said that in the last year of our secondary school education everything is dictated by the exams. Australia is the smallest continent and easiest to learn. Vinod put his hand up and said in a childish voice, "Miss, Australia is the only continent we study in detail. So could you please organise a school trip to Australia to help us with our Geography exam?" It was like an explosion as many voices joined in.

"Please, Miss, could we?"

"We never go anywhere." And so on.

To be heard above the mayhem, Miss Sandhu had to bash the table with the blackboard rubber a few times.

After spending about an hour on Geography I move on to English. Now, that I enjoy. "Friends, Romans and Countrymen, Lend me your ears." And so on. I memorise and deliver the whole of Mark Antony's speech in front of a mirror, until I hear a shuffling noise outside. I guess it is

Lalita Auntie listening outside the door. I stop, as I feel a bit self-conscious.

Then I read a few poems from Palgrave's Golden Treasury. That is strictly speaking not revision, but more for pleasure because our school does not do the poetry section of the syllabus. But I like the imagery.

First, I turn to Thomas Gray's *Elegy Written in a Country Graveyard*. It is Papa's favourite poem. "It should be recited whenever people pray," he says. "Or when there are political meetings." It is really about how many a talent is wasted due to lack of opportunities and inequalities in society. I must remember to ask Ramesh about his views on the poem - its sentiments are clearly socialist.

I go on to read a poem about a cat, which drowned in a fish bowl. I have heard that in the UK some people keep gold fish in large glass bowls. Not much good as pets. Not like dogs, cats or one of our neighbour's parrot, *kasuku*, with its red head and grey feathers, and who talks more than anyone else in their family and can whistle better than anyone in the town.

The next poem I read is *The Daffodils*. It starts *I wandered lonely as a cloud*. An interesting image - the poet portrays clouds as loners, shy and reclusive. And although there are some lonely clouds, they soon join others to form huge, overpowering and mischievous gangs, dark and menacing with their thunder and lightning. They pile up and advance like an unstoppable army. One just does not think of comparing a lonely person to a cloud. That is what makes poetry stimulating, the caffeine of imagination. There, I just managed to get a poetic image in my narrative.

Last term I was asked by Miss Roy to present the Literary Reading in the Wednesday assembly and I chose to read

The Daffodils. I think it went well, though hardly anyone commented on it. However, later that day, Miss Roy asked me why I chose the poem.

"I like images flashing upon my inward eye when I lie on my couch." I told her, referring to the lines:

> *'For oft when on my couch I lie*
> *In a vacant or in pensive mood*
> *They flash upon that inward eye*
> *Which is the bliss of Solitude.'*

"So, do daffodils flash upon your inward eye?" Miss wanted to know.

"Actually, no," I told her. "What flashes upon my inward eye is the image of the poet lying on his couch, with images of daffodils flashing upon his inward eye. The poet deriving such keen pleasure from his memory of flowers has a greater dramatic impact on me than the flowers." And I was not being facetious.

Miss laughed at first and then said, "Surely *'ten thousand flowers, fluttering and dancing in the breeze'* should make a bigger impression.'

I explained my reasoning to her. "You see, I have never seen a daffodil. I suppose they are yellow because the poet talks of a host of golden daffodils."

After a pause, Miss gave a short laugh and said, "Actually, come to think of it, I have only seen pictures of daffodils. I wonder how fragrant they are."

*   *   *

After dinner I have a long chat with Papa. He tells me about a meeting he went to at the temple, where he dissuaded people from spending money on yet another shrine.

"So," I comment, "Isn't it strange that people, who are

mature and intelligent, can still make unwise decisions?"

"Wisdom is not the same thing as intelligence," Papa says.

Just then Natubhai's Himat from across the road comes round with a plateful of colourful sweets - penda, burfi and mohanthal.

"We are celebrating," he says with the big goofy smile he has. "We got Visas for UK. The letter came today."

I must admit that I would have been very envious if I did not know that I myself would be going there to study in a few months' time. Himat then turns to me and says, "I will also go to a school in London from next year. We could be in the same class again."

I am about to reach for a penda, but Papa pulls the plate away from me. He does not allow us to eat sweets at night before bedtime. "Bad for your teeth," he says.

"Tell your parents we are very pleased with their good news," Papa tells Himat, as he is leaving.

We have applied for the UK Visas, too, but only a few months ago. Himat's family had to wait for over two years. His father works in a petrol station and they are not well off. So, I tell Papa that I can understand them wanting to emigrate. But I haven't been quite sure why many middle class families have also applied to go to the UK.

"Prosperity is not enough. Security is paramount. And if a leader of a country lacks discernment, you cannot be sure of receiving fair treatment." Papa sometimes comes up with these high-flaunting statements.

"Discernment?" I have never heard discernment being placed in the top league of virtues.

"You have heard the saying, '*Takke sher bhaji, Takke sher khaja*', haven't you?"

"Yes, of course," I reply. "Roughly speaking, a place where

a *khaja* costs the same as vegetables." The saying has not meant much to me, partly because even with my sweet tooth, I am not too keen on *khajas*. They are too light and crumbly. I only vaguely remember the story behind the saying. So, instead of explaining the meaning of discernment, Papa tells me the folk-tale about it. He is a storehouse of tales. That is Papa for you.

A *sadhu* and his disciple wandered from place to place, spending their time meditating and giving discourses on religion and scriptures. As they had renounced all material possessions, they relied on kind people giving them alms.

One day they arrived in a town and settled down under a big *peepal* tree. The guru asked his disciple to go and buy some provisions for their lunch with the money they had collected that day.

The disciple came back in a short time with a bag of *khaja* (a sweet). "What's this? Was the shop owned by a devout and generous man, who let you have this?"

The disciple was all excited. "I suggest we give up our wandering ways and settle down here."

The guru said, "Calm down, young man, and tell me why."

"Well, you see, in this town everything costs the same. The same coin buys you a kilo of khaja or a kilo of vegetables. In fact everything is worth a coin in shops. It is great."

"Hurry. We must leave right now," the guru said as he started packing his meagre possessions.

The disciple was flabbergasted. "B-b-but we have found the right place. A paradise. And you want to leave?"

"Yes. And immediately. It is important in life to have discernment."

"Discernment, chiscernment! What rubbish." The disciple murmured under his breath, and then declared his intention of staying on in this town.

The guru moved on, leaving behind the disciple, who had a sweet tooth and so rapidly gained weight, eating masses of sweets each day.

A year later the guru, still worrying about his disciple, came back to the town to check on how he was doing. He was met with the news that his disciple had been taken to the prison that very morning.

The guru visited the young man in the prison and discovered the reason for his internment. Apparently a murderer had been tried and found guilty and sentenced to death. When they took the man to the gallows they found that the hangman had made a knot that was too large for the murderer's neck. The judge, who like all in the town had no discernment, then said, "Oh, well, in that case go and find someone who has a fatter neck. It is all the same." The disciple, who had grown plump on a diet of *khaja*, had a fat neck.

Papa explains the moral of his story by saying, "One is never safe in a country where there is no rule of the law. Or even more important, where there is no discernment." Then he adds, "If you go and kill some innocent man here, you would be sentenced to death after a trial. If you criticise the President, then also you get sentenced to death. Except, in that case, there will be no trial. It would be a summary execution. It is like *takke sher bhaji, takke sher khaja*."

I have just finished writing my journal for the day. It is late now - after 11 p.m. There is silence in the house. And outside, too, apart from the shrill squeaks of fruit bats flying just outside my window. Before I switch off the lights, just a last thought - can I describe myself as a journalist because I keep a journal? Or is a diarist the correct word? Or perhaps just a sixteen year old scribbler aspiring to be a writer?"

Part 3: After the Announcement

Chapter 30
Day 1:
Saturday 5th August 1972
Devji: The Sages

About a year ago I learnt from Shashi that the people of Jinja have dubbed our gang, I mean, our group, *The Sages*. I believe it is done rather fondly and not sarcastically. At least I hope so! After all, the society respects older people and our group consists almost exclusively of men in their fifties and sixties. We lead active lives despite many of us being semi-retired.

Our chief interests are social and political events, though many business deals are struck informally but efficiently during our gatherings. We have contacts spread out widely over many countries. People say we are like the BBC of the social world. Our finely tuned antennae pick up news of births and deaths and especially about who is looking for a suitable wife or husband for their offspring, not just in Jinja but all over East Africa, India and even in the UK. We keep in touch with our wide social network through letters and increasingly by telephone. Numerous arranged marriages are conceived in our meetings. And it is not just the social gossip that we pick up. We listen to the BBC overseas news and the All India Radio, and read the *Uganda Argus* and several foreign papers. We are considered to be the best-informed citizens of Jinja.

*   *   *

Just before dawn, at about six o'clock, I knock on Velji's door. He steps out of the house and we go to call on Motilal, who lives near the end of our street. Motilal emerges from his door before we get to it. The three of us hurry through the narrow alley to Main Street. We chat amiably as we walk along the deserted road, past the shuttered shops. The sky is now getting lighter with a red glow on the edges of the clouds on the horizon.

On the pavement outside the post office, there is already a group of eight or ten men chatting in hushed tones. We greet each other briefly, or just nod at each other, and set off on our daily walk along Bell Avenue West.

*   *   *

We can see the Goan Club House and next to it the Catholic Church, with its spire reflecting the red sky. We then pass the main gate to the temple compound. A few early worshippers enter the grounds, and are walking along the path leading to the main building. Its spire is glowing in the morning sun and casts a giant shadow over the shrines surrounding it. Dew drops on the lawn in the temple grounds sparkle.

We pass the Rugby Club and then arrive at the Coronation Park, where we head for our usual spot near the bandstand; its circular structure shining golden in the rising sun. We spread our hankies on the grass, which is nearly dry by now, and sit in a circle. From our position we can clearly see the rail bridge over the Nile, its criss-crossed metal struts reflecting the morning sun. And just then a train passes over it, and we can hear it going choo...choo...choo...choo... sounding just like the noise children make when pretending to be a train engine.

We have barely settled when Karim announces, "Did any of you hear about an announcement by Amin about Asians? It might be a rumour but apparently he has ordered us all Asians to get out of Uganda? I am not sure about the exact deadline but it is not long. I think it is in the next few months."

153

"Somebody mentioned it at Madhvani's party yesterday," Haribhai recalls. "But no one else knew anything about it. Not even Mr Deva."

"Mr. Deva?"

"You know, Mr. Dharma Deva, the Indian ambassador."

"Where did you hear it?" I ask Karim.

"My cousin Salim telephoned me last night from Tororo. His African business partner, Matthew Olawango apparently heard about it from his contacts in the army."

"And how reliable is Mr Olawango's source?" Motilal wants to know.

"I have no idea," Karim admits.

Just then, Malkit Singh arrives. The circumference of the circle expands a little as we shift to accommodate him.

Malkit Singh starts his day with a prayer and then listens to the well-trusted BBC before coming out to our gathering of *The Sage*s. He spreads his handkerchief on the grass and lowers himself down carefully onto it. "Guess what the World Service reported only half an hour ago?" he informs us. "Amin has given us ninety days to get out of Uganda."

There is a hush. Radio Uganda has not mentioned it but it has to be true if the BBC said it. We sit in stunned silence. In the past we have often discussed the worsening position of Asians in Uganda and have been expecting our lives to become increasingly difficult in the country. But this is wholly unexpected.

Velji breaks the silence. "We all know what Amin's pronouncements are like. He rarely follows them up or else he changes his mind."

"According to the BBC report, God spoke to Amin in his dream and told him to throw us all out," Malkit says adjusting his turban, which he obviously tied in a hurry this morning.

154

"Maybe He will appear in a dream sequel and instruct him differently," Velji has a tendency to sweep all difficulties under the carpet.

"Even if Amin does not go ahead with the threat this time, he probably will sooner or later," I predict. Many of the group nod or make assenting noises and I continue, "We can't deny the fact that there is growing *Indophobia* here. The emerging African middle class view us as an obstruction to their own advancement."

"But that is surely not true," Motilal objects. "We are developing the commercial and industrial sectors and so creating opportunities and new jobs for everyone." However, despite being a successful builder's merchant, employing many people in his business, he is planning to leave Uganda. He has already received British Visas for his whole family.

"I know it. And you know it. But do they? We come and settle in their country and before they know it we dominate the economy. We live in big houses, drive plush cars and employ them as servants. They naturally resent it."

"The middle-class Africans also have servants," Motilal points out.

"And Isa, my driver, tells me that the servants prefer to work in Indian households as the African employers do not treat them as well," Motilal says.

"Look, those may be subjective opinions. No one has done a comprehensive survey. But no survey is required to find out that we are generally the prosperous class and Africans on the whole are not." Chandu Shah, the youngest member in our group at fifty-one, has studied actuarial science at University and prides himself on his down-to-earth approach. "Uganda has been independent for only ten years. And in that time things have already changed a lot. We have had a policy of Africanisation for some time now. And we all know what that means." He doesn't mince his words. "We appoint African directors in our businesses. They accept their newly elevated status as figureheads and their fat salary cheques as a well-deserved perk. But they would not remain in those positions were it not for the fact that we are obliged to have an African on the board of directors."

"They are not all like that. Some of them are capable and astute businessmen," I point out.

"Of course, they are. We all know of some excellent appointments. But come on," Chandu sticks to his point. "You must admit that the majority of those appointed have little idea about business. They just haven't the experience. To be good at it, you need to start on a lower rung and then work your way up."

"They haven't had the opportunity."

"I agree but it does not change the fact that many have been appointed because they are Black Africans, and not because they are the best candidates."

"I came here when I was eleven and I think of myself as a Ugandan - an African. All my children and grandchildren were born here. In fact, several of them just over there." Karsanji points in the direction of the Jinja Municipal Hospital.

"Almost all the young folk were born here and this is their home. They may happen to be brown in colour but they are as African as anybody else."

"Yes but we are a visible minority," I point out. "Cultural changes occur gradually and, historically speaking, we have lived here for a very short time. Only two or three generations. And the main problem is we have not integrated well. And it is not surprising. In India we had a caste system with its hundreds of sub-divisions. Our society is used to having a

156

large number of communities existing harmoniously without intermarrying. So we had no problem accepting the semi-apartheid system here under the British, where we lived in separate areas, and our kids went to segregated schools until a few years before independence. But now we stand out due to our economic success and different skin colour.

"Also, we do not intermarry even amongst ourselves. Gujaratis and Punjabis do not intermarry." There was a sad note in Malkit Singh's voice. We need no reminding that Malkit had tried in vain to prevent the marriage of his daughter to a Gujarati boy. She went off and married him anyway in Kenya.

"Nor do Hindus, Muslims or Christians marry each other," I say. "It is an inevitable consequence of having arranged marriages. The parents are never going to arrange their son or daughter's marriage with someone from a different community - for differing backgrounds greatly reduce the chances of a marriage working."

They all nod silently. They make no comment. I wonder how many of them know about Ramesh's *friendship* with Rehana.

"And even if the girl and the boy are both Hindu and Gujarati we oppose the match unless both are from the same community. Do you know of many inter-marriages between Patels, Lohanas, Brahmins, Vaniyas, Vanzas and so on? So what chance is there for inter-marriages between Indians and Africans?" Chandu asks.

Karsanji clears his throat before stating, "In a free society, parents must have the right to choose a spouse for their son or daughter." I wonder what Ramesh would make of this particular interpretation of freedom.

"Well, we had the freedom and now we pay the price for our self-imposed isolation."

In the brief silence that follows I become more aware of the birdsong from the branches in the trees surrounding us and watch a group of crows hopping near us. "Even if we were more integrated, we would still stand out due to our brown skin," I say, turning my attention back to the group. "And by our Indian cultural traditions. We are like the Jews were in Europe."

"Do you think we could be placed in concentration camps?"

"No, certainly not," I say.

"You sound very certain."

"Judging from Amin's behaviour so far, I believe he wouldn't waste his time and effort on building camps. No, he would shoot us and toss us into the river for crocodiles to eat."

"That is reassuring."

"That is what he has done to his opponents so far."

"And some of them were not even opposing him. He just thought that they could, under certain circumstances, be a thorn in his side."

"In that case, our weakness is our strength. He knows we are no threat to him and so he is more likely to just exile us," Chandu points out.

"Well, if it is true, then, some of us have been through this before. You could say we are no strangers to being exiles." Malkit sighs. "My parents left Lahore for India at the time of partition."

"At the same time, mine moved from Delhi to Karachi, in the opposite direction," Karim remarks dryly.

"And we chose to come here - self-exiled, one could say."

"And now maybe we are destined to move on."

"When we were born we brought nothing with us and we will leave with nothing," I quote the common wisdom.

"People normally say that about life; we could say that about our stay in Uganda. Most of us came here with maybe three sets of clothes and we will probably leave with three sets."

"Whatever is written in our fate will happen. It is all in our *karma*. Our deeds in past lives have mapped out our current lives, anyway. All we can do is live a righteous life now," Karsanji says and then adds his favourite phrase, "Life must go on."

"There is nothing we can do about it now. It's all in Allah's hands." Karim agrees.

There are several assenting voices. Most of the group are Hindus and evoke their karma, while Muslims talk about surrendering to the will of Allah.

I watch the crows. Fascinating creatures.

Chapter 31
Day 1:
Saturday 5th August
Devji: Confirmation of the Rumour

After hearing the rumour of Amin's announcement, I wonder if it will be reported in today's *Argus*. As usual the paper is delivered to my office around mid-morning. But I am with a client then. And as soon as he leaves, I pick up the paper.

Uganda Argus
THE FUTURE OF ASIANS IN UGANDA.

... The President had decided to visit the soldiers because he had received good news that there is now discipline and co-operation between the soldiers and civilians in Tororo since the incident in which a Kenyan Air Force pilot was shot dead by a Uganda soldier earlier this year. ... He has lifted the order confining the soldiers to their barracks after the incidence.

The General also directed them to arrest any Israelis who attempt to enter Uganda ...

The General called on every soldier to train himself to be an instructor of the people, and appealed to them to keep fit and not to be taken by surprise like members of the Malire Mechanised Battalion who were beaten by members of the Cabinet in a tug-of-war this week ...

Sandwiched between these disparate items was this ultimatum to Asians:

... he said that there was no room in Uganda for the over 80000 Asians holding British passports who are sabotaging Uganda's economy and encouraging corruption. I want to see

160

*that the economy of Uganda is in the hands of Uganda citizens,
especially 'black Ugandans'...*

*I want you to assist me in defending the public against those
people who are sabotaging the economy of Uganda and confuse
the people.*

Then the article went on to other matters:

*On the way back the President also stopped at Musita Mosque,
some 22 km from Jinja to attend Juma prayers. At the end of
the prayers the President donated 400 shillings towards the
completion of the mosque.*

I am not sure what to make of the news. The headline does
say *The future of Asians in Uganda*. But the article meanders
around many irrelevant items before mentioning the issue.

To begin with, you would think that if Amin wanted to
make an important announcement, which has a dramatic
impact upon nearly eighty thousand people, the least you
would expect is that it would be announced at a large press
conference, possibly in Kampala or on television and not while
addressing the cadets of the airborne division in Tororo, a
small border town. You would expect a parliament to discuss
an important issue like that. But under Amin's dictatorship,
there is no functioning parliament any more.

The bulk of his speech is about other matters, like how the
cabinet minsters defeated the soldiers of Malire Mechanised
Battalion in a tug-of-war contest. However, unlike the BBC,
the *Argus* makes no mention of God telling Amin in his
dream to expel the Asians from Uganda.

The manner of his announcement leads one to believe
that Amin does not really mean it and that it is yet another
one of his announcements, which he will not follow up.

We will have to wait and see.

Chapter 32
Day 1:
Saturday 5th August - Morning
Shashi: Beginning of the End

Nothing exciting happens here. Certainly not in our lives. One day is the same as the other. A slurp of time.

I know we had a military coup and it is said to be a repressive regime. But, you know what? Most people mind their own business. Life goes on as normal. You don't see any signs of unrest. Except on rare occasions, in the dead of the night, you hear rifle fire from the direction of the army barracks. Sort of phut, phut, phut and then silence. Most people stop for a moment. Their foreheads get furrowed with a few more lines. Then they shake their heads, not like a wet dog but almost imperceptibly, before continuing with whatever they were doing. They look worried but they don't comment. Silence is incredibly vocal. (Mr. Banerjee would approve of the last sentence, for after reading one of my essays titled *A Breathtaking Luminescent Sunset*, he told me to *use images, not flowery prose*).

Today it is Saturday and it is school holidays. Papa and Ramesh are at work, and Lalita Auntie and Ba have gone to the Nutan Fabric Store where women are flocking to view the new stock of silk saris.

Since I am supposed to be revising for my exams, Ba does not ask me to run little errands any more. In a way, I wish she would for I quickly got bored after spending about an hour on *King Henry the Eighth* and *the Tudors*. So, I decide to go to collect our post. It is a walk I like because you always bump into friends on the Main Street - either idly lolling about or on some errand.

I notice Vinod casually ambling along - he is obviously showing off his new purple trousers with flares so wide they flap over his shoes. I catch up with him and we walk together towards the post office. It is only ten in the morning but it is already getting hot. So we stroll on the pavement in the shelter of the covered walkway as far as the Sunshine Studio. That is when we come across the body.

It is sprawled on the pavement just before the post office. My first thought is *the man must be drunk*. Who else would lie down on a busy footpath on the Main Street in the hot sun? He is on his side and until you get nearer you cannot see the brown patches of dried up blood on his face or the couple of flies buzzing around him. There is a faint musty smell coming from him. Although I have never before seen a dead person, I just know he is dead.

It is a young man's body. His black trousers and white shirt are torn in places. His hair, long by African standards, is covered in red dust. The face looks vaguely familiar. So I stop to have a better look but Vinod grabs my elbow and firmly nudges me forward. I notice that people in front of us slow down a bit. But no one stops. No one comments. It is possible to walk by the body on the footpath but everyone, without exception, steps right off the footpath on to the road and gives it a wide berth.

There are a few other friends hanging around outside the post office. They are talking in hushed tones and not about the usual things like school and cricket and girls and movies.

"Hey. Did you see the body?"

"Some poor man. Killed by the army I am sure."

If it were not the army, the police would have already been there. It is almost as if the body is left there for people

to see. A warning: *Do not mess around with the government.*
As if anyone needs reminding.

I hardly speak to any of my friends. Instead, I pace around
trying to remember who the dead man reminds me of. The
long rather lean features, handsome even in death, the wide
forehead. It is familiar and yet it is not. John! That's it. John
Ngala. I only met him a couple of times when he worked
in Ramesh's firm till recently. He was very good and was to
become one of the partners in the law business. But then for
no apparent reason, he resigned and left. That is who the
corpse reminds me of.

I walk back again past the body, this time more slowly. He
does look very much like John. Except there is a dark slash
on his neck just below the ear. Of course it could have been
caused by the army when they killed him. But it looks more
like an old scar. I do not want to stop and stare at a dead
person for long - it somehow feels disrespectful.

From there I go to Ramesh and Kumar's office on Iganga
Road. I think it is amazing the way they have worked out
their business arrangement. Best friends from when they
were in school together, they are now partners in the law
practice. And, Kintu, another chum of theirs, who did not
get University education because of his poor background, is
now their business secretary.

Kintu is in the reception area typing, noisily jabbing the
keys with his forefingers. Before looking up, he finishes the
sentence he is writing. A broad smile spreads on his face
as he leans forward to shake my hand. "Shaashi, how are
you?" He is the only person, who pronounces my name as
Shaashi. And before I can answer, he goes on, "To what do
we owe this pleasure? No, don't tell me. I know. You want to
divorce both your wives." I join him in his laughter. Then
he informs me, "Ramesh is with a client, but they should be

nearly finished now."

We talk about a few general things before I ask him, "Oh, by the way, do you know where John Ngala works now?"

Kintu says that he has no idea and adds, "John has been involved with a political organisation opposing Amin." He shakes his head as he adds, "Very unwise."

Just then Ramesh emerges from his office with his client, an elderly man, whom I do not recognise. Ramesh shakes hands with him and says, "Please come back next week to sign the Will."

Ramesh is surprised to see me there, as I rarely go to see him in the office. He nods at me, indicating I should follow him and goes back to his room.

I close the door behind me as I enter. Ramesh stands by his desk. I blurt out about the body by the post office. The smile on his face fades, and is now replaced by a pained expression.

"Wait here," he says as he leaves the room.

I sit on the comfortable chair for the clients as I wait for him. A long minute - or two - passes before Kumar limps into the room, followed by Ramesh, who closes the door behind him. They stand next to each other behind Ramesh's desk and face me. I feel like a criminal being interrogated by two serious solicitors.

"Tell Kumar what you just told me," Ramesh says.

"There is the body of a dead man lying on the main street - just outside the post office."

"And?" Ramesh prompts.

"And I think it is - it looks like that of John Ngala, who used to work with you."

"Are you sure?" Kumar asks.

I feel more and more like I am the accused. "No, not quite sure. But it could be him."

"Did you notice a scar under his ear?"

"Yes, I definitely saw it. Below his right ear. So it is John?"

"Damn. Damn. Damn." Kumar says as he collapses in the chair facing me and Ramesh places his hand on Kumar's shoulder to comfort him. Both Kumar and Ramesh suddenly seem to be enveloped in gloom.

I feel like I need to say more, and so add, "I had only met John a couple of times and certainly had not noticed the scar. And then he stopped working with you. So I was not sure if it was John's body."

"Well, it is not John," Ramesh says. His tone is subdued.

"But Kumar just asked me if there was a scar below the ear. And there was. So, how did Kumar know about it, if it wasn't John?"

"Well, you see - -" Kumar started to explain, but was interrupted by Ramesh.

"No, Kumar. Shashi does not need to know the details."

"But I do," I say.

Kumar looks up at Ramesh and pleads my case, "He needs some sort of explanation."

Ramesh places both his hands on the desk and leans forward towards me. "OK, Shashi. I'll tell you. John had no scar, but his brother Patrick, who bore a striking resemblance to him, did. John introduced Patrick to us before he left us. We only met him once. That's it." He then straightens up and adds, "It is lunch hour now. You better go home. I'll join you later."

I wave at Kintu and just as I am leaving, a door to the third room opens. A pretty young lady leads a couple out of her office. I figure that this must be Rehana, the woman Ramesh is in love with.

It is lunch hour so I head home. Just Lalita Auntie and I are at the dining table. Ba cooks fresh warm rotli for us. They tell me that when they were out shopping, they heard rumours about Amin ordering Asians to leave the country. I switch on the radio news but there is no mention of it. I can't check it in the *Argus* as Papa brings the paper with him when he comes home for lunch. But today he is delayed. So I go to my room to lie down and do some revision. I start reading my History notes but soon doze off. Almost everyone in the town has a siesta on Saturday afternoon and I wonder if drowsiness can be transmitted by telepathy.

Chapter 33
Day 1:
Saturday 5th August
Yusuf: Love is a Dirty Word

My mind was in turmoil after I learnt about Rehana's friendship with a Hindu boy. I had a fretful night, tossing and turning in my bed. Zubeida lay motionless, but I am sure that she was awake, too.

In the morning I declined breakfast and went off to the shop in an angry silence. Business is always brisk on Saturday mornings and by mid-day I had sold two bicycles, several spare parts and had served a steady stream of people wanting their bikes fixed. Normally, I would have been pleased with the business. Instead, I was in a daze.

"Are you not well today, *bwana*?" my assistant Ali asked.

I evaded the question. "Time to close. Let's bring the display bikes back into the shop."

*   *   *

I am home now. A heavy gloom hangs over the family as we eat our lunch. I barely respond to the conversation before retiring to my room for a siesta. I lie on my bed staring at the ceiling.

Less than twenty-four hours ago there was hardly a cloud in my sky; the future looked secure and my world was trouble-free. I have no financial worries as my business is booming.

We have found suitable husbands for our two elder daughters. There is only one responsibility left - Rehana. I thought that I had taken care of it twenty odd years ago, when I promised her hand to Hussein.

The old saying goes: *Man proposes, God disposes.* Now it feels more like: *Man proposes, his daughter disposes.*

How can Rehana be so thoughtless, so foolish? Does she not realise the grave consequences of her proposed action? An intelligent girl like her. They say that these days the young are showing signs of rebellion. But what is Rehana rebelling against? Have I not been a liberal parent? I even sent her to study in England, a Western country - and on her own! Some of my more orthodox relations did warn me of my folly. *You cannot give a girl unbridled freedom. You will lose her.* And now they will smugly remind me, *We warned you.*

When Rehana came back from UK, she did not want to settle down straight away. She asked if she could establish herself professionally before she gets married. Did I object? No, I certainly did not. I even spoke to Mehboob to suggest that we should wait, as if it was my idea. And this is how she is paying me back. Talking to us, her parents, about love for a kaffir boy. Shameless hussy. Maybe those relations were right. I should perhaps never have given her the freedom or exposed her to the Western liberal ways. Then she would have demurely agreed to her marriage and there would be none of this foolish talk about love.

Bollywood movies and Western influences are the real culprits, infecting the minds of the young with all that nonsense about romantic love. After the initial excitement when the rosy glow fades, there is little to sustain the relationship. I have heard of similar cases, which end in divorces.

I sigh and sit up, prop up my pillows and lean against them. I intertwine my fingers and support the back of my head with my hands.

How times have changed! In my days this kind of shameless

behaviour was unheard of. I wouldn't have dreamt of going to my parents and announcing that I had found a girl to marry.

I remember my experience clearly.

It was Saturday. I came back from the shop. It had been a long day and I was tired and hungry. I washed myself, taking care to scrub my forearms carefully from elbows down to my wrists. I sat cross-legged on the wooden 'patlo' on the floor. We did have a small table with chairs but it was only used when we had guests. My mother served me the meal. I was so busy wolfing down the food that I did not hear my father come in and sit on the chair by the table, until he spoke.

"We have guests for lunch tomorrow."

I nodded and took another bite of the delicious chicken makhani, my mother's speciality.

"Do you remember I told you that we are expecting my cousin Amama from India to visit us," Father reminded me. "Well, she is coming to see you tomorrow."

"Hmm." I mumbled with my mouth full.

"Dress smartly because she is bringing her daughter with her. We are doing a nikkah ceremony for you and Zubeida tomorrow."

I nearly choked on the chicken. Had I known I was to get engaged tomorrow afternoon, I wouldn't have arranged to play cards with my friends.

Did I tell my father that I was looking for romantic love? Of course, not. You trust your parents. Your happiness is foremost in their minds.

I had not set eyes on Zubeida before the day of our engagement. I came to love her after we were married. I accepted my parents' choice and have not for a moment regretted it.

I shake my head as I emerge from my reverie after what seems like an interminable time and look at the clock on the wall. It is only 3 p.m. I spring to my feet and walk towards the living-room, shouting in the direction of Rehana's room, "I want to talk to you two." But the women are already in the living-room. Zubeida is holding both Rehana's hands in hers as they talk. There is a momentary look of panic in their eyes as I stride purposefully into the room.

I sit down facing them. "I have made up my mind. You, miss, are not leaving the house, unless accompanied by your mother or me." For the first time in my life I use the English word miss to address my daughter.

Zubeida exchanges a quick look with Rehana. "She has already decided to stay at home with me today," she says.

"You do not understand. I don't mean today or tomorrow. I mean until she gets married."

Rehana looks stunned. She is trying to contain her tears. "Please Abba. Don't be so hard. I need to go out to work and ..."

"To hell with your job," I tell her. "Today was the last day at work for you." Tears are now rolling down her cheeks and she makes no attempt to wipe them.

"The whole trouble started at work. Until you are married, you will stay at home and be a dutiful daughter and when you are married you will be a dutiful wife. Hussein's family is well off and does not require your salary. You will only work if your husband wants you to."

"And who would employ me if I quit just like that? What sort of a reference would I get?" She fumbles to find a handkerchief as she sobs. Zubeida reaches out and embraces her.

"You have other references and excellent qualifications."

"I would be letting my clients down. I am the only one familiar with some of the cases."

"Too bad! You should have thought about that before getting entangled in this Hindu boy's web," I respond but relent straight away. "Alright. You can have three more days at the office. You stop work after Wednesday. And that's that. Sort out your cases in that time or pass them on to the others in your firm. But you are not going out anywhere else. Your mother or I will drop you at work and pick you up. You will not bring shame to our family." Then I stand up and announce, "I am going to Kampala,"

"At this time?" Zubeida looks at her wristwatch.

"Yes, at this time. Don't worry. I won't travel back in the dark. I'll stay tonight at Mehboob's. We will set the date for the wedding. I've made my decision. There is nothing to discuss."

"But, Abba, I don't love Hussein."

"You should be ashamed of mentioning *that* word in front of your parents."

Chapter 34
Day 1:
Saturday 5th August
Rehana: Ending the Engagement

A few minutes after Abba leaves, I tell Amma that I want to go out.

"I promised your father that I won't let you out on your own," Amma says, looking worried.

"I'm not going to see Ramesh, so don't worry. I want to speak to Jyoti - just a short chat." My best friend Jyoti lives only a few doors away. I can ring Ramesh from there.

Amma still looks doubtful.

"I promise I'll be back in half an hour. Please, Amma."

Amma nods and I rush out.

Jyoti's parents are out. So, as soon as I get there, I ask Jyoti if I could use her phone. She leaves me alone in the living-room where the phone is situated. I ring Ramesh and inform him about my parents' reactions. We agree that we will discuss our next step when we see each other at work on Monday.

Then I go to Jyoti's room and tears well in my eyes as I talk to her. She puts her arms round me to comfort me. "I've said this before and I repeat, our society is not yet ready to accept mixed marriages and so the solution is to go somewhere else. Elope to Kenya. Get married there and then inform your parents about it. They will have to accept the situation then."

"Not my father."

"I've known Yusuf*chacha* all my life," Jyoti remarks. "He is a gentle and kind man. Surely he will agree in the end."

"He is one of the kindest persons I know. But he will not

change his mind over this. Why do men object so vehemently when their daughters break the conventions?"

"I've got it." Jyoti claps her hands excitedly. "Since sons get away with it but not daughters, ask Hussein to call off the engagement. You two are very close - he's almost a brother to you. He'd do it for you."

"He'll be hurt."

"He'd have to be told one day. Also, didn't you tell me that he was hanging out with an English girl when he was in the UK?"

"I did hear the rumours. But you know it does not mean anything. Our men use their freedom when they are away from home. Once they are back here, they suddenly become champions of old traditions."

"So, when are you going to tell him?" Jyoti wants to know. "When the wedding cars bedecked with flowers and streamers are driving through the town with their horns blaring? Or are you going to broach it on the wedding night?"

"Oh, stop. I was hoping to break the news face to face the next time I see him."

"But you have no choice now. Your father will get there any minute, and the longer you leave it, the more complicated it will get."

"I know, but ..."

"But, nothing." Jyoti stands up decisively and drags me by my arm to the phone in the living-room.

I hold my breath as I dial the number. Hussein answers the phone.

"You just got me. I was about to go out," he says.

I blurt out my situation.

"Boo...hoo...hoo," he sobs, "you cruel heartless woman."

I have dreaded this moment. "I am terribly sorry to hurt you like this."

His voice now sounds amused. "Listen Rehana, my dear, I am going to give you fantastic news. I am in a similar situation myself, but did not know how to break the news to you. You see, I am seriously involved with a girl."

"You have a girlfriend?"

"Yes, that's what I said."

"Oh. Oh. I can't believe it." I laugh and wipe tears of relief from my eyes with my free hand. I had never imagined that hearing the news of my betrothed's love for another woman would make me so happy. "That's wonderful news," I sniffle.

"You are crying. That's why I dreaded breaking the news to you," he jokes.

"Stop being facetious. Have you told your parents yet?"

"No."

"And why not? Are you not serious about her?"

"I am. I am."

"Then why not tell your parents? You know it's so much easier for men in our society."

"I know. I know. But it's just that she is a journalist and she is ..."

"What's wrong with her being a journalist?"

"I'm glad I'm not marrying you." Hussein laughs. "You never let me finish my sentences. Even when we were kids, you used to boss me around."

"All right, you poor oppressed man, I'm listening."

"She's English. She's called Sally Markham."

"Is that the girl you were seeing when in the UK?"

"What? You know about it? You lawyers are like detectives."

"Everyone in our circle knows. And you have obviously kept in touch with her."

"Yes. And what's more she has been working in Uganda for the last couple of months."

"You won't be able to keep it secret for long now. You better tell your parents right away."

"On the other hand, I could let you take the blame for breaking our engagement and then who would blame a poor heart-broken male for finding solace in the arms of another woman?" But then his tone changes. "I am sorry. I shouldn't be teasing you like this when you must be desperately worried. I will go and break the news to my parents right away. Before your father arrives. Then, I will be blamed for breaking the engagement. Happy? Honestly. The things one does to help one's betrothed's love affair with another man!"

I then ring Ramesh again.

Chapter 35
Day 1:
Saturday 5th August
Ramesh: Ups and Downs in Life

I have led a happy, carefree life so far. A couple of months ago, here was I, young, fit and healthy, successful in my profession and financially secure. My parents were introducing me to girls with a view to marriage, and, had I continued, I would have met someone I fancied enough to marry.

Then I met Rehana, and I felt I was in the Seventh Heaven. (If I say this to Shashi, I can well imagine him putting on a childlike innocent expression on his face and asking me, *"Does it mean you were in the Sixth Heaven until then?"* He would then argue, *"Since the Universe is infinite, why is the hierarchy in Heavens limited to only seven - why not infinite?"*)

They say there are ups and downs in life. Today has been like a roller-coaster.

First thing in the morning, I learnt from Rehana that, as she had predicted, her mother was amenable, but her father is totally opposed to our relationship. I know it was wishful thinking on our part, hoping that he would accept the situation. Rehana fears that he will never change his mind on this issue. Of course, we will get married, but we have not had time to discuss when and how.

And then we got the tragic news about Patrick's death. When we left Patrick in Kumar's uncle's property on Oboja Road, we had agreed at his suggestion that we would not contact him there. He said he had friends who would help him find his way to Tanzania. But somehow the Army

177

managed to get him. I am almost certain that before his death he did not reveal the fact that Kumar and I had helped him because, if he had, then by now the army would have descended on us.

Then there is the Amin's announcement reported in the paper today. The headline in the *Uganda Argus* says, *All Asians Must Go*.

And, finally, there were two phone calls from Rehana this afternoon. As she was using her friend Jyoti's parents' telephone, she kept it brief. When she rang the first time, she said that her father had decided that she must resign from her job with a mere three days' notice. And she is not to go anywhere without being escorted by one of her parents. And then she will be forced to marry her cousin Hussein. I tried to assure her that on Monday we will plan our next move and we *will* find a way.

Later Rehana telephoned again, this time with a piece of good news. After speaking to me, she rang her cousin Hussein to break off the engagement before her father reached Hussein's home in Kampala. And guess what? Hussein told her that he was involved with an English girl and had not told Rehana about it yet, as he dreaded the task of breaking the news to her.

Oh, one other piece of good news. After all these dramatic happenings on a single day in my life, I have not gone insane.

Chapter 36
Day 1:
Saturday 5th August
Yusuf: More Bad News

Normally it takes me about an hour to drive to Kampala, but today a lorry has broken down just outside the city. There is a big traffic jam, and it is another half an hour before I pull up outside my brother Mehboob's house in Old Kampala.

My sister-in-law Shirin answers the door and asks me to go to the living-room, where Mehboob is sitting. He rises to his feet and embraces me but something is definitely wrong. He looks troubled and subdued at the same time. He asks after Zubeida and Rehana. When I enquire after his family, he does not answer but looks out of the window at children playing cricket on the street. Just then Shirin comes in with a tray with tea and snacks. After serving us, she pours herself a cup of tea and sits down next to Mehboob.

I am about to broach the subject of marriage, thinking it is best to come straight to the point, when Mehboob raises it. "I am afraid we have really bad news." He hesitates before continuing, "Just half an hour ago, Hussein dropped a bombshell. He informed us that he has been seeing a female friend and wants to call off the engagement with Rehana."

"We are still reeling from the shock," Shirin adds.

I am stunned and sit mulling over the news, feeling wretched.

"Sorry, brother." Mehboob apologises again. "Poor Rehana. I can't bear to think of the effect it will have on the girl. I am so sorry. If Hussein was just a boy, I could slap him and tell him to stop being foolish. It is so very upsetting but what can you do with a grown up son? Perhaps you can talk some sense into him. He respects you. I told him the scandal would make it difficult for me to show my face in public."

"It shouldn't cause a scandal." I feel theirs is a relatively minor problem compared to what I am facing. "We never publicly announced their engagement. It was a private understanding within our family."

"But I haven't told you the full story yet. He has been snared by a white girl."

"What?"

"Yes. A white girl, called Sally." Shirin interjects. "Someone he met in London, and now she has followed him here. Apparently she is a newspaper journalist."

Mehboob sighs. "We sent him to UK to get a degree, but he also got someone's *dikri* (daughter). Today's generation! They will not be told. You know, I could almost accept his decision. But then I try to imagine the effect it will have on poor Rehana. I can't bear it. How could he even consider it?"

I clear my throat. "I came here today so that we could set the date for the wedding." I clear my throat yet again. "But let me confess. I am in a similar situation to you."

I then tell them about Rehana's friendship with the Hindu boy. "However, I will do all in my power to stop her from doing anything so foolish," I announce. I certainly intend to put a stop to that madness.

We discuss our predicaments for a long time. We brothers have not talked so frankly to each other for years. Sharing our problems has a therapeutic effect on us, and the oppressive cloud that darkened our moods gradually lifts.

"It is very likely we will never face as traumatic a situation ever again in our lives," Mehboob comments.

"And the crisis is caused by our younger generation because they refuse to be bound by centuries-old conventions," I ponder aloud. "The society has changed so much since we were little boys in Kampala. Wonder how many more changes we will witness in our lifetime?"

We get our answer a couple of hours later when Radio Uganda reports Amin's announcement for the first time.

Chapter 37
Day 1:
Saturday 5th August
Devji: Gathering Storm

Velji and I do not go for our usual walk by the lake in the evening. But that is because it looks as if it is going to rain, although the dark thunderclouds have moved on. Instead we spend the evening sitting in Motilal's shop, discussing the events of the day with other friends. There is a lot to discuss.

There was the dead body found lying outside the post office in the morning. But, with all due respect to the dead man, the news that will affect us a great deal more was the President's announcement ordering us to leave the country.

Also, it seems strange to think that yesterday at about the same time when President Amin made his announcement, which could destroy our lives as we know it, here we were, only about eighty miles away, arguing about how to spend the money raised by the Temple Committee. Should we spend the money on a shrine, and if so, to which god should it be dedicated, or would it be better spent on a scholarship fund? We had no idea that what appeared to us to be so important was only a minor issue compared to the President's order. People get so carried away by events nearer home that they lose a sense of proportionality as far as the bigger, more significant events in the world are concerned.

I can well imagine that when the bombs were dropped on Hiroshima and Nagasaki, quite likely, at that very moment, there were people haggling over the price of fish, or couples arguing about what colour to paint their kitchen walls, or whom to invite to their daughter's wedding.

One needs to put life's trials and tribulations into perspective. Because one minute life is normal, and the next - boom!

Chapter 38
Day 1:
Saturday 5th August - Evening
Shashi: Rumour or Fact?

I first heard about Amin's announcement at lunchtime and I thought that someone might have started the rumour so that people would stop thinking about the body of the man on the footpath next to the post office. But how wrong was I.

After siesta, I go to the sitting room and find the *Uganda Argus* with its headline: *All Asians Must Go*. But the papers sometimes report false stories. And I do not give it much thought.

At about five o'clock as it gets a bit cooler, Anver comes round and we call on Vinod, who emerges from his door even before we knock on it. He has changed from his purple trousers into maroon ones, which are just as widely flared. He comes out rocking, swinging his shoulders and singing the Drifters' song, *Another Saturday night and I ain't got nobody*. He clicks his fingers to provide a beat to the lyrics.

"How come you sound so happy?" Anver enquires.

"Just because it's Saturday," Vinod sings, though not quite managing to maintain the same tune.

"What's so special about Saturdays?" I ask.

"Ah, Saturday is the *walk-day*."

"It does not have to be. During holidays one day is the same as the other. We could just as easily play badminton or cricket today and go for a walk on a weekday."

Vinod sighs as if mustering patience to explain an obvious point to an obstinate child. "Because Saturday evenings are so lively - there is an 'electric' charge in the atmosphere."

"Yeah," Anver agrees and adds, "Also, we meet other friends and not just guys we play with."

"Come on be honest." I tell them. "You see most of the other friends in school, or bump into them on the streets anyway. So, don't give me that. Tell me the real reason."

"What else could it be?"

"Girls." I say. "Those *champoodi* girls put on their lovely dresses and prettify themselves before going for a walk and boys derive great pleasure just looking at them."

They giggle. "We will have to revise our opinion of you," Anver says.

"To think that all along we thought you are such a *sharif* boy."

I say, "We use the word *sharif* for a 'goodie-goodie'. But it really means honest. It is you guys who are not being honest." At the same time I make a mental note to look up the origin of the word. It sounds Persian or something. (Maybe Mr Joshi knows the origin; he is a mine of information on languages.)

They do not want to admit that they are not being honest with themselves, and to hide the fact they start to giggle. Uncontrollably. I restrain myself even though their giggling is rather contagious. So they start to tickle me and we end up walking along the main street all gripped in this giggling fever. (I have read somewhere that there was such a thing in Europe in the middle ages. Wonder if it is true? Must ask Mr Nayyar.)

We stop giggling abruptly as we approach the post office, remembering the body. But the body has disappeared. One could say that the body is buried. In the society's collective memory. It will not be reported in the news. I know it was John's brother but that's all I know. Ramesh does not want me to be involved in it, and refuses to give any more details. It feels unreal.

We walk to the Pier and then along the lakeshore up to the temple. Our usual walk but it feels different today. There is quite a buzz. The body should have been the main topic of conversation but it isn't. People are discussing the President's announcement yesterday ordering all Asians to leave the country in ninety days.

It is now just before nine in the evening, a few minutes before the news commences. All our family are in the sitting room. Vinod and his family are here, too. Kamlamasi squeezes in between Ba and Lalita Auntie. Maji refuses the offer of a seat and sits cross-legged on the floor. Sunita cuddles up to her grandmother. Vinod and I sit on the dining chairs. We all watch the screen in silence.

I can imagine everyone in the town sitting in front of a television set with the same question in their mind: *is it just a rumour or is Amin serious about his threat?*

Ramesh switches on the television. The reception is rather poor but he fiddles with the TV until he gets a reasonable picture. A bit crackly, but clear enough for us to get the message.

Evening TV News:

President Amin wants all Asians holding British Passports to leave the country in 90 days. He will ask the UK High Commissioner, Mr. Richard Slater to arrange for their repatriation.

There is a short clip of Amin on the screen. He flashes a smile before he starts to speak, and after he finishes.

"Just shows how appearances can be misleading," Papa

says. "If I had met the man socially, I would have quite likely come away thinking, *A charming fellow. Looks like a jolly good chap.*"

But we are all aware of his ruthlessness and his bloody rule. We hear how his opponents regularly disappear and we have heard of, and occasionally seen, bodies floating down the Nile.

What Amin says is mind-numbing, assuming he carries his threat out.

"But it is not as bad as we were led to believe," Papa suggests. "Apparently BBC reported that he wants all Asians to leave Uganda in ninety days. Instead, in this announcement today, he referred to Asians who hold British Passports."

Normally, after the news they play a short clip of music. Today it is an American singer by the name of Mahalia Jackson. She has a beautiful voice but I still get up and switch off the TV.

We have a short discussion, but it is low key and subdued, considering the explosive content.

Papa points out, "In the past Amin has issued many a decree. He blurts out whatever comes into his head as there is no Parliament to consult or Commissions to examine an issue, before eventually coming up with recommendations. He is whimsical and we should wait and see."

I say, "But what if he means it?"

"Amin is bad and he is mad," Ramesh announces before leaving the room. "Even if he does not carry out his threat, we should seriously consider moving to a land where there is democracy and one's life is not controlled by a power-crazed dictator."

It looks as if our days in Uganda are numbered. To ninety. And the first day has just passed.

Chapter 39
Day 1:
Saturday 5th August
Shashi: Neither Black nor White

We are living in historic times. A drama is unfolding around us. This could be the beginning of my writing career and I have decided to write about the news today like a journalist writing an article for a magazine. Of course, I will use fictitious names for the characters appearing in my report. But I will try and capture the spirit of the time. So, here it goes:

Today starts like any other day. Kanti wakes up early, gets ready noiselessly and his silent shadow slips out of the house just before half past six.

He knocks gently on his friend's door and Ali emerges immediately. They chat amiably as they walk in the semi-darkness along the deserted street with its shuttered shops. When they arrive at the Pier, the twilight is just being edged out by the dawn. Silently, they watch the calm blue surface of the lake mirror the golden sky with its rose-tinted clouds. They listen to the excited twitter of the freshly awoken birds. This is a daily communion and each is immersed in his private thoughts.

They think of their everyday concerns. Kanti makes a mental note that he must order some new stock for his shop, especially woollen suit material. He must also make enquiries about Naranbhai's nephew, who sounds just right for his eldest daughter.

Ali hopes that his landlord does not turn up today. There have been a few unexpected expenses recently.

They hurry home under the rapidly brightening sky. Kanti is greeted by the heady aroma of *chai masala* and then by his wife, Sudha. She is in the kitchen, humming an old film song, but is thinking of the day ahead: *I hope the yoghurt sets by midday. This afternoon at the WI meeting, I must propose regular sessions to sew clothes for the poor children.*

Ali enters his house and hears his wife Mumtaz giving instructions to their houseboy, John, about shopping in the market today, "A small bunch of *mtoke*. And make sure *karela* are not soft."

They all expect to go through the day attending to the business of living. But today is different. The rumour reaches them.

About mid-morning, Sudha is sitting at the dining table shelling peas when Mumtaz from next-door walks in through the open front door. Sudha knows it is Mumtaz from her shuffling walk. She flicks the sandals off her feet with her usual gentle kick forward and announces herself well before she gets to the kitchen with, "I say, have you heard yet?" She sits down facing Sudha and proceeds to tell her about Amin's speech the night before.

At Kanti's shop, Gurmit Singh comes to collect his suit. He tries it on in the fitting room at the back, turns round to look at his reflection in the mirror and says, "Perfect." That pleases Kanti.

Gurmit adds, "I can wear this when I leave Uganda."

"I didn't know you were planning to leave."

"Nor did I till an hour ago," Gurmit says. And then informs Kanti of the news item in the *Uganda Argus*, though it is sandwiched between other trivial announcements, and so Amin may not be serious. He is known for making proclamations, which are never followed up.

Around noon, it is getting uncomfortably hot. There is a lull in the business and Kanti pops next door into Veljibhai's grocery store. The main topic of conversation is the dead body lying by the post office.

Tapu, the shoemaker, whose shop is not far from where the body was dumped, informs the others, "It has been removed now. An army truck came and picked it up. Poor man!"

Kanti mentions the news about Amin's speech ordering all the Asians to leave. Tapu holds his hands up as he says, "Amin has made many threats in the past that have not been followed up. I wouldn't worry."

When Kanti goes home for lunch, Sudha tells him what she had heard from Mumtaz. He has an uneasy feeling that this might not be an empty threat. But the thick afternoon heat dulls his senses, nips his worries. So, he has a siesta after lunch, as it is Saturday.

The heat mellows in the late afternoon as thunder clouds pile up in the sky. By the time Kanti washes and changes, the clouds have blown away towards the horizon. He goes for his usual walk by the lake. He meets several friends, some of whom could easily be you.

Most of you have heard about the announcement by now, but do not take it seriously. But you all say that the truth will be revealed in tonight's news broadcast.

You can hardly wait to hear the evening news. After dinner you sit down in front of your old television with the rest of the family. The neighbour from across the road arrives with his family. They have no TV. You think, *It would be nice to get a bigger TV*. And then there is a hush as the news starts. "President Amin has this announcement for the nation." You feel emptiness in the pit of your stomach as the president starts talking.

You would think that you would pay full attention to something of such importance to you and your loved ones. But no. You are in a daze. Your thoughts wander. You only hear snippets. 'I want all Asians out in ninety days ... leeches ... sabotage the economy ..." You do not understand what he is talking about. *Me? Sabotage the economy? Really? How?* The ground beneath your feet is being taken away. You may have been born here, always considered this to be your home, but that makes little difference.

The TV reception is rather poor, there is crackling and the images flicker on the screen. But the message comes through crystal clear. Your skin has the wrong colour. You do not belong.

You cannot do much about your identity. Yes, you do belong to a minority group. A visible minority, brown skinned and not black, with origins in India so that you still cling to the Indian culture. But is it a sin? A crime punishable by exile? You have never tried to impose your culture on others, nor tried to gain political power.

You consider your options. You could return to India or Pakistan. But, the governments there might justifiably say, *you left of your own accord for a higher standard of living and now you are homeless you want to come back. We have enough problems of our own*. Besides, you don't wish to go back; life is hard there, which is why you left in the first place.

Many of you still hold British passports from the pre-independence era, but Britain has not been very welcoming in the past. Once again there is that little matter of your skin pigment. You are brown not white. You are being thrown out of one country because you are not dark enough and refused entry into another because you are too dark!

Chapter 40
Day 2:
6th August 1972
Devji: A Tyrant

It is a grey, cloudy morning as Velji and I walk in silence to the Park to join the other *Sages*.

Today there is a big crowd there. People have quite sensibly formed two circles rather than one large unwieldy one.

We hesitate before Velji points at the smaller group, where most of the regulars are sitting. They are already in the middle of a lively discussion. "Shit with them?" Velji says in English. It is something he does when he is excited, despite having only a rudimentary knowledge of the language. And then in his nervous state he pronounces the sound 's' as 'sh'. I have corrected him in the past, but today I let it pass.

Malkit Singh and Karim shift a little to make room for us. We unfurl our hankies and lower ourselves onto the grass, which is practically dry because the sun has come up.

Not surprisingly, Amin's announcement is the only topic of conversation today. On the whole, the *Sages* represent the general view of the community, a majority of whom do not believe that Amin is serious about his ultimatum. But after much discussion, we decide that Amin's announcement is not an empty threat. He means it.

I state the obvious. "We are a minority. A visible minority due to our colour. And we are a more prosperous section of the society."

"Significantly more proshperous," Velji concludes for me. "And so an obvious target."

"Also," I add, "Amin needs to ensure that the Army carries

192

on supporting him. So, if he gets rid of us, who make up the bulk of the middle and the upper class in the country —"

"He can hand over our propertiesh and bishnesses to the Army and his shupporters and that would keep them happy." Velji again concludes for me.

"Precisely." I rest my case.

"But that's not right." Velji objects.

We laugh. Malkit Singh says, "Since when has Amin acted right? He grabbed power in a military coup. That wasn't right. He has killed thousands of his opponents. That isn't right. He is a tyrant and a despot. The people never elected him. What do you expect from him?"

"Being unelected does not mean he has to be cruel and nashty." Velji's voice gets louder in his excitement. "In the old days, there was no such thing as elections. And yet there were many kings who cared for their subjects. They were like patriarchs. We hold many of them in high esteem. Take Rama, for example. He cared for his people more than he did for his own happiness. He was so just and righteous that we actually worship him."

"So you don't think we will build temples dedicated to Lord Amin?" I jest.

"No, unless it is done by people who are so desperate to emigrate to UK and who may think God sent Amin to accomplish the task." Velji has the ability to interpret events in an unusual manner, which is one of the reasons I am so fond of him.

The discussion then turns to where did we go wrong? The same question must have been asked by other communities, who also faced similar situations in the past: Indians in Burma, Chinese in Indonesia. And most notably by the Jews over many centuries and especially during the Holocaust, which was barely three decades ago. For Jews the important factor was a rogue evil leader, Hitler, who led his nation astray. In our case, it is Amin. Whatever our shortcomings, it just does not justify expelling a community, solely identified by their different skin colour. For that's what it is because what about Gyan Singh or Mukhtar Shaikh? They both have African wives and have children by them. But they are both asked to leave along with the rest of us.

One could say that we did not integrate fully with the Africans. But then we had a semi-apartheid system here under the British, when the communities lived in different parts of town and kids went to different schools. Besides, cultural changes occur gradually and, historically speaking, we have lived here for a very short time.

Many people talk about paying for our sins in the past lives. God decides, they say. It all sounds too implausible to me and all I can say is *thank God I am not a believer*.

Chapter 41
Day 2:
6th August
Rehana: A Tryst

It is Sunday morning and Amma and I have no idea what time Abba will return from Kampala. I request Amma's permission to go and visit Jyoti.

"Only for a short time, mind you. Your father will be upset if you are out when he returns."

Jyoti tells me that her family have just left to go to a wedding and will be out most of the day. "You could invite Ramesh round," she says with a mischievous smile.

Ramesh arrives a few minutes later. Jyoti holds her bedroom door open and waves us in. "You will have more privacy here," she says, as she heads for the living-room.

As soon as we hear the door shut behind Jyoti, we turn to each other with a fierce hunger. I cling to Ramesh and then raise my head as my lips reach out for his. We stand there in the middle of the room exchanging a long passionate kiss. Ramesh runs his fingers through my hair, feels my face before relaxing our embrace so that he can place his hands on my breasts. I freeze when he does so but then move away from him and unbutton my blouse. I close my eyes and sigh as he caresses my breasts. It lasts only a couple of minutes. I do not want to break away but I remember that we have a limited time. I gently but firmly extricate myself from the embrace, move his hands away from me and button up my blouse. "We can't," I say. "I've promised my mother not to be long. My father will be back from Kampala soon."

We sit facing each other on Jyoti's bed. There is a short pause. I am sure we are both thinking about the same thing as we consider our situation.

"Oh Ramesh, what are we going to do?"

"You told me that Hussein is going to tell them about his English girlfriend. That lets you off."

"No, it doesn't." I say emphatically. "I know my father. There will be less pressure on me for a while. But I cannot imagine him ever consenting to our relationship. He will now look for another boy for me. Can we just not elope?"

"It seems that is what we will have to do. But, I know, you are still hoping to win over your father's consent."

"I know. I would like to but --"

"Your father's back. I just noticed his car." We hear Jyoti call out from the living-room.

I quickly exchange another kiss with Ramesh before hurrying back home.

Chapter 42
Day 2:
6th August
Devji: Indian Government's Announcement

Velji and I are sitting in our living-room when I switch on the television for the news.

Today's Evening News:

The Indian government announces that Ugandan Asians holding British passports are primarily Britain's responsibility.

Velji is outraged. "How could they? The rotten lot."

I get up and switch off the television. "They are trying to be helpful. They are - -"

"Helpful?" Velji interrupts me. "To shut the door in our face when we might need them? You call that being helpful?"

I explain to Velji that if either the British or the Indian government show willingness to accept any expelled Asians, there will be less pressure on Amin to change his mind. The international community would feel that it is not such a big disaster. We would be considered to be people who were returning home, albeit after having spent most of our lives in Uganda, rather than as refugees being thrown out by a ruthless dictator on racist grounds.

It calms Velji down but he returns to his favourite theme since yesterday. "Why didn't everyone get Ugandan citizenship after Independence? If they had shown that commitment to the nation, this turn of events may never have occurred."

I point out to him that many people did apply but the Ugandan government sat on their applications and never processed them. They are still hoping that the decree does not apply to them.

"Well, I applied straight away, and became a citizen of Uganda a long time ago. Cautious people like you held back. Even Mother thought I was being foolish. The events have shown that I was right," Velji insists.

I do not voice what many of us feel at the moment. Perhaps it is better that we are not Ugandan citizens. Maybe we will be better off away from the cruel dictatorship of a tyrant. The only reason Amin has not turned on us is because we are British citizens. Otherwise he would have been as ruthless with us as he has been with the rest of the Ugandans.

Chapter 43
Day 3:
Monday 7th August 1972
Shashi: The Saboteurs

Radio Uganda News Bulletin:

President Amin: *Many non-Ugandans actively sabotage our economy. They are Uganda's enemies. I command them all to leave at the same time as the British Asians. In ninety days.*

Just Papa and I are in the living-room when we hear the news.

"How are we supposed to be saboteurs?" I ask Papa.

Papa explains to me that probably Amin refers to the people who send money abroad.

"Surely, only a minority of Asians with plenty to spare would be involved in it. Also, Ramesh told me that many of our leaders have Swiss bank accounts. But now I understand," I declare. "You are a saboteur if you are brown and send money abroad."

Papa laughs. "I must admit that sixteen year olds are blunt and see the truth more clearly."

"It appears that now Amin is after other non-Ugandans, as well," I comment.

"He is still really referring to us. Just making sure that all of us are included," Papa says. "You can imagine, can't you? He ordered all the Asians with British passports to leave. But then he realised that some of us have Indian or Pakistani passports. So, now he is telling them to get out, as well. He really wants to get rid of us all."

"Ah, but he can't touch people like Veljikaka, who are

Uganda citizens," I point out.

"No. That is because no other nation would accept them. But mark my word. He will try and make it difficult for them to stay on, so that they leave as political refugees."

"How do you think he will do it?" I ask Papa.

Papa sighs. "He will search for any excuse. And if nothing works, he will just say, '*Oh, get out.*' He is like the wicked wolf trying to justify killing the innocent lamb."

"What wicked wolf?" I ask.

"You remember the story from '*Panchtantra*'?" Papa then reminds me the story briefly. After just a few sentences, I recall him telling it to me when I was five years old or so. But I let him finish it. It is only a short tale and he likes telling his stories. And to be truthful, I enjoy listening to them, even if I have heard them before.

The Story of the Wolf and the Lamb

A wolf saw a lamb drinking water from a stream. He rushed at the lamb, but before he could grab the lamb, it looked up at him and said, "I've done you no harm. Why are you attacking me?"

The wolf tried to think of an excuse and came up with, "As you can see, we drink water from the same stream. And you foul it by putting your snout in it."

The lamb said, "Are you sure it is the same stream?"

"Yes, I am sure it is," the wolf said, getting ready to attack the lamb.

The lamb asked "OK. Show me where your drinking place is!"

The wolf pointed towards the spot where he regularly went to drink.

"But that is upstream from here," the lamb argued.

"Oh shut up," the wolf said. And grabbed the poor lamb.

Chapter 44
Day 3:
7th August
Ramesh: A Lawyer's Job

When I arrive at work, Kumar is already in his room. I go in to say hello. He is scribbling on a document with a red pencil. He looks up. His eyes look tired and there is a troubled expression on his face.

"What's the matter?" I ask. "You don't look well."

"I lay awake for hours last night thinking about poor Patrick. Then this morning, I hear the other news. How long have you known it?"

"Known what?" I try to guess what is on his mind. "About Amin's announcement?"

Kumar flicks his hand, still brandishing the red pencil. "No. You know what I'm talking about. Rehana's resignation."

"She told me yesterday." I stand facing him on the other side of the desk.

"Why is she quitting? Have you two quarrelled or something?" He gets up and limps round the desk. "People say, beware of these office romances. They're fine when they last, but it makes working together very difficult if they don't. And she was getting on so well here. And now she has handed in her notice. Apologising for leaving, but without any explanation. What does she mean by personal circumstances?" There is another flash of red as he jabs the pencil closer to my face and says, "Am I right in surmising that the personal circumstances have something to do with you?"

"Yes, but not ..."

Kumar interrupts me. "I thought so. So you've had a lover's tiff, is that it?"

"No! Certainly not. It's her father insisting that she give up the job to stop her from seeing me."

"Oh dear. I jumped to a conclusion without gathering all the evidence. And I call myself a lawyer." He taps his head with the knuckles of his right hand, notices the pencil in his hand and puts it away. He then limps back round the desk and collapses in his chair. "I'm sorry," he says finally. "It must be really upsetting for both of you. If I can help ... do anything ... please let me know!"

"Thanks. I will." I know I can count on his support.

There is a brief silence. Finally Kumar says, "So what do we do now? Do you think Rehana's father will change his mind? Or do we need to advertise again for a new partner?"

I shrug. "If Amin means what he said, we will have to close down our office soon anyway."

"No-one knows how seriously one should take his announcement. I had a call from Kevin Shuttler earlier. He said that the British Ambassador was going to see Amin today and Amin may withdraw his ultimatum."

"And what if he does not?"

Kumar declares decisively, "We will continue business as usual. Even if we have to leave within ninety days, we will continue practising until the day we leave."

"But, why? If we are thrown out, we'll have to leave with empty hands. So what do you suggest we'll do with the money we earn in the meantime? There'll be nothing to spend it on as the shops will start closing down soon." I can picture in my mind's eye stores getting boarded up as their owners flee the country, town centres beginning to look like ghost-towns, hospital wards lying empty as doctors and nurses emigrate, schools not reopening in September after the August holidays, both kids and teachers having flown to safe havens.

Without any hesitation Kumar replies, "We'll give the money away if we have to leave. Kintu could have some of it. But we'll continue practising as long as we have clients. We are lawyers and our clients need us. We're not in it just for the money."

He stands up to stare out of the window at *Nile Sports House*, *Kisumu Sweet Mart*, *A1 Stationers* and a handful of other stores across the street. A group of giggling girls is walking on the pavement, some in Punjabi dresses, and others in skirts and blouses. A couple of African men ride on their bikes next to each other talking. There is hardly any other traffic on the road. But then that is not unusual for sleepy little Jinja.

Kumar sighs and sits down at his desk. He stares sightlessly at the open folder in front of him.

I turn round and walk out of his room and into Rehana's office. She is sitting with her elbows on the desk and her hands cupping her face. She smiles at me but there is sadness in her eyes.

"Two more days. That's all you and I have." She looks tired. She has obviously not been sleeping well. "After Wednesday I will not be able to leave home without a chaperone."

"Don't let us panic yet. I am trying to sort it out." I attempt to comfort her without revealing the despair I am beginning to feel.

"And then there is Amin's announcement. If he means to carry his threat out, what will happen to us? We may end up in different places. We might not even be in the same country."

"Yes. I know. But we will be together if we are a married couple. So I think that despite all the obstacles, we should marry as soon as possible."

Rehana springs to her feet, goes to the door and gently closes it. She returns to me and puts her arms round my neck. We exchange a long kiss. We stop when we hear some voices outside the door.

"Was that a proposal?" She asks with a smile.

"I suppose that's what it was."

"And I thought you would never propose."

"I didn't think I had to formally propose."

"And why not?" she says archly.

"Well," I try to state the obvious. "We have known all along that we will marry and spend our lives together."

"It is still nice to be proposed to. Some of my English friends used to say that it is more thrilling than an actual engagement party. Oh, I am so happy."

"I wish I could say the same," I say, trying to sound sad.

"Aren't you happy? Why?"

"Because you haven't said 'yes'."

"Yes," Rehana says and then shouts, "yes, yes, yes."

There is a knock on the door. "Are you alright?" It is Kumar's voice.

We break our embrace but remain standing in the middle of the floor holding hands and I call out, "Come in."

Kumar and Kintu enter the room looking concerned.

Kumar asks, "Is everything alright?"

Kintu says, "We thought we heard some shouting - almost screaming - so we thought we should check."

Rehana and I look at each other and she nods at me. I say, "We are engaged now."

Kumar rushes to us and nearly loses his balance due to his weak right leg. He throws his arm round each of us. "I am so very happy for you. My heartiest congratulations to you both."

Then Kintu embraces us. "May God bless your union,

my dear, dear friends."

Kumar clears his throat. "You two have made this momentous decision - at least momentous as far as your personal lives are concerned. The question that you need to address now is *'what next?'* The path ahead is strewn with obstacles and you will need considerable courage and imagination to navigate your way towards happiness. The days ahead will test your love and fortitude and ---"

I interrupt him, "You said we can count on your help. We certainly will need it."

So we all sit down round the table to draw up a plan of action.

We decide that we will get married in Kisumu, where my cousin Subhash lives. It is just across the border in Kenya. We will leave soon after Rehana arrives at the office tomorrow morning so that by mid-morning we will cross the Kenyan border, and around lunch-hour be in Kisumu. I will ask Subhash to book a civil ceremony at 2 p.m. We could then be legally married by half past two. After the ceremony, Rehana will ring her parents to announce our news. We will spend the night at Subhash's house, and arrive back in Jinja the day after tomorrow.

"Tell me how can I help?" Kumar offers. "Shall I come with you to give you moral support? Or drive you there? I could be a witness."

"Thanks Kumar," Rehana speaks for both of us. "We would like you, Kintu, to come as well."

"I would love to. But if we close the office we would raise suspicions. And shutting it down for two days without notice is not good for our practice." As always, Kintu points out the practicalities of any plan.

We gratefully accept his offer to stay behind in the office. "Also, Kintu, please cancel all our appointments for tomorrow," Rehana says.

Then Rehana asks Kumar. "Can Manjula come?"

"It's just not practical with the baby." Kumar points out.

"In that case," I suggest, "Subhash, my Kenyan cousin and you, Kumar, will be our only guests for the wedding - and our witnesses."

"What about your parents?" Kumar is puzzled. "You told me they have dropped their opposition."

"They would even assist us if I asked them to, but I do not want them to be involved in our secretive behaviour. A young couple in love may defy conventions. Our society is already being nudged towards greater freedom for youngsters. But people may not react kindly if their well-respected members are associated with a rebellious act. Besides, not knowing would make it easier for my parents to be on friendly terms with Rehana's family in future - assuming her father accepts our union."

We will have notes ready addressed to our parents. When Rehana's mother comes to collect her at lunch hour, Kintu will give her Rehana's note. And then he can deliver my note to my parents.

I am excited by the plan. We all are.

By the end of the day, I have managed to get in touch with Subhash in Kisumu, and have made the arrangements for the ceremony for tomorrow afternoon.

Rehana comes into my office and quietly closes the door. She looks tenderly at me and we embrace.

"I love you," she whispers.

"And I love you," I say.

Chapter 45
Day 4:
Tuesday 8th August 1972
Ramesh: To Kenya

After a fitful night, I am up early, and get to work earlier than normal. I expect to be the first one in and have the keys to the office ready in my hand, but am surprised to find the door wide open. Kintu and Kumar are standing in the reception area, drinking tea.

"Here comes the Prince himself." Kintu places his cup on his table and bows to me.

"Man of the day." Kumar puts on his BBC accent. He is proud of his ability to do so.

"I didn't expect you guys here so early."

"It's your big day and we are the excited ones." Kintu says.

"I still wish you were coming with us too," I tell Kintu.

"I know. I know. But I will be more use holding the fort here." Kintu shakes my hand vigorously. "Good luck my friend. I pray to God that everything goes well today."

"Ramesh is a great organiser," Kumar says, putting his hand on my shoulder. "I am sure he has covered all possible angles."

"Only things over which I have control. I have no control over the weather, for example. What if there is one of those massive tropical storms and the roads are flooded? The heavy rains have now ended, but you never can tell."

"Or maybe Mount Elgon might erupt after having lain dormant for millions of years," Kumar offers.

"Or there could be a nuclear war," Kintu laughs.

I look at my watch for the fifth time in as many minutes. I pace up and down the room, stop at the window to see if Rehana is coming and then resume my pacing.

"Joking apart, my main worry is that Rehana's parents may find out about our plans and stop her leaving the house." I peer anxiously out of the window again. "There is still no sign of her."

"Of course not. She normally arrives at eight and she will follow her normal routine today so as not to arouse any suspicions," Kumar points out.

"It's already five to eight. Well, six to eight, to be precise." I stand up and sit down again.

Kumar clears his throat. "When you arrived, I was about to tell Kintu about a poem I am composing in honour of today."

"Oh no. Not another one of your poems. I thought you had been cured of your affliction by now. You do remember, don't you, Kintu, how when in school we had to put up with Kumar's poetic efforts. How we suffered!"

"Come on. What was wrong with my poems?" Kumar pretends to be hurt.

"They didn't always rhyme or scan." Kintu suggests.

"Some of them did! Besides, I usually wrote modern poetry. It's free from such old-fashioned constraints. You have to rise above such petty concerns. Mine were flights of ideas, not just words."

"They lacked - how shall I put it? - lofty ideas? Poetic images?" I elaborate.

"One can write about everyday experiences. I am fully aware of glaring deficiencies in my poems, but you did like some of them. Go on. Admit it."

"You're right my friend. Now I remember. I take it all back.

Kintu, do you remember his poem about an old shoe."

"I must have missed that one," Kintu says. "I don't remember it."

"It was about an old shoe belonging to a one-legged man. After long, long use the heel wore down and he had it fixed. But then it got holes in the sole. He replaced the sole. Then the leather top tore. He had that mended. But soon after that the eyelets - holes for the laces - broke. So eventually he threw it away. But someone noticed it on the rubbish tip. Everyone in the town recognised the famous shoe. So the person very kindly brought it back to him. It was a sentimental homage to an old worn out shoe."

"I was making fun of people's attachment to worldly goods," Kumar explains.

"Yes, I know. And it was funny. OK, tell us what you have written about today."

"I haven't put pen to paper, yet. I am still formulating it in my head. It goes something like:

> *Today my best friend is going to elope*
> *It's like balancing on a slippery slope.*
> *It could bring a lot of heartache and pain*
> *But deviating from the path of love is insane.*

And before either of us can make a comment, Kumar admits, "All right, all right. It's trite. But you must agree that it rhymes a bit. And more important, it served its purpose of distracting you. You haven't looked at your watch for several minutes."

I immediately consult my watch. "It's three minutes past eight and she's still not here. Hope nothing has gone wrong."

I hurry back to the window and stare out. "She's coming. I can see her!" I shout gleefully. "I hope her mother does not come into the office."

I move away from the window so as not to be visible to her mother and wait impatiently for the door to open. There is a delay and I move back to the side of the window and peer out. Rehana is standing on the pavement outside the office watching her mother's vanishing form, clad all in white, even her head covered in a white *dupatta*. As she turns the corner and is out of sight, Rehana runs into the office and into my arms. However, she extricates herself quickly as Kumar and Kintu are present in the room. Her face is more animated and her dark eyes are livelier than normal.

Kumar has picked up his cup and is about to resume drinking when I reach over and take the cup from his hand and place it on the saucer on Kintu's table.

"Let's go," I say.

"*Diyo Bwana Kuba*, (Yes, Big Boss)," Kumar says solemnly as he stands to attention. He salutes me.

Kintu clicks his heels and also salutes me, "What are my orders, *Bwana*?"

Rehana reaches in her bag and removes an envelope and hands it to Kintu.

"Please give this to my mother when she comes to collect me and ..."

"Yes, *Mama Kuba*, (Big Madam)," Kintu now salutes her. "And what?"

"And thank you for all your help."

A few minutes later, we are on our way to Kenya. I sit in the front next to Kumar, who is driving. Rehana is in the back seat. There is only light traffic on the Main Street and we are soon at the end of the town. We pass the railway station, with its signboard, *Jinja, Altitude 3,869 feet*. On the right, beyond the workers' quarters for The Kilembe Copper Smelter, we can see a silver streak, which is the lake. A little further, on our left, we glimpse the Mwiri College perched on a flat-topped hill. And soon after that we come to the lush green cane fields of Madhvani Sugar Works.

We relax now. Jinja is behind us and in a couple of hours we will be in Kenya. I stretch my arm over the back of the seat and touch Rehana's hand. She kisses my fingers and then holds them against her cheek before releasing them.

I turn round in my seat to look at her. She has her window half open and she is enjoying the cool breeze. Her eyes are closed and her hair streams back. I think she is so beautiful and lovely in every way. And in a few hours she is going to be mine and I will be hers. My heart feels like it is melting as it overflows with happiness. All other thoughts and worries vanish. I know we will have to overcome her parents' opposition and my parents' reservations. We can surmount any obstacle because we love each other and that is what matters. And all this talk about Amin's threat to the Asians seems so remote. Even if Amin means it and we face exile, who cares as long as we are together?

As we approach the border, Kumar slows down and eventually stops, as there is a long line of vehicles queuing to get into Kenya.

"Why are they so busy today?" Kumar wonders aloud.

I get out of the car and walk towards the border post. I skirt round groups of men standing by their vehicles engaged in agitated conversation, until I reach a man on his own, leaning against his truck, wiping sweat from his forehead with a large blue handkerchief. He is a tall man, his trousers secured round his protruding belly with an orange patterned necktie. He catches my eye. "Can you believe it? No notice. No announcement. No nothing." He shakes his head in disbelief. "They close the border just like that. I have a load to deliver and it won't last long in this heat."

I walk on to the border post. There are military vehicles parked on either side of the metal gates marking the boundary. A group of armed sentries are stationed on the Kenyan side. Barbed wire stretches across from the gates on the road to the woods on either side.

The Ugandan Border Office is a brick building with a corrugated iron roof. A large picture of smiling Amin hangs on the wall behind the counter. A couple of young troubled-looking guards are talking to a group of irate drivers, who are remonstrating with them. Eventually the group decide that they are not going to get any more satisfaction arguing with the guard. I stand aside to let them pass.

I ask the young guard behind the counter what is happening. "Early this morning, the Kenyans constructed the barriers, and announced they have closed the border to all traffic. Indefinitely."

I keep my composure. "It's a bit sudden."

"I know. There were no announcements. The way I understand it, the border will open in a day or two but there will be extra rigorous checks. It seems that they are afraid that people thrown out of here will seek refuge in their country."

I realize that the official is a sensitive young man, who is being diplomatic and has avoided saying that in fact it is the Asians that Kenyans are trying to stop from entering their territory.

When I return to the car, Rehana and Kumar are watching a troop of Colobus monkeys leaping from branch to branch in the trees nearby, the long manes on their sides fanning out like white cloaks.

"The Kenyan authorities have obviously taken Amin's

announcement seriously. The border is sealed." I inform them.

"They can't just do that."

"They can and they have."

"So, when will the border reopen?" Rehana asks.

"No-one seems to know. Closed for an indefinite period, they say."

"What will we do now? My father was going to stop me going out on my own from Thursday but now he will lock me up as soon as he discovers our attempt to elope. And we won't have another opportunity." Rehana struggles to control her tears. "It seems the whole world is conspiring against us."

"No, not the whole world. I am with you," Kumar says as he reverses the car and does a u-turn. "And I will try and get you back in time so that your parents won't find out about this trip."

As we speed back towards Jinja, gloom settles in the car. Rehana remarks, "Nothing seems to be going right for us."

I turn round in my seat and smile at her, "It's not true."

"But it is. Tell me one thing that has worked well."

"The fact that we met and love each other?"

"I know. I know." She places her hand on my shoulder. "But why can't we just marry like most other people. In London, my friend Nancy met the man of her dreams. Both sets of parents welcomed their friendship with open arms. The couple arranged to get married. I was one of the bridesmaids. Everything went like clockwork on their wedding day. Whereas, we have to surmount obstacles at every step."

For a long time we sit in silence, mulling over the situation as Kumar speeds back towards Jinja.

There is a delay near Bugiri as a lorry full of *mtoke* is being unloaded next to the market on the high street. A small group of men are hurrying to-and-from the truck with big bundles of the green bananas on their backs. There is only one lane open on the road. I look at my watch and exchange an anxious glance with Rehana.

"I don't think we'll get back in time," she is worried.

"We may still make it," Kumar tries to reassure her and presses his foot down on the accelerator.

"Even if we do, what then?" Rehana is on the verge of crying.

"Well, we could arrange a secret ceremony in Jinja."

"When? After tomorrow I am going to be a virtual prisoner in my own home. It's hopeless." Tears start trickling down Rehana's cheeks.

I twist round and grasp her hand. "We'll find a way." I manage to sound more confident than I feel.

"What way? Seems we are being thwarted by our fate. If we were religious, we would turn to prayers now."

That gives me an idea. "Let's arrange to have a religious ceremony tomorrow."

Rehana sniffs. "Hindu or Muslim?"

I shrug my shoulders. "Let's go for a Muslim ceremony. Your father might be won over by it."

"I doubt if my father will ever change his mind. I also do not see much hope of finding a mullah willing to perform the ceremony. But we could try. And if that does not work, we go for a Hindu wedding," Rehana offers.

"Sort it out this afternoon," Kumar suggests.

I squeeze Rehana's hand, "See, it's not hopeless."

She smiles through her tears.

At twelve twenty-five, Kumar swerves into the parking space outside the office with a loud screech of the tyres. We burst into the office. Kintu assumes it is someone from

Rehana's family, who has come to escort her home, so he stands up, holding in his hand Rehana's letter to her parents. Rehana sighs with relief to see the note. She puts the letter in her handbag and a couple of minutes later Zubeida knocks on the door for her.

Chapter 46
Day 4:
8th August
Shashi: Kenya's Response

It is lunchtime. Papa has arrived home and is talking to Ba and Lalita Auntie in the living-room. Ramesh is not home yet. I pick up the *Uganda Argus* and go and sit in the smaller living-room. As I turn the page the article inside the paper about Kenya closing its border catches my eye.

Kenya Says NO to Asians from Uganda.

FRONTIER TO BE SEALED

Kenya said it would seal her frontier to bar entry to Asians threatened with expulsion from Uganda.

In his capacity as the Minister for Home Affairs, the Vice-President Mr. Daniel Arop Moi, said in Nakuru that Kenya has no intentions to provide refuge to the 80,000 Asians holding British passports affected by Uganda's President Amin decree to expel the lot from his country.

Mr. Moi said the Kenya Government will not allow Asian British Uganda passport holders to flock into the country since Kenya was not a dumping ground for citizens of other countries.

The Kenya - Uganda boundary would be sealed off against would-be refugees from Uganda using Kenya as a calling station, and maximum border patrols will be mounted to combat any intended influx ... The failure to comply would result to court prosecution.

... Kenya with 140,000 Asians of her own, and Tanzania are believed to be watching developments closely. Both have

considerable Asian minorities.

... Britain has, however, threatened to review her 4 million pounds a year aid to Uganda if the expulsion is carried out.

I put the paper down and look out of the window. Often there are birds gingerly picking at seeds scattered by Ba or Auntie. But now the yard is deserted. Right near the middle, someone has left a green watering can with patches of red rust on its body. It casts a short, sharp shadow in the mid-day sun. Can a nation get rid of thousands of its people like one disposes of a rusty can?

I reflect on our present situation. On a personal level, I think I am a fairly popular boy in the school with many friends. But suddenly I feel unwanted. We all do. Uganda wants us out. And now India, followed by Kenya, say that they do not want us to go there either. Presumably, the Kenyan government is trying to stop the brown saboteurs from entering their territory. No word of support for us. Just, "Keep Out." I imagine that in the past many Ugandan Asians have been welcomed with open arms when they went to Kenya or India to invest money. But now that we will be broke, we are not welcome there anymore.

I can hear the front door open and then Ba's voice summons me, "Shashi, lunch. Ramesh is here."

During the meal I tell the rest of the family the news, "I just read that Kenya is going to close the Ugandan border."

"They have already done it." Ramesh says.

"Already? How do you know?"

"I'll tell you later," he says.

I think, *Why the big mystery? Very likely he heard it from a client and all he has to say is so-and-so told me.*

217

Chapter 47
Day 4:
8th August
Ramesh: My News

After lunch is over, I turn to Ba and Papa and say that I have something very important to discuss with them

Lalita Auntie stands up, grabs Shashi's wrist and pulls him up to his feet, saying, "Come with me Shashi, we can have another game of chess. Maybe this time I will beat you."

But I stop them from leaving. "Stay, please. I would like you all to hear what I have to say."

I then describe all that had happened earlier today. I explain my reasons for secrecy, saying that I was trying not to get the family involved in an action which will have major social disapproval. There is a tense moment of silence as I wait for their reactions.

Ba sighs loudly and looks at Papa, who says, "We didn't realise you would move so fast. We thought you would still carefully consider all aspects of your action. But we forgot that the young are always impatient." He shrugs, looks at Ba and then faces me again. "Tell us how we can help?"

I sigh with relief when Ba smiles at Papa and nods and they both stand up together. I also rise from my seat. They come and hug me one after the other.

Papa says, "I appreciate your reasons for not involving us when you were going to elope. But there is nothing underhand about the religious ceremony you are planning for tomorrow. So, we would like to attend but I fear that Rehana's family will still be offended if we are present, and they are not even informed. So, we had better stay at home, but we give our blessings to you both."

Ba dabs her eyes, hugs me once again and says, "It breaks my heart not to be able to attend my son's wedding, but Papa's right. It will only make things more difficult for you with Rehana's parents if we attend." She then breaks away from the embrace, wipes the tears from her face with the end of her sari, and says, "I must get something sweet for the happy occasion." She then turns to Auntie and asks her, "Do you know if there are any *ladoos* left?"

"No, Bhabhi, they are all finished." Auntie shakes her head.

"I'll get some *jaggery*, in that case," Ba says and hurries to the kitchen.

Auntie comes and hugs me. Shashi stands up and holds out his hand to shake mine but I embrace him and tell him "Now you see how I knew the Kenyan border is closed."

Ba comes back from the kitchen and we all have small pieces of jaggery to sweeten our mouths. There are big smiles on all our faces.

"I wish I could come to help you celebrate this joyous occasion." Auntie says and then turns to Papa and Ba and asks, "Couldn't I go?"

They exchange a quick look and Ba says, "There is no reason why you shouldn't go. Yes, my dear, do go and represent me there."

"Great. Then I will represent Papa," Shashi, who has been listening quietly so far, announces. "The newly married couple can then come and touch my feet and ask for my blessings."

"Who's invited you?" I laugh.

"You can buy my silence with an invitation!"

I suddenly feel a cloud of worry descend on me. "I can't emphasise enough that the news must not reach Rehana's family before we go to the priest. If her father so much as gets an inkling of our plans, he will lock Rehana up in their house. And if she were already in the office, he would march in and take her back to their home by force. Finally, there is one other problem. We haven't yet found a priest, Muslim or Hindu, who is willing to conduct the ceremony."

"I know you do not want us involved directly," Papa says, "but I would gladly come and talk to Shankar Maraj in the temple if you like."

Chapter 48
Day 4:
8th August
Shashi: Aryans

Ramesh is in his room. As the door is open, I walk in without bothering to knock. He is sitting at his desk.

"You have only a few hours to organise everything for tomorrow. Do let me know if I can help in any way," I offer.

"Thanks, I will," he says and smiles.

"How are you going to manage? Marriages are huge affairs," I point out. "People prepare for them months in advance. When Vinod's sister, Ramila, got married, I went to help with writing and addressing the wedding invitations. And that took us a whole day."

"We are not inviting hundreds of guests."

"I know, but you are planning to marry tomorrow. And you haven't even found a priest to conduct the ceremony. And as if that isn't enough, there is a real possibility that the bride's father, if he discovers your plans, will march in and force his daughter to go back home. Yet you seem pretty calm."

"Why? How should I be?"

"Tearing your hair out."

He laughs. "If I did that, Rehana may not want to marry a man with huge bald patches on his head." Then he adds on a serious note, "I admit I was panicky this morning, worried that Rehana's parents might discover our plans and stop her from leaving home. And there were other unknown factors - such as the Kenyan border closing, as we found out to our cost. We hope tomorrow it will be more straightforward."

"But how about the ceremony itself? It takes hours and

hours and involves so many people. How will you get it done in the morning before lunch?"

"You are thinking of our traditional ceremony. We are hoping to have an *Arya Samaj* ceremony, which is brief."

"Isn't *Arya Samaj* just another branch of the Hindu religion?"

"It is. It is a much simpler and basic form of the religion introduced by a saintly scholar called Dayanand Saraswati."

"Where did the name come from? *Arya Samaj*? Sounds like a Nazi organisation."

Ramesh grins. "You are right. It has Nazi connotations. Arya Samaj just means a society of *Arya*. But Hitler adapted the Sanskrit word Arya, which means a righteous person. He even appropriated our symbol of a Swastika and inverted it. *Swastika* is also a Sanskrit word."

"Why did Nazis adapt the word and the symbol?" I wonder aloud. "They surely didn't think of us Indians belonging to the same race as them."

Ramesh looks at the watch on his wrist before replying, "It appears that ancestors of both the Europeans and the Indians originated in Central Asia near the Caucasus Mountains, from where they spread out maybe about ten thousand years ago. One wave came down to India and Iran. The other lot went to Europe. So, we possibly have the same origin."

"But there is no proof. These are just myths, aren't they?"

"Actually, there is some evidence. You see, the two main languages Sanskrit and Latin have many similarities. The philologists group them together as Indo-European languages." He turns his wrist and taps on his watch, as he stands up. "We haven't got time to discuss all that now. Maybe another time?"

I put on a serious face and say in a severe tone, "So you think it is more important to make preparations for your wedding than to explain the history of Aryans to your younger brother?"

Ramesh replies not in words but in action by throwing a cushion at me.

Chapter 49
Day 4:
8th August
Ramesh: Wedding Plan

When we return to the office after lunch, Rehana goes to see the Mullah. Kintu has cancelled all the appointments for today, so we are free and sit in Kumar's room as we wait for her to return.

She is back in half an hour, looking grim.

"Well?" I ask.

She sighs and shakes her head. "No luck. As I thought, the Mullah refused to have anything to do with it. But he is a nice man really. He said he couldn't do it, but he wouldn't let my family know that I went to see him about it. And as I was leaving he said, *May Allah grant you happiness.*"

I immediately rush off to see the Hindu priest.

As I enter the temple grounds, I notice the priest, Shankar Gor, examining the flower shrubs next to the statue of Gandhiji.

As I approach him, he turns and greets me, "Ram, Ram."

"Ram, Ram, Maraj," I respond.

"You are Devjibhai's son, aren't you?" I am not sure how he knows me, but decide he must have seen me at one of the wedding functions.

"Yes, I am his elder son, Ramesh," I confirm. "You have a good memory for faces."

He smiles and runs his fingers through his long grey beard. "I saw your father last week at a meeting here. He made a good case for setting up a scholarship fund for deserving students. Instead of building yet another shrine.

He convinced enough people to support him. I do not vote on these matters but I was certainly swayed by his reasoning."

"Yes, I did hear about the meeting," I say and then come straight to the point. "I am here to ask a favour of you, to request you to conduct my marriage ceremony."

"As you know, my duties in the temple keep me busy and I do not normally officiate at these ceremonies." He shakes his head and locks of his grey hair bob around his face. He hastens to add, "I've occasionally done it. But those have been exceptional circumstances."

"Mine is not a normal situation."

"A love marriage?" he enquires.

"Yes."

A butterfly flits by his face and he gently waves his right hand to encourage it to move away. He watches it as it flutters to a nearby bougainvillea bush.

"I am surprised. Your parents seem to be liberal-minded. I would have thought that they wouldn't object to you choosing your own girl."

"They're not the ones opposing it."

"Ahh. The girl's parents."

"Yes. They are Muslim."

"I see...e...e" he says and there is a long silence as he ponders the situation. He stands there looking across the temple ground towards the Coronation Park and the River. Finally, he nods and turns to me. "Right. I will perform the ceremony. I prefer to have both sets of parents attend to grace the occasion and bless the happy couple. But it seems in your case only your parents will be present."

"They will not come either."

"Listen, son," he says. "I am willing to perform the ceremony. But I like to see all four parents bless the union.

And if they cannot all be there, whatever the reason, at least one parent should be there to grace the occasion."

"So, if we were orphans you wouldn't help us?" I challenge him.

I think he has perhaps not heard me, as he is now examining the bougainvillea blossom. I am about to repeat my comment when he looks up and says with a smile, "If you were orphans, it couldn't be helped. But I can see your point. Your father has a reputation as a good lawyer, and it seems the son is one and a quarter times cleverer than the father. I will perform the ceremony but, for my peace of mind, can you assure me that your parents have blessed the union?"

"Yes, they have." I then explain the reasons behind their not wanting to be present at the ceremony.

"I am free tomorrow afternoon. How about 2.30 p.m.? It is an auspicious time by astrological calculations." He smiles and adds, "But then you young folk do not believe in these old beliefs."

"Any time during office hours tomorrow is an auspicious time for us," I reply, smiling back at him.

Chapter 50
Day 5:
Wednesday 9th August 1972 - Morning
Rehana: The Marriage

I hardly slept last night. And then it was a fitful sleep. It may have been my last night at my parents' home. And today might be the last day on which my parents speak to me. I am about to cause them more pain than they have ever experienced before. Of course, I feel terrible about it. But I am elated at the same time - elated at the thought that in a few hours' time I will be married to Ramesh.

After lying awake for hours, I get up at my normal time so as not to arouse any suspicions. I have a bath and dress in my cream coloured *salwar kameez*, with a matching diaphanous *dupatta* wrapped round my neck. I look at my reflection in the mirror; move the dupatta over my head and throw the other end over my shoulder. I turn around and the kameez twirls around. I never imagined getting married in these clothes, smart as they are.

Amma is waiting for me at the front door. I rush to join her and try to hold normal conversation with her as we walk to my office. But my mind is focussed on the day ahead. Amma stops near the office and before turning back says, "See you at lunchtime."

I am too nervous to do much work that morning.

Amma comes to meet me at lunch hour. We walk home in silence and eat without exchanging many words.

At 2 p.m. Amma walks me back to the office. I rush into the building and find Ramesh hovering near the front door. He looks tense but his face relaxes to see me arrive. The ceremony is due in half an hour and we have planned to go straight away.

Just before we leave, I tell Kintu, "I guess you are once again staying behind to mind the office. I'm so sorry you can't come."

Kintu smiles. "You can't keep me away this time. We have decided to close the office this afternoon."

"What about telephone calls?"

"I'll leave the phone off the hook. People will think that it's just another problem with the telephone line."

Kumar drives the car with Kintu beside him. Ramesh and I sit in the back.

Ramesh's brother Shashi, and Lalita Auntie, Kumar's wife Manjula, and my friend, Jyoti, are waiting just inside the temple gates. We all walk together to the priest's living quarters, behind the main building in the temple grounds. The sun is high in the sky and it is hot. The temple spire casts a short, sharp triangular shadow on the ground, which points the way to the priest's door - and to our destiny.

The priest, dressed in a white dhoti and shirt, meets us on the threshold. He has a red *tilak* on his forehead, and his grey, ash-white, shoulder-length curly hair is oiled and glistens in the sunshine. He has a big smile on his face.

I have never met him before and Ramesh introduces us. I hold my hands together in a *namaskar* and bow. He touches my head with his right hand and says, "May God grant you happiness, *beti* (daughter)." Before we got here, I was not quite sure how I would be received by him. But I am touched to be blessed and addressed by him as '*beti*'.

The priest has recognised Lalita Auntie. "I am glad someone from the family is here."

"I am here to represent Savitabhabhi," Auntie says.

"And I will represent our father," Shashi announces solemnly but then joins the others in their laughter.

The priest leads us into his house. We all remove our

footwear in the entrance hall.

He uses only one room for himself. It has two doors in the wall opposite the entrance. I guess one leads to the kitchen and the other to the bathroom.

The living space reminds me of my room in the YWCA, when I was a student in London, except this is more spacious. It is sparsely furnished, with a small table and four chairs at one end, a bed on the opposite end, and a small settee covered with a white bedspread by the window. There is a small statue of Ganesh in one corner.

The priest asks Ramesh and me to sit next to each other on the sofa and we do so rather shyly. Kumar and Manjula perch on the edge of the bed. The rest sit on the dining chairs.

The priest pulls out a large white sheet from a cupboard near the bed and spreads it on the floor. He then goes into the kitchen and emerges with a large stainless steel plate on which he has painted a big swastika with red *gulal*. Its edges are lined with rice. In the centre of the swastika sits a little clay lamp holder with a big cotton wick soaked in ghee. He places the plate in front of the Ganesh statue.

"If you young men don't mind, could you move a couple of chairs near the statue for the couple? I shall of course sit on the floor."

I immediately say, "We can also sit on the floor."

"So can we," the others chorus.

The priest sits on the left and Ramesh and I on the right hand side of the statue. The rest of the group sit facing the elephant-headed Ganesh.

The priest lights the ghee-sodden wick in the lamp, folds his hands and mutters a prayer, before addressing us. "We always invoke the name of Ganesh for any auspicious occasion," he says, I think, chiefly for my and Kintu's benefit. I have been to a few Hindu ceremonies and am more familiar with it than Kintu, who has never been to a Hindu, or for that matter, any Indian ceremony. He is following it all with keen interest.

Om Ganeshaya Namah (We bow to Ganesh), the priest says, bows his head and murmurs a short prayer to Ganesh.

He then looks up and addresses us. "We pray to God to bless this union between Ramesh and Rehana. To bring them happiness in every aspect of their marriage. There is duality in nature. There is *Purush* and *Prakriti*. Human beings and nature. *Shiv* and *Shakti*. The universe and the forces that dictate its behaviour. And the same applies to life forms. We are part of the *Duality*. Male and Female. Ramesh and Rehana. These two aspects are essential for our happiness and fulfilment as well as for the continuation of mankind."

In my nervous state, I do not take in half the words he says. It does not feel real. I have to remind myself that this is no dream or my fantasy. I am actually getting married. It is really happening – and happening now. I look at Ramesh. He is watching the priest but turns his head and catches my eye and smiles. He shifts to be more comfortable. I can sense that he is not used to sitting cross-legged on the floor. Probably the priest has noticed it, too, for he stands up and motions us to rise. All of us scramble to our feet.

The priest then declares in a solemn voice, "We are gathered here for a happy occasion to unite two people in their journey towards a fulfilling and a happy life. The Arya-Samaj ceremony is simple and brief but that does not make it less important."

He looks at Lalita Auntie and nods in the direction of a large silvery plate with two garlands spread on it. Auntie fetches the tray and stands next to Maraj.

Ramesh and I face each other holding the garlands

in front of us. They are made of mostly cream coloured frangipani flowers, interspersed with bright yellow-orange marigolds. I breathe in deeply, appreciating the bouquet of heavenly fragrance.

I look at Ramesh and feel overcome by the love I feel for him, and from the look on his face I can see that he reciprocates my feelings.

Maraj continues, "In front of God and the society, represented by those present here, you will place garlands round each other's necks. By doing so you will confirm that you are united in matrimony and all it entails. You will place the other's happiness above yours. May God bless you and give you a long and fulfilling married life."

I reach over Ramesh's head and place the garland round his neck. He smiles and then puts the other garland on me. The priest then motions us to follow him to the table, where he has a folder ready. He extracts the legal documentation, and hands us a pen. First I sign it and then Ramesh does.

"Now you are a legally married couple," the priest announces. "Congratulations."

We bend down and touch the priest's feet. "God bless you," he says.

We then turn to Lalita and just as we are beginning to bend down to touch her feet she puts her arms out and embraces us. The rest of the guests take turns and congratulate us by embracing us.

We then thank the priest and start moving towards the door.

"Just one more thing," the priest says. "If I could have a quick word in private with the newlyweds. A delicate matter."

The rest of the group move outside and Ramesh and I sit on the sofa. The priest pulls up a chair facing us. He clears his throat. "I would be failing in my duty if I did not bring up this matter. I know these days you young people, especially the UK returns, are familiar with facts of life. But if you need any advice, I can talk to you, or lend you love manuals for your perusal later at your leisure. I have some of the ancient ones - you know *Kama Sutra* and *Koka Shastra*. Or if you wish, I also have English manuals."

Ramesh looks at me, but I am too embarrassed to say anything. He thanks the priest but declines the offer.

The priest bids us farewell, "Now you are setting out on a journey of life together. May you have a long and happy married life."

As we join the others outside, Shashi asks Ramesh, "What was the delicate matter the priest wished to discuss with you?"

Ramesh ignores the question and turns to talk to Kumar.

"Hadn't you paid him for conducting the service?" Shashi perseveres.

"He has refused to accept a single cent. So I have offered to send a donation to the scholarship fund the temple has set up."

"Then why did he want a word in private?"

"He didn't want a sniggering teenager there."

"I think I can guess," Shashi says and then sniggers, but it is obvious he is putting it on.

Chapter 51
Day 5:
Wednesday 9th August
Rehana: A Married Woman

When I came to work at 2 p.m., I was Miss Rehana Butt. Now it is half past five and I am Mrs Rehana Mitani. I have been a married woman for over two hours.

I stand by the office window, waiting. Ramesh is standing next to me and holding my hand. I can see Amma turn into our street and hurry along towards the office. She is dressed in white salwar and kameez and her head is covered with her dupatta to protect her face from the afternoon sun.

We step away from the window and kiss briefly. I pick up my handbag and move towards the door. "Good luck, my love," Ramesh says. "I still think that it would be better if I were to come with you." We had a long discussion about it and he is still not convinced that I should face Abba without him.

"No, it is better this way," I assure him. "I'll ring you when I am ready."

"I'll be waiting by the phone," he says solemnly.

I pause by the mirror near the front door to look at my reflection. I think I look different. No, I am sure I look different. I wonder if Amma will notice it.

I emerge from the door before Amma gets to the office and we set off for home. She does notice a difference, for she stops and briefly scrutinises me. Maybe there is a hint of excitement as well as apprehension in my eyes.

I was wearing the same clothes earlier when she walked with me to the office, and yet she asks, "Is that a new salwar and kameez you are wearing?"

"No," I reply truthfully, "I have worn them once before."

"Funny, I didn't notice them this morning." Amma shrugs her shoulders and walks on. I hear her sigh. She is no doubt relieved to think that I have now accepted my fate and come to terms with giving up my job and my relationship with Ramesh.

We walk the rest of the way in silence. My mood seesaws between elation at being married and a cold dread at the prospect of informing my parents about it. What I have done feels so underhand and will hurt them deeply. I know Amma would have loved to be present at the ceremony. Her youngest daughter's wedding! She has been looking forward to it and collecting jewellery and clothes for the occasion for years now.

But it is Abba I am most worried about. He will be furious. And I can't see him ever accepting my rebellious act. I know I will be the cause of a lot of pain and heartache. I should feel guilty. And I do. But at the same time I feel ecstatic. I am now married. To Ramesh. The man I love. I would rather have died than not be with him. From tomorrow we will openly live together as a legally married couple. Legally? Are we? I know that in the UK, a marriage is not recognised if it has not been consummated. I am a lawyer and yet I am not sure if the Ugandan law is the same here as in the UK. And if that is the case, we must consummate our marriage soon as possible. I smile - almost snort - as I suppress an urge to laugh. What kind of reasoning is that? Only a lawyer can think like that. That I must sleep with my beloved because it is legally advisable? I want to do it, legal or not. I so badly want to be in his arms and to make love to him. Wild love. I can barely wait to be his. I want him to undress me. And I want to hold him in my arms all night long. And ... We have now arrived home and I pause as Amma unlocks the door. I am still not sure whether to break the news to her before Abba arrives home. We go to the living-room, and sit facing each other.

She looks me in the eye. "What happened today, love?"

"Why do you ask, Amma?"

"I know you, *Beti* (daughter), and I can tell something is on your mind." She places her hand on mine. "Last few days you were upset over having to stop working and the other matter. You just had your last session at work and I thought you would be devastated. But you are not. On the contrary, you seem to be happy. You were smiling to yourself as we walked home."

She waits for me to reply as she sits there, her lips pursed and her eyes anxious and unblinking. The sun reflects from the diamond stud in her nose. I look straight at her and blurt out. "I got married today."

"What? Stop this foolish talk. You have been at work all day. How could you have got married?"

"We had a civil ceremony conducted by a priest this afternoon." There is a look of disbelief in her eyes. "Yes, Amma. Ramesh and I are now married."

She clutches at her heart as she gasps. "Oh Beti, what have you done? Such a foolish action. And why this haste? You didn't rush into it because you are ..." She lets the unfinished sentence hang in the air.

"No, Amma, I am not pregnant if that is what you mean. In fact, I have done nothing to disgrace myself."

"What do you call marrying against your father's wishes?"

"There is nothing disgraceful about marrying the man you

love. Defiant? Yes. Disgraceful? Certainly not."

"Oh *mari butchi* (my little girl). I am so worried about your father's reaction." She comes and sits next to me and holds me in her arms. She gently rocks as she strokes my hair, a comforting gesture that I remember from my childhood days.

Just then the front door creaks open. Amma and I exchange a nervous look and she gets up to fetch Abba. I wait, my heart thumping. She leads him to the seat by the window and then comes and sits next to me, facing him. It feels like *déjà vu*. Abba sat in the same seat exactly five days ago and heard for the first time the shocking news of my *entanglement*. He looks grim, as if expecting more bad news.

Amma believes in a direct approach. She announces, "Rehana got married today."

Abba just sits there. There is no change of expression on his face. It is as if he did not hear it. Amma leans forward, her hands clenching and unclenching. I stare at the floor, my heart beating faster and faster.

When Abba speaks, his voice is surprisingly calm. "I knew it was a mistake to let you go to work this week. It was against my better judgement. I should have forbidden you to set foot outside the house. And now you have acted in this unforgivably rash and foolish manner. Brought us so much pain. And disgrace." He jumps to his feet and his face contorts as he shouts, "And that shameless boy, Hussein, let me down, too. Being snared by a white girl."

He steps forward and wags his finger close to my face as he almost screams, "And YOU. You have not just got involved with a boy, but a Hindu boy at that."

Now he shakes his fist at me. I shrink back, expecting to be hit but he restrains himself. "I wish you had not been born. From now on I will imagine you have never been in our lives. And that I have just two daughters and not three. Get out of my home, and do not ever darken it with your shadow."

"Abba, I am sorry I've hurt you but --"

"I am not your Abba anymore and I know you are not sorry."

Amma tries to intervene, "Please! Listen, let me -"

"No! You listen to me." Abba turns towards Amma and jabs his forefinger at her. "You have always been too soft with her. And spoilt her. And now she has darkened our lives with her shameless conduct. You are not to invite her back to our house."

He grabs my arm and marches me to my bedroom. "Now pick up your belongings and go," he orders. "I do not wish to ever see your disgraceful face again." He gives me a push through the doorway, turns round, and storms off to his bedroom.

I feel numb as I throw some of my belongings in a suitcase and emerge from my room. I stop for a moment by my parents' bedroom and through the open door see Abba sitting on their bed, holding his head in his hands with his elbows resting on his knees.

I go to the living-room and phone Ramesh. After just one ring he answers. I can picture him waiting for my call, all ready with the car keys in his hands.

"Have you told them?" he wants to know.

"Yes." I break down into sobs. "Please come and get me."

"I am coming over right now," he says.

Amma is standing in the hallway with tears in her eyes, and our servant, Musa, is by her side. He picks up the case for me and brings it out to the front of the house. Musa looks sad, too. He shakes my hand and gives me a mournful smile before shuffling back into the house.

Amma waits on the footpath with me. She has been dry-eyed till now but suddenly bursts out sobbing. "Oh my daughter, my darling little daughter," she keeps repeating as she holds me in an embrace. "I hope you have not made a mistake, my love," she says as we hear a car turn the corner.

It screeches to a stop and Ramesh springs out. He bends down and touches Amma's feet. She raises him up and hugs him, and then embraces us both together, an arm round each, and murmurs, "May Allah make you both happy."

Ramesh gets back in the car and waits. I embrace Amma again. We stand there hugging and crying. Then I break away and get into the car and nod at Ramesh.

As he gently drives away from our house, I look back. Amma is still standing there. Her face appears blurred through my tears. The car then turns round the corner and I can't see her any more but her image stays with me until we get to Ramesh's house.

His family is waiting for us at the front door. We approach his parents, who are smiling. We touch their feet and they place their hands on our heads and bless us. As I stand on the threshold of my new home in the fragrant frangipani-laden air in the mellow dusk, with the man I love standing by my side squeezing my hand, I feel more tears cloud my eyes.

Ramesh's mother, Mummyji to me from now onwards, and Lalita Auntie place garlands of creamy-coloured *champa* (frangipani) round our necks. Mummyji makes a red vermillion *chandlo* on both our foreheads.

There is a large stainless steel dish filled with vermilion paste on the floor. I remove my sandals and place my feet, one after the other, in the red paste and then step on a large blank piece of paper to mark my first footsteps in my new home.

There is also a basin full of water. Lalita Auntie washes my feet and helps me to dry them with a little pink towel before I put my sandals back on.

Shashi picks up the paper with red outlines of my feet on the white background. "Welcome to your new home, Bhabhi," he announces with a smile. "The police take your fingerprints, we take footprints."

I smile at him. And then burst into tears. It has been a day of emotional ups and downs and it is all too much.

"Oh, you have all been so kind," I say between sobs, and then add in English, "Thank you so much."

Chapter 52
Day 6:
10th August 1972
Devji: Attempting Reconciliation

I am an early riser. Today I wake up at just after six. Savita is asleep; I can hear her regular breathing as I gently slide out of the bed without disturbing her. I wrap a shawl round my shoulders, and step out into the garden to soak in the sheer beauty of the morning.

Usually I go to the Coronation Park at dawn, and sit by the riverbank with friends. But too much is happening. I need to be on my own to clear my head.

It is still dark, but the dawn will break in a few minutes. I sit on a bench and take a deep breath in the cool fresh air.

There are no clouds and the sky is dotted with stars. Venus is bright and hardly twinkling. Insects are humming and birds are just beginning to chirp. Their songs are still subdued and the chorus to greet the dawn has not yet commenced. I feel overwhelmed by the pre-dawn serenity.

The world is so amazingly beautiful. Who created it? One could ask, does everything need a Creator? Because if that is the case, then one could say who created the Creator? In Sanskrit there is a word to describe God - *Swayambhu* (The Self-Creator). If one accepts the principle that it is possible to self-create, then why couldn't the material universe be self-created?

However, the Universe is mind-bogglingly beautiful. So can it all be by accident? I know I am making a value judgement here. I could say that I find nature beautiful simply because I have evolved to appreciate it. Whatever may be the case, why do we human beings worry so much about trivial things such as material possessions? Even other concerns like honour and pride seem superficial when compared to the beauty of nature.

At this moment I feel at total peace with myself and with the world.

I am shaken out of my reverie by a movement. Savita lowers herself gently next to me on the bench. We sit there savouring the peace together.

The martins are now active and we watch them zooming around and listen to their shrill cries. The horizon has got lighter and is splattered with red.

After a while I interrupt our communion with nature and say, "What a day! Yesterday."

She sighs, "Tell me this is all a dream. Just over a week ago we discover that Ramesh is involved with a girl. A Muslim girl at that. Only yesterday he tells us they are planning to marry. And now she is our *Vahu* (daughter-in-law). And the newly-wed couple are in our house." She stares ahead at the mango tree as she mulls aloud. "I never thought our son's wedding would be celebrated so simply. I imagined it to be a big occasion. You know, at least a thousand guests. And a henna night and a *sanjee*, where I would sing songs with my family and friends till I am hoarse."

"I know," I say. "You would have liked a big splash and you barely got a ripple. Do you mind it terribly?"

She smiles. She twists her hair into a bun and secures it with pins on the top of her head. A strand of her hair, which has not been secured, flutters in the breeze over her cheek. "It would have been nice. But, no. I don't mind. Ramesh is happy and so I am happy. I just hope he has made a wise choice. We hardly know Rehana, but she seems to be a very nice girl."

I gently caress her hand as we sit there in silence a little longer.

With my left palm I shield my eyes from the sun, which has just come up. The chill in the air has lifted. A huge brown moth is fluttering in the shade of a bush. I muse aloud, "There is still one factor that casts a shadow over their happy day."

Savita nods. "Should we go and talk to her father?"

"I would like to, but I doubt if it will make any difference."

Savita gets up and stands in front of me, shielding me from the sun. She narrows her eyes and studies my face. "I can't believe you are saying that. You're not a defeatist. And think of the number of family feuds you have helped to resolve."

She is right. But usually people with disputes have approached me as a respected member of the community. I can't help smiling at her look of determination, one hand resting on her hip, her outline silhouetted against the brightening sky. I am reminded yet again of why I love this woman so dearly. I say, "Shall we go in the afternoon after her father closes his shop?"

She nods.

*   *   *

I ring the bell and stand back next to Savita. There is a sound of shuffling behind the door before it creaks open, revealing a middle-aged woman in a white Punjabi dress. This must be Zubeidaben, I think. I recognise some of Rehana's features in her. She is fair skinned and has large dark eyes, but with circles round them, as if from crying.

"Zubeidaben?"

She looks quizzically at us for a moment.

"We are Ramesh's parents," Savita tells her.

Her eyes light up and she smiles. "Oh, come in, come in,"

she says and then, suddenly, a look of panic spreads across her face.

"Is Yusufbhai in as well?" I ask her. "We would really like to speak to both of you."

We remain standing on the threshold while she goes to check if Yusufbhai is available. Of course we know that she has gone to ask him if he is willing to meet us.

A couple of anxious minutes later, Yusufbhai appears. He is dressed in white trousers and a white shirt. He smoothes his hair with his hands as he approaches us. I have no doubt that he would rather not speak to us, but his ingrained good manners and sense of hospitality prevent him from turning visitors away. He sweeps his arm in welcome and says, "Do come in."

He studiously avoids my eye but waits patiently by the living-room door as we remove our shoes in the hallway. When we go in the living-room he says, "Do sit down."

"I'll get water for you," Zubeidaben says and hurries away.

Yusufbhai smiles at us for the first time and then follows Zubeidaben out of the room. It is an apologetic smile; obviously he does not want to be left alone with us.

A short time later, Zubeidaben returns with a tray with tumblers of water. She places the tray on a large circular table in the centre of the room. The table is really a Zebra skin drum, its top covered with a circular glass plate. She goes out again and returns immediately with another tray with tea and snacks on it. Yusufbhai follows her. He then sits facing us, but avoids eye contact.

"You shouldn't have taken so much trouble," Savita says. I also express the same sentiment.

"It is no trouble," Zubeidaben murmurs as she serves tea.

We make small talk about anything but what is uppermost

in all our minds. We agree that it is rather hot and that a good cup of tea is what one needs on an afternoon like this. We all feel that it is not likely to rain as August is usually rather dry. Zubeidaben gives the recipe of her homemade biscuits to Savita. We wonder if President Amin seriously intends to carry out his threat of expelling us.

It is only when we have finished drinking tea and tasted the delicious biscuits that I broach the subject uppermost in all our minds.

"Now that we are related we thought we should get acquainted with one another."

Zubeidaben smiles and looks anxiously at her husband. After a pause, he clears his throat. "You knocked on my door, and I do not turn away guests. But that does not mean I have accepted the situation."

"What has happened has happened. We cannot change it now," Savita responds.

"And we have to be there to support the young," I say. "It is the happiness of your daughter and our son that should matter to us." I watch his face as I say it. The muscles of his jaws are working and there is a pained expression on his face.

"I have only two daughters. One in Zanzibar and one in Mombasa," he says slowly and deliberately.

Zubeida has refrained from saying anything so far but has been carefully watching her husband's reactions. She looks pleadingly at him now and says, "Your saying so does not change the facts. Rehana is still our daughter and her happiness still matters to us."

"She is not my daughter anymore."

"We cannot change the past." There is a look of determination on Zubeida's face as she continues, while Yusufbhai stares at the window. "She is the same girl you cuddled as a baby. And were thrilled when she called you Abba for the first time. And when she took her first faltering steps, you picked her up and swung her around with joy. She is the same girl who came home with glowing school reports, and each time you proudly carried them in your pocket for weeks on end. And sent her to England to study. *Only the best for my little girl*, you said."

Zubeida dabs her eyes with the end of her dupatta.

"And look how she has shown her gratitude to us." Yusuf stands up indicating he wishes to terminate the conversation.

As we move towards the door, I turn to him and say, "Yusufbhai, I understand how you feel. Both my wife and I were also against this marriage and tried to dissuade Ramesh. But then we realised that without Rehana he would be miserable. So we changed our minds. Their happiness is paramount to us and I am sure you agree that as parents it is our duty to do all we can to make them happy. Rehana desperately yearns for your blessings and it is casting a shadow of unhappiness on her."

"She knew I would not speak to her if she defied me."

"You know the adage, *Chhoru kachhoru thai, pun mabaap kamabaap na thai*. (Children may misbehave but parents don't). Do you want her to feel let down by her own parents when she needs their support most? And what about the future? What happens if Amin carries out his threat? You and Rehana could possibly end up at opposite ends of the world. And then it will be too late to make up."

"She does not exist for me anymore," he says but his voice and look belie his assertion. He is troubled and he is wavering.

Chapter 53
Day 6:
10th August
Turmoil

Uganda Argus

"SOME WILL STAY, SOME WILL GO."

"Asians holding British passports and nationals of India, Pakistan and Bangla Desh- except those in essential occupations- will have to leave Uganda within 3 months. The final order came from the President General Idi Amin, who told a Press Conference at the Command Post, Kampala that he had signed a decree to this effect which came into force from Aug 9."

Devji:

Just a few days ago, I told Shashi that Amin is trying to get rid of all the Asians and not just those holding British passports. The news in today's *Argus* confirms it. And how long before he announces that Asians, who are Ugandan Citizens, should also leave?

I wonder what professions will be defined as 'essential occupations."

After dinner I walk into the main living-room, but find Ramesh and his new bride, Rehana, there. They are talking to Shashi and Lalita. So I head to the TV room and flop down on the settee by the window.

Just as I start to go over the events of the last few days, the door is slowly and carefully opened. Savita shuts it behind her noiselessly. She comes and sits down next to me on the sofa and holds my hand.

She sighs loudly. "Do you ever get a feeling that too much is happening?"

I nod. "I feel like that now. First, Ramesh gets married, which could be a major event in our lives. And now Amin's threat. It seems we have little or no control over our lives at the moment."

"But there are many people who say that Amin does not really mean it." Savita has always been more optimistic than me. "Just another one of his mad announcements, they think. Though I know that you think he is not bluffing."

"I hope I am wrong. Maybe, his decree will be applied to only those who have no Certificate of Residence in Uganda. A very small number of people will be affected in that case. The effects on Uganda's economy will then be relatively small and there may not be any international condemnation of Amin's government."

"When will we find out?"

"In a few days' time, I guess."

Just then the doorbell rings. I hastily release Savita's hand, but leave it to Shashi to answer the door. I hear him welcome Velji and his family, who have come to watch the news. They join us in the TV room.

Shashi leads the neighbours to where we are sitting. Savita and I get up to welcome them. We all are still on our feet, when Ramesh, holding Rehana's hand leads her into the room. There is a shocked look on our visitors' faces, until we announce Ramesh's wedding and introduce Rehana to them. There are gasps of surprise as they exclaim over the secrecy. They would have complained about being kept in the dark, but when they hear the name "Rehana", they realise that the bride is Muslim, and understand why it was all kept secret from them. Ramesh and Rehana go and touch the elders' feet and are blessed by them. Everyone has a piece of *penda* to eat to sweeten his or her mouth to celebrate the event.

But then it is time for the news.

Ramesh switches on the television. The reception is rather poor but he fiddles with the TV until we get a reasonable picture. A bit crackly, but clear enough for us to get the message. It confirms what we have read in *Argus* this morning that all Asians who are not Uganda citizens must leave Uganda in ninety days. But there is more.

There is shocking news for poor Velji, who has all along assumed that Amin's decree does not apply to him and his family.

TV News Bulletin:

> *... He (Amin) also announced that "It is true that there are about 23,000 Asians, who are Ugandan Citizens. But I see no more future for them than for others who are not citizens. If all of them go, I will be very, very happy.*

There is a hush. Maji wants to know what that 'nasty man' said. Vinod tells his grandmother that Amin wants all Asians to leave. Even those who are Uganda citizens. Maji sighs loudly, hits her forehead with an open palm and then sits there with a vacant look on her face for the rest of the evening.

Velji says in a flat voice, "A lot of us applied for and got the Ugandan citizenship, as soon as it was possible. And most of our children are born here. We are as Ugandan as any other person in Uganda. Surely, he can't mean that his decree applies to all of us. That would be racist. These days it cannot happen. The world won't allow it."

Ramesh comments, "If only the world was like that."

Chapter 54
Day 9:
13th August 1972
Britain Accepts Responsibility

BBC News Bulletin:

Mr Geoffrey Rippon, Chancellor of the Duchy of Lancaster has told a press conference in Kampala that Britain has decided in principle to admit some 50,000 Asians, who hold British passports, if they are expelled from Uganda. "However, we are referring the dispute to the United Nations," he said.

Devji:

It is reassuring that at least Britain has accepted its responsibility for its citizens, even if they are of Asian origin. And there are many who think that the international pressure applied through the United Nations may force Amin to withdraw his ultimatum.

Personally, I am not hopeful.

Shashi: Not that bothered

When I jotted down my thoughts about a week ago, I made a couple of statements, which I need to withdraw. First, I said nothing exciting happens here. Time has proved me wrong, very wrong. There is a lot happening. On a grander scale, there is President Amin's announcement. It will totally change our lives. And within our own little world of family life, there has been the excitement of Ramesh getting married.

Also, I mentioned a *giggling fever*. Well, there is no such thing. I bumped into Mr Nayyar yesterday and asked him. He said maybe I was thinking about a *dancing fever*, which did occur in the middle-ages in Europe. Apparently people started dancing in large groups and could not stop until they fell down exhausted. He asked me if I was thinking about it because of the mass hysteria that will increasingly grip us in the next ninety days. "We can see history in the making," he said. He sounded completely calm and detached. His tone suggested *Aren't we lucky to witness this historic event?* Typical of a history teacher.

The day after Amin made his announcement, I made a mental note that I would keep a diary and record our last days here. Like Anne Frank. But then I did not keep my promise. Maybe, subconsciously I was afraid that I might meet a similar fate as Anne, and that my diary would be found after my tragic death in one of Amin's concentration camps. (I know Miss Roy has told us several times that it is 'similar to' and not 'similar as', but the latter being a literal translation from Gujarati sounds better to me and this is my narrative, so I can break a few rules).

A lot seems to have happened in the last week and yet in a way nothing much seems to have changed, except our future. People are still getting on with their lives although now their efforts are directed towards creating a future outside Uganda. It reminds me of the time when there was a power failure at a wedding function in the *Lohana* Community Hall. It suddenly became pitch dark. People fumbled around to locate alternative sources of light. My friends and I thought it was great fun because we felt our way to where we had seen some primary school kids sitting in a group, and made sort of *hooooo hooooo* noises, trying to sound like ghosts, or what we thought ghosts sound like.

It is a similar situation now. People are fumbling in a fog of ignorance and misinformation. *Fognorance*. There, I have coined a new word, like some authors do. (Miss Roy told us about a book called 'Clockwork Orange', in which the author has coined a whole new vocabulary; our library has not got it, so I have not read it yet.)

At first, we thought all Asians have to leave. And now Amin has announced that genuine Ugandan citizens will be allowed to stay. But that would be a small number.

As for the rest, the majority would like to go to UK, if they are admitted. Most of us have passports, issued when Britain governed Uganda. Mine says that I am a British Protected Person. But apparently, a few years ago the British Government passed a law stating that those with Protected Person passports did not have an automatic right to settle in the UK. And now India and Pakistan have announced that they will not accept people who are not their citizens.

I overheard Papa and Shantikaka talking about it yesterday. And I heard Kaka say, "We have not made any demands on the British Government so far. Now when we need their protection, surely they will not turn us away. After all, our passports state quite clearly that we are British Protected Persons."

Both Papa and Kaka agreed that they were most concerned about the future of their children. "We have lived our lives. We have been fortunate so far. But it is our children's future we need to secure," Papa said. And then added, "I am most concerned about Shashi. If only we could stay here for four more months! Then he can take his O Levels. Whereas now his education will be disrupted."

I think it would make no difference because as we do exams in December, I would have had to wait to next September to start studying for my A Levels because the UK school terms start then. I will now do exams next June and still do my A Levels in September, as originally planned.

"You don't need to worry about Shashi," Kaka assured Papa. "I often talk to his teachers and they all say what a precocious child he is."

I just tried to look up the word 'precoscious' in the dictionary and could not find it. Then I found it under 'precocious', without an s (this is the correct spelling). Well, I must say in all humbleness that I am not precocious enough if I did not know the word. (I must tell Ramesh about this logical twist, he will appreciate it. He reckons we have inherited a 'twisted logic' gene.)

I have been looking forward to going to UK for a long time. Now it seems it may be a few months earlier, and I await the day with rising excitement.

Ramesh and other UK-returns talk about what life was like in London. Apparently, after returning from the college in the evenings, they used to get together in one of their rooms and either cook a meal for themselves or end up going to a restaurant. They then played bridge into the early hours, or went to the West End (I still haven't figured out why in London they have their cinemas and theatres at one end of the town and not in the centre).

Sometimes, Ramesh used to get back to his room after having been out and remember that he had no clean underwear and socks for the next day. So he and his roommate Kumar went out to a launderette, even if it was well past midnight. Fancy having launderettes! And them being open all night! Imagine anything - apart from cinemas - being open after 6 p.m. From listening to them talk, I had pictured myself having a similar life to them, including going to the West End and to launderettes late at night. As I am nearly seventeen, so really a grown-up, I would have lived in a bed-sit somewhere near the West End, either on my own or sharing with a friend, but now I realise my student days in London won't be like that.

Instead, now I will stay with the family. Ba will make sure that there is no washing to be done late at night, and if I offered to do the family laundry, either she or Papa would say, *Don't you worry about it. You surely have homework or revision for your exams to do.* Thanks to Amin, no laundry pleasure for me. (I better clarify that this is only a joke, should someone read my diary.)

I am not totally self-absorbed and I do appreciate that it will be hard for my parents (and for many people in the community). They will lose all their possessions, house, car and even their savings, which are in Ugandan banks. We will be poor. Poverty does not sound romantic when you are the one who is poor.

I mentioned this to Ramesh yesterday. He nodded in agreement and then added, "But don't forget that many of the less well-off folk have been trying to get Visas to go to the UK."

"So, this news isn't like a bolt from the blue for them."

"No. It is more like a blessing from the heaven."

"But they will leave behind the little they have. They will be even poorer. Being homeless in cold weather sounds dreadful."

Then he explained that the UK government provides council houses and *dole* money for the poor and the unemployed. It had never crossed my mind that there could be poor people in the UK. I have never seen a poor white person. Or come to think of it, I have never seen a white person doing any menial job, except in films.

"Wow!" I said.

"And everyone gets free health care and education, including in the universities!"

"Wow!"

"So, the poor do not have to beg for help from family, friends or charitable organisations."

"Wow!" I repeated, more for the effect this time.

"What you call 'wow' is called socialism," Ramesh said with a smile.

Ba, who was also listening at the time, said, "It is like *Rama Rajya*. (The golden era under the reign of Lord Rama.)"

Ramesh, who is very westernised, and often criticises some of our customs, agreed readily. "In the west they call it *The Welfare State* and it exists now and not in the fabled past."

"Well, our current community is not that far from an ideal society," Ba said. "Most people have a reasonable standard of living. There are no real poor folk. Everyone helps everyone else. We live like a large, happy family - Hindus, Muslims, Christians and Sikhs. There is no friction between communities and there is a lot of good neighbourly feeling."

"But, Ba, can't you see when you say *the community* you are referring to the Indian community." Ramesh pointed out. "What about the Africans? Many of them are very poor."

Ba started to protest but Ramesh quickly added, "Oh I am not blaming you. I know. I know. It is from the time of the British rule, when we had semi-apartheid and we lived in separate areas. But it suits us and we have made no efforts to change it. We do keep ourselves to ourselves. And now we are paying a price for it."

"But even if we had integrated with the local African population, how would things be different?" I tried to side with Ba because I thought Ramesh was almost blaming her for the existing order. "We would still be a visible minority."

Ramesh laughed. "You know what? If we had integrated better, Amin would treat us like he treats our black fellow-Ugandans. And we are more prosperous. So, he would kill us rather than exile us."

"Are you saying that it is better that we did not integrate?" I asked.

"Well, there is no justification for not integrating. However, it happens to have worked out in our favour." And then he added with a mischievous smile, "In fact, I think we guys should start wearing *dhotis* to emphasise we are different."

I tried to visualise the image of my friends sauntering along the Main Street or going to school with a long white dhoti wrapped around their waists. The very idea of anyone under the age of sixty in a dhoti is hilarious.

Oh, by the way, I have decided that, like Ramesh, I am a socialist.

Chapter 55
Day 9:
13th August
Devji: More Attempts at Reconciliation

I have been musing as I sit in my favourite chair in the living-room. Rehana brings a glass of *lassi* and places it in front of me. She smiles before leaving but it is a wan smile. A newly married woman should be floating on a cloud. Instead, a sad shadow hovers around her. She is about to leave the country, and would like to bid farewell to her parents.

I wish I could help but there is not much I can do. When we saw her parents, I clearly remember the hurt but obdurate expression on her father's face. And his words still ring in my ears, "I am sorry but nothing that you say will change my mind. I guess an angel will have to descend from heaven to persuade me to accept the girl's rebellious behaviour."

He left us in no doubt that no way he was going to change his mind. His decision could not be any clearer.

I must have been frowning when Savita walks in and sits down on the chair facing me, because she asks, "What's the matter?"

"Rehana just brought me the lassi. And she looked sad. I couldn't help wondering if —"

Savita interrupts me as she, too, has obviously been thinking about the gloom that envelopes Rehana. "Shall we go to her parents and try one more time?"

"But you remember her father's parting words."

"I am surprised at you," Savita says. "You are the

one always telling the boys, *If you fail, try and try again.* Remember?"

I get up and march into the hall and slip on my sandals. Savita joins me.

Fifteen minutes later we stand outside Rehana's parents' home, and I ring the bell.

Zubeidaben answers the door. She gives us a welcoming smile, but her eyes are puffy with circles round them as if she has not been sleeping well, or crying, or both.

While we wait in the living-room, I rehearse in my mind about how to present our case. You know, *life is too short. The traditions change and we must not assume them to be inviolate. It does not matter what religion one follows as long as you are a kind human being. Your daughter's happiness should be paramount in your mind* ... and so on. But I find there is no case to fight when I hear Yusufbhai's voice. The words are indistinct to start with until he shouts out, "No. No. And NO."

Zubeidaben returns to tell us that Yusufbhai will not be able to talk to us today as he has a headache. So we are back home in less than an hour.

I feel there is nothing we can do now to reconcile him to Rehana.

Day 11:
Tuesday 15th August 1972
Devji: Yet Another Attempt

I feel I cannot give up trying to reconcile Rehana with her parents. Mr Butt has had two days to think about it and maybe is willing to accept the situation. So I telephone him to invite them for dinner, but he has not changed his mind. He declines in a polite but firm manner, "Thank you but we cannot come." Then he puts the phone down.

Chapter 56
Day 11:
Tuesday 15th August
Ramesh: Getting Visas

Uganda Television News Bulletin:

President Amin: *"I am not changing my mind. Asians who are British will have to go to England and he, Mr Rippon, has accepted that. My decision of ninety days still stands."*

Day 12:
Wednesday 16th August

BBC News Bulletin:

The British Government has started making preparations for an airlift of British Asians from Uganda.

Day 13:
Thursday 17th August

BBC News Bulletin:

Mr John Ennals, Director of the United Kingdom Immigrant Advisory Service, says that Asians expelled from Uganda could be a benefit for Britain. Many of them speak English and have skills that could be very useful in Britain.

The situation is becoming clearer now. Amin is determined to exile us.

Papa and I have decided to go to Kampala tonight. We will stay at Harikaka's house and go and join the queue outside the British Embassy well before sunrise.

Both Rehana's and my passport expired when we were students in London. Our new passports were issued there. So we have 'proper' British citizenships, and we are free to enter the UK. But Papa, Ba and Shashi have British Protected Persons' statuses, which the British government is going to accept, but they need to apply for Visas.

However, it is Lalita Auntie we are worried about. She is an Indian citizen. She can go back to India, but we are her immediate family. And we do not want to be separated from her. So, we will explain her situation to the British Embassy staff and we hope they will give her the Visa on humanitarian grounds.

When Shashi heard about our plans, he said, "I'll come with you to keep you company." But both Papa and I said at the same time, "No." I guess our tones had that finality in it, which tells you *don't waste your time or ours arguing about it.* So, he did not pursue it any further.

Chapter 57
Day 13:
Thursday 17th August 1972
Shashi: Ordinary Folk - 1

Today as I flick through my papers, I see my essay *The Dark Side of Jinja* about the Subedar family. It crosses my mind that should anything happen to me, and if this journal were to fall in the hands of strangers, they might get a totally false picture about the people of Jinja. They might think that there are a lot of nasty people in the town - and that is just not true. Most of the people here are gentle, and hospitable, with human frailties, but on the whole, very nice. (Sorry, Mr. Banerjee, I know you told us that the word *nice* is, "An overused, bland adjective that one should avoid like a plague." And I remember Vinod saying to you, "So, what should we say if we want Nice biscuits?" And you gave us another lecture on the difference between a Proper Noun and an Adjective. I wonder, Mr. Banerjee, which part of the world will you end up in? I hope it is somewhere *nice*.) Anyway, I think *nice* describes the people of Jinja very well.

So, I have decided that every now and again I will describe the ordinary folk in my journal, even though there may not be exciting tales associated with them.

I will start with our neighbours.

On our right live Veljikaka, his wife Kamlamasi, their son Vinod (who is my best friend), their young daughter Sunita and Veljikaka's mother, Dahimasi, whom we call Maaji. She is a spirited old lady who makes a great fuss of us youngsters but can be tough as a nail.

Veljikaka is a builder, a good one, people say. I also know that he often does small jobs for the less-well-off people for free.

Papa helped the family to settle in Jinja when they came from Bugiri, a little village not far from here. Veljikaka knows Papa from his childhood days in India, and he often goes to the *Sages'* meetings with Papa at dawn.

Next to Veljikaka lives Motikaka, (another *Sage*), who is a prosperous builders' merchant. He had applied for UK Visas a long time ago and eventually got them about a month ago. And day before yesterday Motikaka and his family emigrated to UK. Motikaka rang Vinod's family to say that they had arrived safely in UK. They are staying temporarily with his cousin in Harrow but hope to move out soon.

Only today Papa told me about a business deal that Veljikaka and Motikaka struck a few days ago.

It is an intricate story. I have described it below, having had to imagine a few scenes, though the outline of the events is as Papa described it. I have tried to narrate the tale from different perspectives, even though Ramesh told me that a writer should tell a story from just one person's point of view. But, hey, this is not for publication. This is my own record of our lives in Jinja.

A Deal
Day 4: 7th August 1972

Velji spent the sultry afternoon indoors, filling in cracks, which had recently appeared in the back wall and then covering them with plaster. When he heard a firm knock on the front door, he wiped his hands on his trousers as he went to answer it.

"Glad to find you are still here," Motilal greeted him. "Coming for a walk?"

"Sure. I need a breath of fresh air."

They walked along Main Street. As it was evening, all the shops were shut. They stopped outside Motilal's shop, *Jinja Builders Merchants*. Motilal placed his hand on Velji's arm. "Look, Velji, since you are determined to stay on in Uganda, why don't you take over my business?" Motilal had rehearsed what to say several times in his mind. He spoke in a soft voice to make it sound deeper and therefore more convincing. "I would rather you got the business than anybody else. You're a good friend and I have done business with you for years. Many, many years. Of course, others are interested. But I am giving you the first option."

Velji had often toyed with the idea of cutting out the middleman by running his own building materials depot. Lack of capital had been his main obstacle. But now he was being offered the possibility of owning his own business. Velji seriously doubted if anyone had expressed an interest in buying Motilal's business, even though it was the prominent outlet for building materials. He was aware that he had the upper hand and could drive the price right down. So he deliberately showed little enthusiasm for the proposal.

"I am no businessman. You know very well that by tradition we are carpenters in the *Mistry* community. And I have been a carpenter since I was fourteen. I only know about building and not about running a business."

Motilal cleared his throat, but before he could say anything, Velji added, "Besides, Motibhai, I haven't got that sort of capital."

"You could have it at a rock bottom price even though I could get a higher price from some of my African customers, no?"

"But even if I managed to raise the money, what use would it be to you?" Velji watched Motilal's face carefully, but there was no change in his expression.

"Ugandan shillings are not the only currency. We can find other means for our transaction."

"This is a business deal. We have to be clear about the terms."

Velji had little formal education but he was a shrewd man.

Motilal at last revealed what was on his mind. "OK. In that case, how about a small price, but in pounds in UK?"

"What sort of talk is that?" Velji protested. "You know me. I'm an ordinary builder. Unlike you rich folk, I have nothing outside Uganda."

Motilal was not convinced. *What? A shrewd man like Velji and no savings in sterling?* With foreign exchange restrictions, anyone planning to send their children to England for further education made provisions in the UK. "Surely, you must have some savings for your son's further studies."

"No, I am afraid not. I spent all my savings on Ramila's wedding earlier this year. I was hoping to save towards Vinod's further education in the next two years, while he does A Levels in Kampala."

"But we have known for a long time that things could get bad in Uganda. We all saw the writing on the wall and sent out what we could."

"Exactly. What we could. You forget that a lot of us live hand-to-mouth and therefore can't build up a jackpot in sterling."

Motilal had expected Velji to drive a hard bargain and had planned other strategies. "Listen, Velji. This is a golden opportunity for you. I have a stock of over four hundred thousand shillings and you can have it at half price. I would've preferred a payment in pounds but I could accept gold jewellery. Of course, time is short but it may be a few days before we get bookings for our flights. You do not have to answer today. Think about it tonight and let me know tomorrow."

They walked in silence, each lost in his private thoughts. As the light was rapidly fading they took the shorter route instead of the usual one by the lake. They walked to the post office and then to the *Odeon* cinema. From there they strolled back via the *Town Talkies* and the *Lido* cinema.

When Velji got back home, he could hear his wife and mother

talking in the living-room. Like everyone else they were talking about their uncertain future. It was a warm night, and Velji wiped his face with a handkerchief as he sat down. Radha immediately went to the kitchen to fetch him a glass of water. He drank it in one gulp. He did not normally discuss business with the women folk but these were extraordinary times, and he decided to sound out their opinions. Besides he needed to think aloud.

His mother, Dahiben reacted as he expected. "Have you lost your senses? Buying a business when everyone's talking of leaving the country?"

"Not everyone. Quite a few people are Uganda Citizens and will remain here."

"How many? Very few. Apart from Vajiben, none of my friends are staying. And Vajiben's son is talking of going to the British and saying that he has lost his papers."

"They'll just say it's too bad, then."

"The British are not heartless. They know that Amin is not going to issue new papers. He wants us all out. When they are accepting thousands, they are not going to make a fuss about a few more."

"We should thank God that we are allowed to stay here. We had the foresight to apply for the Ugandan Citizenship at the beginning."

"Foresight, boresight." Dahiben sniffed. "You and your foresight. If you had not decided to be wise-and-a-half we would still have the British passports, and would be going to settle in a better place with the rest of the community."

She never gives me any credit, thought Velji. "We don't know if it is a better place. They don't want us, either. There is a lot of colour prejudice in UK."

"Here they definitely do not want us. They're bound to make the life of those who stay behind a misery. You just can't stay here hoping that Amin will not have another dream where God tells him to throw us out as well."

Velji looked at Kamala, hoping for some moral support. But

she voiced the same feelings as his mother, though in a more restrained voice. "This will not feel like home anymore. Most of our friends and relations will have left so that Uganda will feel stranger to us than UK will to them. It would be like us being exiled from them. And isn't it a bit hasty trying to acquire a business when the situation is still unclear?"

Encouraged by her daughter-in-law's support, Dahiben became even more vociferous. "It's madness, I'm telling you. To sell family jewellery to buy sacks of concrete! You have gone raving mad, my son. I'm not giving up my jewels. I shall give them to Vinod's bride, when he gets married." Apart from her personal collection, Dahiben had retained some more of the family's jewellery for future use.

Velji was hoping to get some support from the women and instead ended up having to defend his decision. "We will make so much money from this deal that next year we'll be able to go shopping in India and buy twice as much jewellery. Besides, gold earns you no interest. If we had sold the jewellery when we came here, it could have earned us a great deal of interest by now."

Dahiben was not convinced. "That interest in Ugandan Shillings would be no use to us. And what will we do when your friend Amin Dada asks us to pack and leave as well? Will I fill my suitcase with cement bags? Listen, son, this is not the right time to sell family jewels - the only valuables one can carry easily." Dahiben pushed her glasses further back up her nose and then thumped her fists on her lap to indicate that she was not going to change her mind.

"You women do not understand business. This may be a calamity for our community but for those who stay behind, it could turn out to be a golden opportunity that comes once in a lifetime," Velji declared and then got up and left the room as he decided further discussion was futile.

Day 5: 8th August 1972

Velji knew how strong-willed Dahiben could be, so next day he finalised the deal with Motilal promising only Kamla's jewels. Motilal clearly thought they were not enough, but knew his weak bargaining position. He had assumed he would get little or nothing for his business. Now he had a few more valuables besides his own that he could take with him to the UK. They shook hands on the deal and arranged to meet in the afternoon at Devjibhai's law firm.

After lunch Velji called Kamla into their room and asked her for the jewels he needed.

"Oh God, so you are going ahead with this wretched deal after all." Kamla struck her forehead with her palm and sat down on the bed.

"It's only about half of your jewellery. We'll buy you more and better jewellery next year. This is an amazing deal. Acquiring the entire stock at a fraction of its price." Velji sighed at the obvious lack of foresight in his wife.

"You could have it free when Motibhai goes."

"No, it is not that simple. You just do not understand it. If I turned down the offer, Motibhai would approach some of his African customers and one of them might just have transportable valuables, like jewels. He made me the first offer because of our friendship. And its real value is many times all the gold we have. We are not even touching *Ba's* gold. Now, come on, I have to go soon, so hurry up and get it out."

After unlocking the safety deposit box, Kamla tied the jewellery in a handkerchief and placed it on the bed. Velji picked up the bundle of jewels, and slipped it in his pocket. "I am telling you: we will not regret this," he announced as he left the room.

*   *   *

Velji and Motilal went to Devji's office and asked him to produce a sales document transferring Motilal's business to Velji.

Devji was concerned and advised Velji against risking whatever meagre savings he might have in buying a business in the present uncertain political climate.

But Velji was determined. "Don't worry," he assured Devji. "I am getting it at a knockdown price and I am not risking much."

Motilal smiled and said, "Look, Devji. We are friends here. I'll tell you. I am practically giving the business away. We don't need to keep secrets. Velji is giving me a few jewels, and they are worth a fraction of the price of my business. What with Amin announcing a new dictat every day, there is too much uncertainty here. Especially for non-citizens. And as you know, I got our UK Visas a couple of months ago. So, I am leaving as soon as I can."

Day 8: 12th August 1972

News: Sale of Businesses

Uganda Argus

ALL SHOPS OWNED BY ALIENS TO BE SOLD

President Amin has announced that he is going to instruct the ministers concerned to start selling all shops owned by Asians who have been asked to leave the country.

Once the shops have been bought by Ugandans the owners will be asked to leave the country and go anywhere they like in the world except Ugandan territory ...

The shops will have to be bought by Ugandans only and not Asians remaining here.

When Velji heard the news that the businesses of departing Asians could only be sold to black Ugandans, he realised he would not be allowed to own Motilal's business, even though the transaction had been completed before the announcement. His heart sank at the thought of the huge financial loss. But he was even more worried about his mother and wife's likely reactions. And they were very much as he expected.

Whenever Dahiben was agitated, she would sit on her comfortable red chair, pull up her legs, as if she was sitting on the floor, with her arms draped round her knees, her head covered with the end of her white sari, and carry on a monologue for what seemed like an infinitely long time.

She had discovered from many years' experience that the best way to be heard was by starting one's complaint with, *"Nobody listens to what I say."* Having gained their attention, she went on with her monologue addressed to an imaginary listener, possibly her dead husband. "Velji thinks I am too old and that he knows best. Always a headstrong boy. First, it was *we must get Ugandan passports.* I said *the British have just left. Why not see how it all settles down.* But does he listen? Listen to his old mother? No, our clever son knows best. So, he goes ahead and gets Ugandan citizenship not just for himself but for the rest of the family, too. *Talk to the elders in the community,* I told him. *If it was such a good idea, why isn't everyone else rushing to get the citizenship? But, he knows best."*

Velji and the rest of the family knew better than to interfere. They left her alone as her comments were not addressed to anyone in particular. They carried on with whatever they were doing, talked in hushed tones and were silent if they entered the room. It was not possible to ignore her monologue, but it was also not easy to speak to her when she was possessed like that.

"What craziness has affected my son? He kept saying, like the chant of a possessed, *I want my own business. I want my own business.* Even if it meant giving away all his wife's jewels. There. He got his business and has already lost it. And the jewels are gone, too. I tried to talk sense into him, but he says *you women don't understand business.* And now look what a mess we are in."

Vinod had a special bond with his grandmother. In the end he went and sat next to her. "*Dadima*, you are always telling me it is all in God's hands," he reasoned with her. "Also, a few days ago you were saying that you wanted to leave this place. So maybe God has answered your prayers."

At first it was almost as if she did not hear Vinod. But a few minutes after he spoke to her she abruptly stopped, looked calmer and went to the little, colourful shrine in her room. She sat cross-legged in front of it and started chanting Lord Rama's name.

Velji was cowed by Dahiben's outburst and moved around the house sheepishly. Kamla's reaction was much more restrained. "Motilal is still here. You should go and tell him the deal is off."

"How can I? A deal is a deal. We even signed it in front of the lawyers."

"These are unusual circumstances. There is nothing to lose in asking." Velji was spurred on more by Kamla's sad, resigned tone than by Dahiben's outburst, and he went to see Motilal, even though he had little hope of succeeding.

Motilal's wife Sona answered the door and ushered Velji into the living-room, "We heard only an hour ago that we have got tickets on tomorrow's flight," she said.

Motilal was sipping tea from a saucer. He carefully put the saucer down on the table as he stood up to welcome Velji, who could tell from the look in Motilal's eyes that he had guessed Velji's mission.

Motilal had a big pile of papers in front of him. "One collects these," he said, and then added pointing at a nearly full bin next to him, "but most of them really belong in there."

Sona came into the room with a cup of tea for Velji and placed it in front of him. "What a trying time for all of us!" she said, giving him a sympathetic smile.

When Sona left the room, Velji decided to come straight to the point before he lost his nerve. Motilal listened to him with a sympathetic expression. At crucial points, he waggled his head, indicating he agreed and sympathised.

When Velji finished, Motilal said, "Brother, your tea is getting cold. Do drink it."

"Well, what do you think about our deal?" Velji asked as he reached out for the cup.

"Whatever is written in our fate, we have to bear it."

"But cancelling this deal is not in the hands of the fate. It is in your hands. Besides, I have not even taken possession of the business."

Motilal just shook his head. "But, brother, you know that in business, a deal is a deal. We shook hands upon it and even signed legal documents to confirm it."

A wry smile hovered on Velji's face. "A legal document. True. But when there is no law in the land, what value is a piece of paper like that?"

"There are still laws in the country," Motilal said.

"Which piece of legislation allowed Amin to make his announcement and send thousands of people packing their bags for no justifiable reason?" Velji argued, but he was already resigned to accept defeat.

"There is a much higher law than that." Motilal maintained his affable tone but refused to budge. "The law of one's word. We are followers of Lord Rama and we believe that once you give your word, you keep it."

Just as Velji was leaving, Motilal made a conciliatory gesture, "I know what. I will pay airfares for you and your family, if you decide to leave as well."

Velji gave a hollow laugh. "I have enough Ugandan shillings for flights. And one can't take them away from Uganda. We are going to leave them here anyway."

Velji stood up to leave. He had not expected to succeed, but he had promised Kamala that he would try and he had fulfilled his promise.

After Velji's departure, Motilal remained in his seat lost in thoughts. Sona walked into the room and her voice brought him out of his reverie. "It's not right to keep his jewellery." She had obviously overheard the conversation.

"That's business. You win some, you lose some." Motilal had never discussed business with his wife and was surprised at her intervention.

"Old rules surely do not apply in the present circumstances."

"Velji took a risk and it did not work out," Motilal pointed out. "In normal times he wouldn't have been able to buy a business like ours at such a low price,"

"But you must make allowance for the times. And taking money off the poor does not please God. With His Grace we will get much more in our new home. Also they are our friends. And if they are forced to leave as well, they will need all the gold they have to help them through early days in a new country."

In the end, Motilal announced that he would think about it. That was a standard ending to any arguments they had. It signified that there was no point in discussing the matter any further. *He might change his mind, but then he might not.*

      *   *   *

Later that day, Sona announced, "I am going to see a couple of friends before we leave."

"Don't be long," Motilal told her.

"I'll be only a few minutes," Sona said, as she hurried towards Kamla's house.

Kamala looked worried and depressed but she welcomed Sona and they sat in the kitchen sipping tea.

After a short time, Sona stood up and announced, "I must go. I promised I wouldn't be long." From her handbag she pulled out a little pouch decorated with black sequins and handed it to

Kamala. "Here. Please take this."

The troubled look in Kamla's eyes was momentarily displaced by a joyous glint, until she saw what was in the purse. "There is some mistake. These are not my jewels," she said in a sad tone.

"Please, just take them."

"But, Motilalbhai told my husband that the deal was sealed."

"You know what men are like - stubborn as donkeys, and then they suddenly change their minds. They do not like to go back on an agreement. So my husband feels he cannot hand back your own valuables. Instead he has sent these."

"He definitely sent these, did he?" Kamala had noticed a little hesitation in Sona's response.

"You don't imagine I would bring these without him knowing about it, do you?" Sona laughed. "But, please promise not to tell your husband about this at least for a couple of days. It is important. Promise?"

"Yes. Yes. I promise." Kamala pulled a gold ring from her finger and gave it to Sona. "But please take this as a token of our love and friendship."

At first Sona refused.

"Upon my life, take it," Kamala said.

Sona reluctantly accepted the present. The two friends hugged each other with tears flowing freely from their eyes.

Day 9: Sunday 13th August 1972

The next morning, Motilal and his family were up early. By eight they were ready to leave for the airport. Motilal looked troubled and paced up and down in the living-room. Sona looked in to tell him they were waiting for him, but decided to leave him alone. After a few minutes he stopped pacing, sat down on the coffee table in the middle of the room and rubbed his forehead with his fingers. He sat there struggling with his thoughts for a couple of minutes and then sprang to his feet.

"Be back very soon. Make sure you are all ready to leave," he called as he rushed out of the front door.

He hurried to Velji's house and knocked on the door loudly and rapidly.

Velji answered the door. "Are you all right? What's the matter?"

"We are just leaving," Motilal blurted out. "Forgive me my friend, but here are your jewels." He thrust a jangling bundle into Velji's hand. The two men hugged, and Motilal hurried back to his home.

"Thank you and good luck," Velji shouted after him, holding his hand above his eyes to shield them from the early morning sun.

* * *

Later that afternoon flight BA 117 left Entebbe for London carrying Motilal, Sona and their children.

"Look at the fluffy clouds. Flying in a plane is so exciting," said their youngest daughter Saroj, who sat by the window.

Sona stroked the girl's hair affectionately. Then she put her hand on Motilal's arm and said in a soft voice, "Whatever was destined has happened. We must now look towards the future."

"Yes, what matters is that the children are fine and we came through unhurt."

"That is the most important thing." Sona held her hands together to thank God for getting them safely to their flight. "One should not be too attached to material goods."

"I agree." He smiled in affirmation. "We should be thankful that even though on the way to the airport the soldiers took everything we had, at least they weren't violent." He looked pleased about something. After a pause he revealed the reason. "I did not tell you, but this morning, just before we left I went to see Velji, and returned his jewels."

"You did?"

"Yes, I did," he beamed. "Just imagine. If I had not done so, the army would have taken his jewels along with all our valuables."

"Well, not all." Her smile had a hint of mischief.

"What do you mean not all? The soldiers found the bundle with all our jewellery under the car mat."

She undid her hair-bun and extricated a gold ring carefully woven in the strands.

"I don't recognise that ring," he said.

"It's the ring Kamala gave me, but I did not want you to see it yet."

"Why not? And why did Kamala give you her ring?"

"Well, you'll never guess what I did yesterday." Sona smiled and then informed him of her visit to Kamala.

Chapter 58
Day 13:
Thursday 17th August
Shashi: Rehana Bhabhi

Rehana Bhabhi stepped through our front door only a week ago, but it feels as if she has always been part of our family. I know that Ramesh and she are madly in love because they defied the world to get married. I have also noticed them stealing loving glances at each other when we are sitting round the dinner table.

Bhabhi has won our whole family over in the short time she has been with us. She talks freely and easily to all of us. And the way she and Lalita Auntie chatter away, you would think that they were old friends.

My friends are terribly impressed that Ba and Papa accepted Ramesh's love marriage without any major opposition. Vinod told me he thinks my parents are 'fantastic'. I agree and I would tell them that I was proud of them, except it might sound presumptuous. A son does not pat his parents on their backs, as the English would say.

But I have noticed a shadow of sadness hover over Bhabhi. Yesterday, I knocked on her door to ask her something. After a brief pause, she said, "Come in."

I think that she had been crying, even though she had wiped her tears by the time I entered the room.

I mentioned this to Ba later and she nodded sympathetically and said, "Not surprising. Poor girl. She would so love to be reconciled with her parents. It is such a shame."

I do feel sorry for poor Bhabhi. She is just settling into a new family and soon she will have to adjust to a new country as well.

Today about mid-morning, I am about to go out to see my friends. I crouch down in the hallway, tying my shoelaces, when Bhabhi asks me if I could do her a favour.

"Sure," I say, glad to offer my services.

"I have left a few of my things at my parents' place. I could manage without most of them, but wouldn't mind having my dressing gown." I have seen her emerge from the bathroom wearing Ramesh's gown, which swamps her.

"I'll get it," I say.

*   *   *

I ring the doorbell. It has a tinkling sound like a bicycle bell. There is a shuffle of footsteps behind the door. The door opens slowly as if the lady answering the door is in no hurry to do so. She is dressed in Punjabi style clothes and has big dark eyes like Bhabhi's, except Bhabhi's glow and sparkle, whereas this lady's are expressionless.

"Oh, hello Auntie. Rehana Bhabhi asked me to get her dressing gown, if it is OK with you."

The transformation is instant; the eyes, which looked dead, are suddenly lively and interested. A smile spreads on her face as she opens the door wide and beckons me in. "You are Rehana's *diyarji* (young brother-in-law). Welcome."

She leads me to the living-room and asks me to sit and says, "I'll get you tea."

I tell her that I had breakfast only a short while ago and repeat that I have just come to collect Bhabhi's gown.

"I'll be back in a minute," she says and leaves me there.

I perch on the leather sofa and look around. Facing me is a television, covered with a white embroidered cloth. There is a large circular drum in the centre of the room with a zebra skin top. On the wall is a picture of a large mosque with Arabic writing underneath it. I guess it is a mosque in Mecca. I have seen similar pictures in some of my Muslim friends' houses.

Zubeida Auntie returns, carrying a tray with a large glass of freshly squeezed orange juice and a plate of biscuits. "It's the first time you have come to my house and I can't let you go without having something."

I protest, as it is polite to do so, but then accept the juice and a couple of biscuits, which are obviously homemade and mouth-wateringly delicious.

"How is my daughter Rehana?" Auntie asks as soon as I stop eating.

I try to put Auntie's mind at rest. I tell her that Bhabhi is just fine and that we are happy to have her with us. I think I am reassuring Auntie but then I notice that her eyes have started glistening with tears. When I go on to describe how we all get on smashingly well, tears start running down her cheeks. I guess it is because she reckons that Bhabhi does not miss them, as she is happy with us.

So I tell her I am sure that yesterday Bhabhi was crying, and that Ba said that it was because she misses her parents. I think that being told that Bhabhi has not forgotten them would cheer Auntie up. Instead she bursts out crying.

I wonder *now what have I done wrong?* I decide to leave before I upset her any more.

So, I get up and say, "Bhabhi will be waiting for her gown."

Auntie goes into one of the bedrooms and returns with a holdall. "I have put a few more of Rehana's things in here. I hope it is not too heavy to carry," she says.

I lift it with my left hand to show her that I am stronger than I look. At the door, just as I am about to leave, she squeezes my arm affectionately and says, "Thank you for coming and for bringing me Rehana's news. You have made me so happy." This is the same lady who was sobbing a few minutes earlier because of something I had said.

I think *She is just being polite.* But then she adds, "*Beta,* please come back often and let me know how she is." I realise that I cannot have upset her if she calls me *beta* (son). So, I resolve to go back soon.

When I get home, I hear laughter from the living-room. Bhabhi is in there talking to Ba and Lalita Auntie. I give her the holdall and she wants to know about her mother. I tell her that Auntie was fine to start with but that she shed tears when I gave her Bhabhi's news. And then Bhabhi starts to cry. I notice Ba's eyes are shiny as well and Lalita Auntie dabs her eyes with a hankie.

I am a bit miffed. I had only tried to be helpful and instead seem to be a carrier of a crying epidemic.

So I go to Vinod's place and we listen to Jimi Hendrix's album, *Are You Experienced?*

Chapter 59
Day 14:
Friday 18th August 1972
Shashi: Saying Thank You in English

About mid-morning there is a knock on our front door. I get up from my desk, but then I hear our servant Okello let the visitor in and announce in his deep voice, *"Mama ya mama-dogo iko hapa."* (The young mistress's mother is here.)

Ba instructs him to bring water and tea before she goes to welcome Zubeida Auntie.

"I'm so glad you have come," Ba greets Auntie and then calls out as they pass the bathroom door, "Rehana, your mother's here."

I quietly go into the small living-room, from where I can overhear them through the slightly ajar door. I am curious to discover if they would discuss my making them all cry yesterday.

Ba holds Auntie's right hand in both of hers and leads her into the living-room. "I hope you don't mind me coming without letting you know first," Auntie says as soon as they sit down.

"What sort of talk is that?" Ba replies. "Your daughter's home is your home, too. Rehana is in the bathroom and will join us soon."

"I have this gold pendant for her hair," Auntie announces. "It belonged to my mother. But poor Mother died a few years ago. It was God's will. However, she had always said that it was for her little Rehana when she gets married."

"Does Yusufbhai agree with Rehana still being given it?" Ba wants to know.

280

I can hear Auntie give a nervous laugh. "He does not even know I've come here. Or brought this with me."

"How much longer is he going to fight against it?" Ba asks. "Ramesh and Rehana are married now and there is no going back."

"I know," Auntie sighs. "I tried to tell him that but he does not want to talk about it. I know he is suffering, too. But men can be so stubborn."

There is a short pause. They are both probably lost in their own thoughts until Ba speaks. "Once my husband told me a story about how some women changed their husbands' behaviour. They refused to let their husbands touch them until the men stopped fighting each other. And it worked. It was some European story, I think."

"If only it worked in real life!" Auntie sighs again.

There is the noise of the bathroom door opening in the corridor and Rehana Bhabhi running to the living-room. I catch a glimpse of her. She is wearing her towelling dressing gown, the one I fetched yesterday. And her hair is piled on top of her head and tied in place with a big white towel.

I hear Bhabhi greet her mother in English, "Oh, Amma, thank you for coming."

And I also hear her mother laugh and say, "You and your English ways. Thanking your own mother for coming to see you!"

It does not seem right to peep in and so I do not. But I can picture the scene in my mind. I bet Thomas Hardy wishes he was alive to witness this scene. *Mother and daughter embracing each other for a long time as they stand in the middle of the living-room. A crow hopping on the windowsill, tilting its head curiously, to see what the human beings were up to. Tears flowing freely. Ba standing by them dabbing her eyes. And Mother teasing her daughter for thanking her in English.*

Chapter 60
Day 15:
19th August 1972
Shashi: The Wings of a Party

These days there is only one topic of conversation. After glancing at the *Argus*, Papa says, "It looks as if Amin is not likely to change his mind. We are lucky that the British are happy to have us."

"I wouldn't put it that strongly," Ramesh clears his throat before reading out the latest news. ***The BBC reported today that Mr. Heath is under great pressure not to allow any large-scale immigration to the UK.***

"Pressure from whom?" I want to know. "I thought you told me that the opposition party, Labour, is likely to be sympathetic to us anyway."

"It is members of Mr. Heath's own Party. A group called The Monday Club is totally opposed to our settling in the UK. They are reminding the Prime Minister that in its last manifesto Tories had given a pledge to the nation that they will not allow any large scale permanent immigration to the UK."

"How can just a few members of a Club challenge a government's decision?" I am at a loss to understand it.

"It's not like your Satyawadi Team," Ramesh laughs.

Rehana Bhabhi explains to me that the Monday Club consists of highly influential members from the Right Wing of the Tory Party. They are often from the upper echelons of the society.

Soon after, Vinod comes round and I give him the news.

"What about the other Clubs? Do they support us?"

Vinod wants to know.

"What other Clubs?" I do not know what he is talking about.

"The Tuesday Club and the Wednesday Club. And especially the Sunday Club. Surely they are a powerful Club."

I explain to him that it is only a name. "It is a club to which Tory MPs from the Right Wing of the party belong."

"Tory Party is surely not a bird with a left and a right wing," Vinod muses aloud. "This is all too confusing."

He then goes home, shaking his head as he steps out of the door.

Chapter 61
Day 19:
23rd August 1972
Devji: Uncertainties

People do not know what exactly Amin has in mind. First, it was all British Asians had to leave. Then he announced that his decree also applied to those with Indian, Pakistani or Bangladeshi passports.

Then, the day before yesterday, on the 21st he changed his mind, as reported in the papers:

Uganda Argus

"ALL ASIANS MUST GO".

"President Idi Amin said at the weekend that all the 23,000 who hold Uganda citizenship will also have to leave the country in addition to the 60,000 who have already been asked to quit. Addressing a mass rally in Rukungiri, Kigezi District he said that the second phase of the exodus resulted from sabotage and arson the Asians had started or were planning to carry out."

The news was like a thunderbolt for people like Velji, who had acquired Ugandan citizenship as soon as it was possible and therefore thought that they are allowed to live here. Now they find themselves in the same boat as the rest of Asians.

However, today the *Argus* reports:

"THESE ASIANS CAN STAY".

"Asians who are Uganda citizens will not be required to leave the country, President Amin said yesterday when he briefed the visiting Sudanese Foreign Minister Dr. Mansur Khalid, on Uganda's policy on the British Asians during a lunch at Command Post."

Velji said to me, "I knew there was some mistake. He wouldn't throw out people who became Uganda citizens."

I replied, "I very much hope you are right. But I do not trust Amin. He may have made the statement because a foreign dignitary was present."

Chapter 62
Day 19:
23rd August
Shashi: Ramesh, the Rebel

I am tormented by curiosity. I want to know how life will be different in UK. I have heard many stories from Ramesh and other UK-returns about their experiences. I have read plenty of books by English authors - Jane Austen and Thomas Hardy, and almost all the Dickens novels I could find in our school library. I have seen quite a few English movies. But I still can't picture life in the UK clearly enough. I bombard Ramesh with questions. He answers briefly and says that I will soon find out. That doesn't satisfy me. I need lots of details to form a vivid picture.

"What is the country like? Is it full of big buildings and factories?"

Ramesh shakes his head vigorously. "The cities are like that but even they have parks. And the countryside is green and very pleasant."

"What colour is the soil there? Not orangey red like here in Uganda?"

"Red in some counties like Devon but black in most parts."

"And the sky?"

"Don't be silly - sky is the same everywhere. On second thoughts, no, that's not quite true. It's often overcast - grey and not always blue."

"That does not sound very nice." I make a face.

"I don't mind it. It makes light gentler to the eye. Soothing and not glaring. But then there is a feature of the day that we do not have. It is the length of the day."

I laugh. "Are you kidding me? The day has to be twenty-four hours long everywhere on the earth, as the earth rotates as a whole."

Rehana Bhabhi is in the room and has been listening to us. She and Ramesh join me in the laughter.

"Of course it is twenty-four hours long," Rehana Bhabhi says. "That is not what Ramesh means. He is talking about the daylight hours."

"Surely it is twelve hours day and twelve hours night. Like everywhere else," I say.

Ramesh and Rehana Bhabhi then tell me that days are long in Summer, it gets light as early as five in the morning and the night nudges in at 9 or 10 p.m.; and in Winter it is light only from about eight in the morning to four in the afternoon. That comes as a real surprise to me. That fact has never been mentioned in any of the Geography books that I have read. No UK-returns have told me about it. And it is one of the most interesting features of UK and all the non-tropical countries.

"Do they have different working hours in winter?" I want to know.

"They do change the clocks by an hour. And it does take some time to get used to the long hours of twilight in summer months," Bhabhi says.

"So the night does not spread its dark cloak over the land in a matter of minutes at dusk," I say. Ramesh and Bhabhi smile and I am pleased to see them appreciate the poetic image.

But I still want to know more. "And the people? How are they different?"

"On the whole the natives are friendly. And before you ask, no, it's not true that they only bathe once a week. Most people have a shower or a bath every day."

I want to know how the English feel about us not eating meat. I learn that a vegetarian society has existed in UK since the beginning of the century, and that George Bernard Shaw was their champion. I am pleased to hear that more people are becoming vegetarians.

I ask Ramesh to recount his anecdote about explaining vegetarianism to his first landlady.

"You have heard that a dozen times before."

"Tell me again," I plead.

Rehana Bhabhi is there and she urges him, too. So, he recounts it again for her benefit.

Ramesh's first landlady was a kind and gentle woman and he was very fond of her. When he informed her that he was a vegetarian, she wanted to know, "So, will you have chicken?"

"No, no meat, red or white. I do not eat food that involves killing animals."

"Do you like fish?"

"How can one not like fish? They swim so gracefully. Yes, I do like fish and that's why I don't eat them."

"Where do you get your proteins from then?" she wanted to know.

"Pulses, beans, yogurt, etc."

"You can get yogurt there?" She was impressed. Yogurts were still a novelty in the UK then. "Pretty advanced, I see."

Ramesh did not have the heart to tell her that yogurt was a traditional dish amongst Indians, and that almost every household made it at home.

He mostly ate out in restaurants but had an occasional meal with his landlady. She had no idea what to serve him instead of meat. So, the first time he ate with the family, the rest of them had *meat and two veg*. On his plate she had left a gap where the meat was supposed to be. So, he used to say that he likes a meal of *a gap and two veg*.

"And tell Bhabhi about the party where they wanted you to smoke dope."

"You do not want to hear that."

But Bhabhi says, "Oh yes, I do."

"You see," Ramesh explains the background first. "Papa is the best father one could hope for. He is kind and generous."

"And he is a great story-teller," I add.

"Yes, that, too, but he is — "

"But most important of all," I point out, "he does not embarrass you in front of your friends."

Ramesh smiles. "Yes, he is great that way. But he is very cautious and terribly protective, almost pathologically so. And that means there are certain things he has absolutely forbidden us from doing."

Ramesh now leans back, stretching out his legs, and takes a sip from his glass, as if that is all he is going to say.

"What things?" Bhabhi asks, her face glowing with expectation.

Ramesh smiles again, clearly enjoying having a captive audience. He turns to me and says, "What do you think, Shashi? Can we trust her with our secrets?"

"Hm." I hold my chin, as I consider the difficult question, before saying, "Yes, I guess so."

"There is another problem. I can't just list them because there are stories attached to them," Ramesh informs Bhabhi.

"Good!" Bhabhi rubs her hands together. "Tell me. I love stories."

"Well ..." Ramesh clears his throat, for dramatic effect, I

suspect. "Well, a long time ago, before Shashi was born, a boy, the son of one of Papa's friends, had climbed a *jambuda* tree to pick some of its delicious fruits. But he lost his footing and fell down. His back was broken and he was crippled for life. So ... Papa's first commandment was *Thou shalt not climb trees*.

A few years later our cousin, Girish, was injured when a van knocked him off his bicycle. He was not hurt badly. Jinja has very little traffic and that is the only incident that I know of where a cyclist was injured by a vehicle. But that resulted in the second commandment: *Thou shalt not ride a bike*.

And finally a couple of boys have drowned swimming near the Rippon Falls. Almost every parent in the town has forbidden their kids to go into the river or the lake. But Papa has gone a step further and turned it into *Thou shalt not swim*.

Most of our people can't swim anyway. It's not surprising as the river and the lake are not safe. And as you know, till recently there were no public swimming pools for Asians. But the Madhvanis are our family friends and we often went to their place to play with their kids. So I learnt to swim secretly in their private swimming pool."

"And so did I," I say proudly.

Ramesh puts his arm round my shoulder, grinning at Bhabhi. "And both of us also rode friends' bikes and climbed trees."

"You naughty boys." Bhabhi laughs. "Does Papa know?"

"No, he is still not aware of it. And don't you dare tell him." Ramesh wags his finger at her.

"My lips are sealed," she assures him, and then asks eagerly, "Are there no more commandments?"

"You haven't explained yet about the dope party in London," I remind him

"Aah ... yes, I got sidetracked," he admits. "Well, I am sure by now you have realised that Papa and Ba brought up Shashi and me to lead as abstemious a life as possible. No smoking. No stimulants - not even tea or coffee, let alone alcohol. And yet no one ever stopped us from going to the temple for the festival of *Shivratri* and drinking *bhang*. It is better known by its English name 'Marijuana'. Everyone in the town drinks the tangy green drink with a strong taste of fennel seeds. Madhvani's chef also makes the *bhang*, which is famous in the town for its potency. I suspect he probably adds some other drugs to his concoction. So - do my parents not realise that *bhang* is a drug? Or does Papa make an exception once a year on this religious festival? Not very likely as Papa is not religious.

Anyway, one year the drink was particularly strong and I had a generous portion. Later that day, when I sat down for dinner I found the table was slanting. Then the walls started leaning at different angles. I rushed into my bedroom clutching my head, which seemed to be spinning. And I had a terrible headache. The experience has put me off *bhang* for life."

Ramesh rubs his forehead - grimacing, as if the memory is bringing back the migraine he suffered.

"The party," I prompt him, growing impatient at his long-windedness.

"I'm getting there," he says amicably.

"You see, it was one of those parties in London, Rehana, where alcohol flows freely. But, as always, I stuck to either orange juice or Coca Cola. My friend Steve told the rest of the gang, 'Ramesh is like a hermit. A vegetarian. Doesn't smoke or drink.'

'How about marijuana?' Another friend asked jokingly, hoping to raise a laugh.

'Oh that,' I said nonchalantly. 'I gave that up when I was twelve.' Of course they thought I was joking but then I told them of my experience with *bhang*.

The friend then asked me, 'So if you are not into drugs or alcohol, what do you do to rebel against the establishment?'."

Ramesh then turns to me, holding his hand like a conductor's baton. And on cue we both shout in unison,

"I swim, climb trees and ride a bike."

Chapter 63
Day 20:
24th August 1972
Shashi: The British and I

BBC News Bulletin:

There was a noisy demonstration in Smithfield market in London today against the immigration of Ugandan Asians. It was supported by the National Front Party.

Day 21: 25th August

A full-page ad in the *Uganda Argus*

An Important Announcement On Behalf Of the City of Leicester, England

The City Council of Leicester, England, believes that many families in Uganda are considering living in Leicester.

If you are thinking of doing so, it is very important you know that PRESENT CONDITIONS IN THE CITY ARE VERY DIFFERENT FROM THOSE MET BY EARLIER SETTLERS. THEY ARE:

HOUSING: several thousands of families are already on the Council's waiting list.

EDUCATION: hundreds of children are awaiting places in schools.

SOCIAL AND HEALTH SERVICES: already stretched to the limit.

IN YOUR OWN INTERESTS AND THOSE OF YOUR FAMILY YOU SHOULD ACCEPT THE ADVICE OF THE UGANDA RESETTLEMENT BOARD AND NOT COME TO LEICESTER.

BBC News Bulletin:

Further opposition against letting the Ugandan Asians into the UK has emerged from within the Community Relations Commission. Mr Bernard Perkins, one of its twelve members has handed in his resignation as a protest against the UK Government's decision to accept Ugandan Asians who are British citizens.

After reading the news that some British people are opposed to us settling in UK, I am not sure what to expect when we go there.

When I was a child, Papa told me a story about the Parsi community in India.

Parsis are Zoroastrians, who migrated from Persia to escape religious persecution. They sailed to India and arrived at the port of Surat in Gujarat. They sent an emissary to the King to ask his permission to settle there. The King sent a pot of milk back with a message saying, "Ours is a pure society - like milk." The Parsis sent the pot back with sugar stirred into the milk with a reply, "We will mix into your society like sugar dissolves in milk - you wouldn't be able to tell us apart from your own citizens and at the same time we will contribute to the society - like sugar improves the taste of milk."

And now Parsis are an integral part of the Indian society.

I suddenly recalled the tale a few days ago and referred to it when talking to Papa. I told him, "We obviously forgot its moral when we settled in Uganda."

Papa smiled, as he was pleased that I remembered the story. He said, "I daresay that if we lived here longer we would have integrated more. I hope we will in the UK."

*   *   *

For years I have been eagerly awaiting to go to UK. So when Amin made his announcement, I thought that it only meant that I would go there earlier than planned. It also meant that my family and friends would also move there. I really wasn't that bothered about the fact that we were being kicked out.

But now I am not sure about the future. The context has changed. Instead of going as a student with a generous allowance from my parents, I will be a poor immigrant. And judging from the articles in the British papers, which Ramesh has occasionally managed to get, many people in UK are opposed to us settling there. There have been demonstrations in some towns and speeches in Parliament from MPs who are urging the government not to honour their commitment to British passport holders.

Leicester City Council has even placed an ad in today's *Uganda Argus* urging us not to settle in Leicester.

My feelings towards white people have varied in the past. There is a small community of them in Jinja and they keep themselves to themselves. Until a few years ago, the only two decent clubs, the Jinja Golf Club and The Amber Club, which has the only public swimming pool in the town, both had signs near the entrance proclaiming "Whites Only" with a smaller sign below it: "No Dogs Allowed." So although I had occasionally seen white people around the town, I had never actually met a white person face to face until I was ten.

After a holiday in Mombasa, we were coming back to Jinja by train. I was making my way back from the restaurant car to our carriage, where my mother was sitting. I was more than half-way along one of the carriages when a couple of European ladies appeared at the other end of the corridor. Rather than go back to the end of the carriage, I flattened myself against the window. I was only a slight little boy and the passage was certainly wide enough for them to pass me without touching me. But before they got near me, I was suddenly and unceremoniously hauled into a compartment behind me by a European man, who held me by the scruff of my neck until the ladies passed us. He then roughly shoved me into the corridor without a word. I have tried to make sense of his action. All I can think of is that he did not want the white skin of the women to be tainted by even a mere touch of the brown skin of a ten-year old boy.

It was a whole year later before I met another white person. I was in Junior Secondary School.

A new English teacher, Mrs. Bartlett, joined the staff and she became our Form Tutor. She was very nice. I was her favourite and she used to ask me to call out the Register as she found it difficult to pronounce the Indian names. I remember how once I came to my own name in the Register and just read it out aloud without thinking about it. As I did not reply *Present, Madam*, she marked me absent. I realised my mistake only when the class burst out laughing.

She was also very patient. Once, Abdul, who lived just outside Jinja, explained his late arrival with *I came footing because our car broken*. We all thought it was hilarious, but Mrs. Bartlett patiently corrected Abdul's English for him. Another time Abdul said *my sister is a typewriter*. We bent over double with laughter, but she explained the difference between a typist and a typewriter, without even a flicker of a smile.

Then there was a nice friendly lady at a fair in our school grounds. She had a bookstall and talked to me amicably and charged me only one shilling for a thick hardback book. I thought it was a story about a shepherd because it was called *My Good Shepherd*. It turned out to be a religious book and I am afraid I did not read it beyond the first few pages.

And how can I forget Mr Louis Van Aardt? An ex-RAF man who had been shot down over Germany during the Second World War. The famous film *The Great Escape* was apparently about the camp where he was held a prisoner. He was a client of Papa. In December last year, when he heard that I was planning to go to Nairobi, he offered me a lift. He said he had to go there anyway on business.

I have never seen a more impatient driver or one who swore so much. He broke all speed limits, and he started swearing the moment he spotted a car in front. *Get out of my bloody way. You, bloody fool, can't you see I am behind you? Why do you need to slow down now, you bastard?* And so on until he overtook the car and then went through the same performance when he reached the next car.

He used the same offensive language when he dealt with petrol pump attendants and fruit vendors on the way. But despite his language, he was a very nice and friendly man. I thought that maybe his swearing was a result of him having spent time in the prisoner of war camp, until I came across some more Europeans when on holiday in Kenya, and their talk was peppered with *Bloody this* and *Bloody that.*

Then a few days later, I found myself on the receiving end of a white man's offensive language. My three cousins and I had arranged to meet my uncle in a Nairobi car park. He was slightly late so we waited by his car, talking to each other. Two of us leant against his car and the other two against the vehicle next to it.

A few minutes later, a white man, wearing shorts and a wide sun-hat, strode up to us and started swearing profusely in Swahili for leaning against his precious car. He assumed that we would not understand English, although my UK-return cousin was clutching a copy of The Times. We were taken aback as we are not used to being sworn at, and certainly had not come across such abusive and aggressive language. Indians rarely swear. And grown up men never wear shorts.

These limited number of experiences seemed too trivial to matter when I thought I would only be a temporary visitor as a student in England. But now I am going to spend the rest of my life there, it suddenly seems important to know if people on the whole are like the man who hauled me out of the train corridor or if they are nice like Mrs Bartlett.

*   *   *

Ramesh has started reminding me that I should be able to take my O Levels in UK in December. He is turning into a tyrant. It is mid-afternoon and today for the second time he comes to my room to check that I am studying and not sleeping.

"Studying?"

I am reading in bed and hold up my History notebook.

"Good." He turns round to go back to his room.

"Did you like History in school?" I ask him.

He stops and frowns. "It was OK," and adds after a pause, "actually, come to think of it, it was boring. How do you find it?"

"Also boring," I say. I am pleased to learn that he feels the same way about it. "I enjoy it when Mr. Nayyar gives us the alternative versions of History. But what's the point of learning about, say, Henry the Eighth and the Tudors?"

He pulls up a chair and straddles it, resting his arms on its back. "I would have agreed with you in the past. But now, as you are going to adopt the UK as your new homeland, knowing its history is important."

"OK," I say, "but do I have to be proud of its colonial past?"

He laughs and reaches over to ruffle my hair. "Is that bothering you? You know, England has hardly any colonies left. And gone are the colonial attitudes, too. However, you can be proud of its achievements in literary and scientific fields. And especially of its democratic institutions. There are a large number of liberal-minded people and it is one of the best places to live in now."

Ramesh stands by the window. There are no clouds and the sun is harsh in the light blue sky.

He tells me things about the UK, which I wish were in our History syllabus. I had never heard about a man called William Wilberforce, who long time ago led a movement against slavery and even persuaded the British parliament to make slave trade illegal. How enlightened and ahead of his time!

"And do you know where the main international opposition to the South African Apartheid now comes from? Britain. A large number of people there boycott South African goods and the sporting ties with South Africa are broken now. I remember when Springboks, the South African Rugby team, came to play there. A huge group of anti-apartheid protestors invaded the pitches and the matches had to be abandoned. I remember keeping a cutting from a newspaper. Mind you, newspapers being what they are, the front page had a picture of a pretty young blonde protestor in a miniskirt being carried away from the rugby pitch by the police."

I laugh, "I bet you kept the cutting because of the pretty blonde girl in it and it had nothing to do with the anti-apartheid movement." And before he can reply I add, "But then what about the demonstrations in England against letting Ugandan Asians settle there?" I refer to the article in today's *Uganda Argus* about it.

"Of course there are some who are against us going there.

In fact, there is a political party called The National Front, which would like only white people living in the UK. But they are a small minority and the fact that they exist just goes to show the strength of the British democracy - you are allowed to express an opinion freely. The majority of the British are fair-minded and liberal in their outlook. You could say *the natives are friendly*." He smiles.

I believe him because of the reports we hear from the people who have already gone to UK. They ring back and say how the government gives them accommodation and "dole" money until they are on their feet. But even more important, they say that the local people are friendly and offer to help. So it seems that thankfully they are more like Mrs. Bartlett.

"That is reassuring to hear," I nod my head and then add in a serious voice, "Just one more request."

"Yes?"

"So that I can be easily assimilated, could you teach me to swear like the British men do?"

"No, I bloody well won't," Ramesh says in English, turns around, and marches out of the room.

Chapter 64
Day 25:
28th August 1972
Shashi: Logistics of Exodus

Radio Uganda News Bulletin:

*President has ruled that all non-citizens are to fly by
East African Airways.*

The President has really ruled that? Seriously? I thought
Amin wants us out as fast as possible. I have just done some
quick mental calculation. I don't know how many EAA
planes could be made available, but are there enough to carry
between sixty and eighty thousand people in three months?
We have sixty-five days left to flee from our mad President.
That means about a thousand people will have to fly out
every day. I will have to check, but I think maybe about one
hundred and fifty people fit into a plane. So we are talking of
six or seven planeloads per day. I will be surprised if the EAA
has got the capacity to provide so many flights.

Besides, it is just not possible for a plane and its crew to
fly from Entebbe to London each day. A plane takes almost
a whole day to fly to London, a few thousand miles away.
The crew then must have a day of rest before returning to
Entebbe on the third day; then another day of rest before the
plane or the crew can make another trip to London. In other
words, a plane can only fly to London once every four days.
So they need four times more planes. And pilots.

And what about the airport capacity? We have only one
international airport. And it handles maybe two or three
flights a day. How will they cope with this sudden surge in

passengers? When our president says he wants us all to fly by East African Airways, does he imagine some of us clinging to the outside of the planes - like you see pictures of rail passengers doing in India?

Day 26: 29th August

BBC News Bulletin:

Mr. Henry Brind, British Deputy High Commissioner in Uganda, has announced that 485 Asians have been processed with entry permits to date.

Shashi:

485! I can't believe it. I know that there are some people, like Ramesh and Rehana Bhabhi, who already have rights of entry to UK, but they are a small minority.

If in a month about 500 are dealt with, it will take 120 months or 10 years to issue permits to us all. The countries, which are willing to accept us, need to speed up their procedures. I guess now that British Government has agreed to accept us, they will move fast. One expects them to be efficient. They will have to employ more Embassy staff. And I hope they do.

Day 37: 10th September 1972

BBC News Bulletin:

The Government has announced that plans for airlifting British Asians to the UK by East African Airways, in collaboration with BOAC and British Caledonian Airways are finalised.

Shashi:

Phew! It seems someone has pointed out to the President that his demand for everyone to fly by the EAA was not thought through properly.

Chapter 65
Day 37:
10th September
Devji: No One is Safe

Many of the *Sages* have left Jinja, but the few remaining ones still continue going to the Coronation Park for our pre-dawn meetings.

When Velji and I reached the Park this morning, the red dawn was beginning to seep around the edges of the dark clouds on the horizon. There were only five of us today and I was the one with the most shocking information.

The moment we spread our handkerchiefs on the lawn and lowered ourselves down on them, I broke the news, "Manubhai was arrested by the army yesterday."

"You don't mean ..." Chandubhai did not complete his question as he guessed from my serious expression that his worst fears were justified. He finished his sentence with, "I see you do mean Manubhai Madhvani."

The group sat in stunned silence. They know that Madhvanis are our close family friends. I did not go into details about how Jyotiben rang last night to ask for our advice and sympathy. She was deeply worried about her husband's safety.

Manubhai is the head of the richest family in Uganda. Their business, which includes production of sugar, beer and textiles, is based in Jinja because their sugar cane plantation is just outside the town. They employ about fifteen thousand people in their various enterprises. The Madhvani Group represents more than ten percent of Uganda's exports earnings. And they are highly respected and liked because, despite being fabulously rich, they are gentle people, who are known for their charitable work.

The silence of the group this morning was finally broken by Velji, who stated the obvious, "If the Madhvanis are not safe, then who is?"

Chapter 66
Day 37:
10th September
Shashi: The Ordinary Folk - 2
Life Goes On

Earlier in my journal, I said I will describe the people of Jinja, and talked about Veljikaka and his family. Now is the time to describe some more people.

As is the custom, whenever someone cooks something special, they send a little of it round to the neighbours to taste. When Ba wants to send food to the neighbours, I am the one who takes it to them. Once we had guests and one of them asked me, "What do you want to be when you grow up?" When I hesitated, he said, "Tell us what you are good at." And I replied, "I am good at transporting food to the neighbours. So I think when I leave school, I will open a transport business, specialising in delivering food." They all thought it was funny. Even Ba laughed.

I even recognise several households' specialities. For example, Vinod's mum, Kamlamasi, makes delicious *samosa*. Poojamasi cooks great *batetawada*. The tastiest sweets come from Radhamasi, who lives four doors away from us on the left. It is not surprising as her husband, Karsanjimaraj, runs the best sweetshop in the town. Chefs are highly respected in our society and so the suffix *Maraj* (short for Maharaj-King) is often used after their names. Karsanjimaraj owns Jinja Sweet Mart, the popular food shop, near the Madhvani Office. He is the main caterer at many weddings in the town. He is also one of the *Sages*.

His family consists of his wife, Radha*masi*, their son,

Shyam*bhai* (who works in a bank) and daughter-in-law
Sharda*ben* and five grandchildren (two boys and three girls).

A dramatic event occurred yesterday in their family. Papa
was called by them early this morning and he came back
looking grim and sad. He told us about what happened and
I am back in my room trying to record the sad tale. As with
my other descriptions about the folk of Jinja, I have once
again taken the liberty of imagining the details.

Life Goes On

"It is our last day here. Let us all eat together." Karsanji*maraj*
told his family when it was dinnertime. So the whole family sat
down for their last supper together. The adults, Karsanji*maraj* and
his wife Radha*ben*, their son Shyam and daughter-in-law Sharda,
mostly ate in silence. But the children, who knew that they were
going to fly in an aeroplane next day, were excited and chattered
away.

After dinner Shyam announced, "We leave at sunrise tomorrow
morning. So, children, off to bed right away." When his eldest
daughter looked at him enquiringly, he said, "That's right. I am
asking you not to clear up. Yes, the sun must have risen in the
west today!"

Both the boys ran to their rooms laughing and the girls left
quietly. The three-year-old holding her two older sisters' hands
turned back to smile at the adults as she was led away.

Shyam then addressed his wife and parents, "That applies to
us as well." Sharda still picked up the children's plates to take
them to the sink. "I mean it," he told her. "Leave it all as it is. If
the army wants to live in our home, they can clear up the mess
before they occupy it. Not a large price to pay for a house."

Sharda turned to her mother-in-law to see if she agreed. Radha
nodded at her. Sharda placed the pile of plates back on the table,
washed her hands in the washbasin and silently went to her

bedroom. Shyam got up to follow her. He turned round at the door to see if his parents were also retiring to bed, and noticed that Karsanji had taken the pile of plates to the sink.

"Father, who are you trying to impress with our tidy house?" he gently chided.

"Son, *Jindagi Emaj Chale* (Life goes on)."

Shyam smiled and quietly closed his bedroom door. He had heard his father say this phrase a million times. Shyam had even persuaded Sharda to embroider the sentence *Jindagi Emaj Chale* and had it framed before giving it to his father as a present.

"He is right, you know." Radha told her husband as she got up stiffly to go to bed. "Why do you bother? We will be gone tomorrow."

"One has to do one's duty. Our karma decides it all." Karsanji was going to expand his theory but remembered that he had bored his long-suffering wife with his philosophy many a time in the past. And his family. And his customers.

He believed there were two streams of life - external events beyond our control, and an internal spiritual flow, which we can control. One just has to do what is right. That includes not criticising others for their follies. When he prayed, he often told God, *I cannot decide how others choose to live their lives. But I live my life as I believe you would like me to.*

He told Radha that he would join her later. She knew that even at work, after all his assistants had gone, Karsanji always did a bit of final tidying up and then sat for a while lost in his own thoughts. Meditating, he called it.

He sat in the kitchen surveying the room. He saw the gas cooker with its blue gas cylinder by its side. He smiled as he remembered how, before gas cookers became available, he had used a large coal stove and filled up the house with smoke. He had started his business cooking from home, when he had used that kitchen for several years and only moved to commercial premises after his business grew.

Despite feeling a sudden weariness descend upon him, he

stood up after a while and decided to take a last look around at what had been his home all his life. Radha had left their bedroom door half ajar.

The other three bedroom doors were closed. One of the doors, where his three granddaughters slept, had a new door. It had been badly chipped a few years ago and one of his customers had offered to fix it. But as he prevaricated, Shyam went ahead and had it fixed. Karsanji was pleased that Shyam was now taking over as the head of the family.

Karsanji slowly shuffled into the living-room. There were light rectangular patches on the wall where some of the pictures had hung. They had decided to take only the family portraits and a painting of the Goddess Kali. The empty frames lay in a pile beside the television.

He walked around looking at the pictures that still hung on the wall. There was Lord Shiva, the God of Destruction, looking serene despite his job. Next to it was the framed motto, *Jindagi Emaj Chale* (Life Goes On), which his daughter-in-law Sharda had embroidered for him. After much thought, he had decided to leave this behind. But now he took it off the wall and sat down with it on the new brown comfortable sofa. He smiled as he read *Life Goes On* sewn in bright red and orange thread on a light cream background. He read it aloud a few times and then hugged the frame to his chest.

Next morning Radha found him lying on the sofa, clutching the frame. He had passed away peacefully during the night.

Chapter 67
Day 39:
12th September 1972
Devji: My Prayer

Velji and I hurry to the park just as dawn breaks and mellow orangey-yellow glow seeps into the atmosphere. There are only six *Sages*, attached to their long shadows, sitting on the grass. We can hear their voices from afar, but not the actual words. It is an animated discussion, which is interrupted by our arrival. I can guess what the topic of conversation is today.

We spread our hankies on the ground and lower ourselves on them. I leave a little space for latecomers. As I greet the others, I try to think who is still missing and the sad reckoning dawns on me. We have lost three of our group. Both Karsanji Maraj and Philip De Souza died of heart attacks within last week and Inder Singh has left Uganda for India. "I want to spend my remaining days in peace," he told us before he made his decision.

The group resume their discussion. Of course, they are talking about Amin's announcement yesterday that he will put any Asians left after the deadline into concentration camps.

I miss a lot of what is being said because I am lost in my own thoughts.

Here is a group of people I call my friends. They represent a cross section of our community. There are Hindus, Muslims, Sikhs and Christians amongst us. We have shop-keepers, teachers, a lawyer, an accountant, a builder and we even had a chef, in our group. And we are all being banished from this land, the land we have thought of as our home for most of our lives. It is a collective punishment and for what? For having a different pigment in our skin, for having a different background? The world has shrunk in recent times. There have been relatively small conflicts like in Korea and Viet Nam, but no World Wars for over a quarter of a century. America and Russia, because of their fear of the bomb, will hopefully learn to coexist peacefully rather than mutually destroy each other. I have often imagined that in not too distant a future, human beings will cast aside their narrow divisions and think of themselves as a single human race, and live under a single world government. Wars will be a distant memory of the past. People will strive to create a just society where all human beings will be cared for, and there will be no huge discrepancies in living standards within a nation or even between nations. It will be like *Rama Rajya*, the society under Rama's rule as described in the ancient scriptures.

Ramesh says socialism will deliver it. The young are gifted with optimism. But I am beginning to wonder if it will ever be achieved. Is our human psyche so constructed as to make it always impossible to achieve this utopian dream?

I am shaken out of my reverie as a pair of large crested cranes land not far from me and flutter their wings noisily. People stop talking as they watch the magnificent creatures strut around for a minute or two before taking off.

"Crested cranes. A symbol of Uganda," Mohanbhai says. "Our present homeland."

"Does UK have an animal as its symbol?" Babubhai wonders aloud.

"I was looking at a book about UK and in it there was a picture of a horse-like creature rearing on its hind legs. It had a long thin horn on its head. But I don't know what it is called." Karim says.

"I believe it is a mythological creature, a bit like we have *Airavat*, the elephant with several trunks," Mohanbhai says.

I drift off again into my own thoughts.

In Hindu mythology, life under Rama's rule is referred to as an ideal society. But will such a society always be a dream? Will we always have this tendency to go one better than our neighbour, to exploit others to achieve that dream and to never be satisfied. Surely, that can't be true. I think I was satisfied with my life. And so were most of the people that I know. We would have liked life to continue as it has been since we settled in Uganda. We should count ourselves lucky that we have been happy here. But then things change.

Buddha preached that life is in a constant state of flux and change is part of it. And accepting the change and adapting to new circumstances is what we mean by accepting the will of God. And for atheists like me I suppose the *mantra* should be *Take life as it comes*. Try and change it for better for humanity at large, but do not be surprised if the task proves impossible because each human being is trying to change it. And pull it in a different direction to what one wants. So my motto is: *I do my duty and other things trouble me not*. I shall continue to strive to make it better for all human beings and for all life forms. These thoughts actually make me feel calm or even, dare I say, happy?

I am suddenly aware of movement near me and I notice people are scrambling to their feet. The sun is stronger and apart from a few gold-rimmed clouds the azure sky is bright with the new dawn. As we start walking back towards home, Velji puts his arm on my shoulder, "You hardly said a word, *Bhai*." There is concern in his eyes. "I know we have difficult times ahead but don't let that get to you. It is all in God's hands. If only you believed and prayed like the rest of us, it would make it easier for you to accept your fate."

I smile at him. "I was quiet," I tell him, "because I was praying. In my own way."

*   *   *

When I get home, I am still in my 'praying mood'. I go straight to the living-room and sit in the chair by the window overlooking the garden. I am there for a long time reflecting on my life.

Another chapter in my life is about to end.

This one commenced just over twenty-eight years ago. In 1944, in Rajkot, a town in Gujarat. I remember it like it was yesterday.

I was at my desk writing my diary. Did I say desk? I suppose you could call it that if you wished to flatter a rickety wooden crate, which was just big enough to support a pad and an ink holder.

About mid-morning, one of the street dogs started to bark. "It's only me. Dhanu. You know me." I could hear the postman calming the creature down as he approached our compound.

"I say, Masi, where is your Devji?" I heard Dhanu asking Mother. "I've a letter for him. A *foreen* one." The English word foreign has become part of Gujarati vocabulary.

As I scrambled to my feet, I heard Mother shouting, "Devji, Hurry. A *foreen* letter. Come out. Quick."

"Coming," I said and then repeated it loudly, in case I was not heard the first time. I put the ink well safely on a shelf and went to the sink to wash my stained fingers.

When I emerged in the compound, Mother was sitting cross-legged on a straw mat on the ground with a big flat basket on her lap. She was removing grit from *moong dal*. Dhanu was squatting on his haunches facing her and blowing on the tea in a saucer before noisily slurping it. When he saw me emerge, he hastily put the saucer down and scrambled to his feet. Reaching in his brown leather bag, which looked like a school satchel, he pulled out a thick envelope and held it proudly in front of him. "Here. Post from abroad for you."

I grabbed the letter and tore it open eagerly with mounting excitement. When I finished reading it, I looked around. Mother sat motionless, gazing at me patiently. Dhanu had picked up the saucer again and held it in front of his face, but he had forgotten about drinking the tea. And several neighbours had gathered around us. Even the dog had joined us and was wagging its tail. Someone had gone and informed Father and I could see him hurrying towards the crowd that surrounded me.

"Well?" Dhanu asked. "Is it good news?" There was a murmur of support from the crowd.

Father who had now reached us said, "Tell us, son."

"It's an offer of a job in Africa. In Uganda," I announced.

There was a sudden hubbub. "That's good news," several neighbours' spoke in unison. I bent down and touched father's feet, and he blessed me before pulling me up by my shoulders and embracing me.

Mother approached me and as I started to bow to touch her feet, she held me and hugged me for a long time. She was crying and laughing alternately. "Oh, son. May God bless you."

Little Lalita, only three at that time, could not understand what was happening and burst into sobs. I picked her up and comforted her.

For the rest of the day, we had a stream of visitors, who came to congratulate me. Mother kept a big bowl of *ladu* to

314

sweeten their mouths. Mostly there were joyous greetings but not all. There were a couple of cautioning voices.

Ramji*kaka*, the old uncle, still steeped in his traditional ways, cautioned father, "Our scriptures forbid crossing of oceans. It's just not wise."

Father placated him by saying, "But you know very well that we can appease the seas with an offering of a coconut. These days, sailing across to faraway lands is nothing new. Many people have gone to settle in Africa."

Then there was Vaji*masi*, my aunt. She was my mother's sister and lived across the road. She was always dressed in white, having been widowed at a young age. I was very fond of her. She sat next to Mother, her head covered with the end of her sari, and started to cry. "Going all the way across the ocean to Africa. When will we see him again?"

"It will be all as God wishes." Mother tried to comfort her. "The young have to do what is good for them. We must not stop them. Just give our blessings."

Vaji*masi* smiled through her tears. "I know. I bless him with all my heart. May he always be happy. But so many of them don't return for ten or even twenty years. I think I will have gone to sit at God's feet by the time he comes back. I can't help feeling that I may never see him again. You may, but I am too old."

As the two sisters wiped their tears I went and sat next to them and said, "I promise I'll come back to visit you as soon as possible."

*   *   *

Since then so much water has flowed under the bridge. And now as I sit in my favourite chair in the living-room and think about my life, I realize that I had no way of knowing what the circumstances would be like. I could not have foreseen that I would not be able to keep my promise. I supported my family financially but could not visit them till 1948. Vaji*masi* was dead by then. I tried to persuade my parents to join me in Uganda. But they declined the offer, partly because Lalita had just started in *Aryakanya Gurukul*, a prestigious Girls' boarding school in Baroda.

After that, I only managed a few short visits to India: to do rites for my father after his death; to attend Lalita's wedding and a year later, when she was widowed, to bring her to Uganda. That time, I tried to persuade my mother to join us. But she was already frail. "I don't want to start anew in a faraway land at my age".

My last visit was in 1969 to perform religious rites after my mother's death.

Chapter 68
Day 39:
12th September
Shashi: It is Getting Worrying

Events are moving fast. I am not a historian trying to chronicle our last days in Uganda, but I have decided to keep a separate section of my journal to record the political situation as it develops.

If you were to chance upon my journal, I would not want you to walk away with the false impression that people are calmly packing their cases, and leaving all they own behind with a stoical acceptance of their fate. It is true that there is no wailing or beating of their chests. But people are deeply worried. Wouldn't you be if you were leaving everything you own behind in what you thought was your homeland and are exiled to distant shores with no more than your personal possessions in a suitcase?

I raised this point after dinner a couple of days ago and everyone in the family came up with different explanations. Ramesh said that perhaps people are too numb with shock to react in a visible manner. But they agreed that on the whole it was truly remarkable that there was no mass hysteria.

Ba said that it is at times like this you realise that what matters most in your life are your family and loved ones and you just want to escape with them. Material possessions are of little importance, she stressed. Lalita Auntie said she could not think of a single object she owned that she would miss particularly. But if she was told that she would be separated from our family she would be heartbroken. Rehana Bhabhi said she felt the same. Her main worry is she may be separated by a huge geographical distance from her parents and may not have a chance of reconciling with them. Ramesh and Papa expressed similar sentiments.

And today there has been a worrying development. After lunch Ramesh produced a news item from a British paper he had managed to get hold of. It seems that Amin has sent a telegram to Kurt Waldheim, the UN Secretary-General, and sent a copy to Golda Meir, Israeli premier.

"There is a part of the message here. Just listen to it." Ramesh said. He cleared his throat and read out aloud,

> *"Germany is the place where when Hitler was the prime minister and supreme commander, he burned over six million Jews. This is because Hitler and all German people knew that Israelis are not people who are working in the interest of the world and that is why they burned the Israelis alive with gas in the soil of Germany.*
> *Signed, Idi Amin, President of Uganda."*

Lalita Auntie shook her head in disbelief, "How could anyone make a comment like that? You would have to be totally heartless."

"It sounds unbelievable. Do you suppose it could be a made-up story?" Rehana Bhabhi asked.

"It is possible but very likely he did say it," Ramesh answered. "Ever since Amin has been on close terms with Colonel Gaddafi of Libya he has made several anti-Semitic remarks. And only a few months ago, as we know, he ordered the Israelis in Uganda to leave the country in twenty-four hours. At least we have got ninety days."

Papa said in a grave voice, "Since his announcement, Amin has said a few times that Asians are sabotaging the economy and that we are the enemy of the people. Like

Hitler thought Jews were. We know how Amin's mind works. In the telegram, he clearly states that Hitler was right to kill the Jews and by implication he would be equally justified in getting rid of us. Why else would he send a telegram to the UN Secretary General expressing these sentiments? He is preparing the world for it."

Day 40: 13th September 1972

Concentration Camps

Uganda Argus

President Amin has announced that he is not going to change the deadline. He will order the construction of Concentration Camps to lock up any Asians who are still in Uganda after the deadline.

Today's announcement is just what Papa predicted yesterday. Amin admires Hitler and given half the chance will follow in his footsteps. After I heard the news, I wondered if it was possible for all of us to get away in time. There are only fifty days left before the deadline. Things are moving rather slowly and it is getting worrying.

Chapter 69
Day 41:
14th September 1972

Radio Uganda News Bulletin:

East African Airways and several international airlines have made a joint announcement: They will charge £70 per person to fly Ugandan Asian Refugees from Entebbe to London.

Shashi: Shree Charso Bis (Mr. Four Twenty)

I listen to a lot of Western pop music, Elvis and The Beatles and Jimi Hendrix. So, I will be well catered for when we go to UK, but the older folk, like my parents and Lalita Auntie, only listen to Indian music. And since we can take very little luggage away with us, I decided to record a cassette of Bollywood music for them.

I was just recording the song *Mood moodke na dekh, mood moodke* from the old movie *Shree Charso Bis*, when Vinod marched into my room.

"Recording songs from *Shree 420*, I see." Ever since the film was released, the phrase Mr 420 has been synonymous with a cheat or a crook. "Apart from Amin, I will tell you who the real Mr 420s are," he announced.

"Who?"

"The airline companies," he said. "They want £70 per person for tickets and there are six of us in our family."

"Five," I corrected him.

"Well, six. Ramila may live with her in-laws but she is our

320

family, too. So altogether they want £420 from our family. And the figure of 420 shows them in their true colours."

I was about to say that the fare was slightly lower than the normal price. But then thinking about it, for a family who can barely make ends meet, it is not an insignificant sum. The price of tickets could be almost half of Veljibhai's annual income.

I mentioned this to Papa at dinnertime and he said that he had already offered to buy tickets for Veljibhai and his family. "Also, the rich folk like Madhvanis and Mehtas have already passed the word around that they will help anyone who needs it."

I snorted. "Now that Ugandan money is not of much use to them, they help the poor." I do know that these families support many charities. In fact, they are known for their philanthropic acts. But I was deliberately trying to provoke Papa.

"You sound more and more like your socialist brother," he remarked.

"We can't help it," I said with a broad grin on my face. "It is how we have been brought up."

Papa struck his forehead with his open palm and turned to Ba, "As always, we are the ones to blame."

Chapter 70
Day 41:
14th September 1972
Velji: My Ugandan Citizenship

I have to get my family's right to live in Uganda confirmed at the Uganda Passport Office.

I leave Jinja at just after eight thirty in the morning and I am outside the Office in Kampala by ten o' clock. After queuing for about half an hour, I enter the building, where I have to wait yet again. People sit in a row of plastic chairs, placed in the corridor outside the main office. I stare at the large picture of smiling Amin on the wall.

When it is my turn, I am admitted into a big room, where two officers sit behind large desks. I am directed to a large, round-faced man, wearing a blue striped shirt and a silver tie. The officer is sifting through some of the papers on his desk with his huge hands and does not even glance up at me for what seems like a long time, but perhaps is only a couple of minutes. I clear my throat to announce my presence. But he ignores me until he has sorted the papers to his satisfaction. Then he glances up and points at the chair in front of him. I sit down and wait once again.

"Yes?" the clerk says at last.

"I have come to register my family as permanent residents of Uganda." I place all five passports and the application forms in front of him. Devji has checked them all for me and assured me that all the documents are there and that they are all valid.

The officer picks up the top passport and the application form attached to it with a paperclip. "Hm. So ..." He glances through the form. "... I see you were born in India."

"Yes, Sir. But I have lived here for forty years. Most of my life, in fact."

"And you are a builder?

"Yes, sir."

He opens the passport and looks at my picture and then glances at me. He shakes his head. "The passport is not valid."

"But it was re-issued only a year ago and does not expire for four more years."

"No, the picture is not valid. It is an old picture."

"The picture was taken only last year when I applied to renew my passport."

"See. That's what I mean. It is an old picture."

I remain silent, as there seems little point in arguing.

The clerk lifts the open passport high up in front of his face, looks at me, and back at the passport, shakes his head, and then with a sudden jerk tears it in two with his powerful hands. "It is also not valid because it is torn." He throws the passport in the cane wastepaper basket with a flourish. His face betrays no expression as he picks up the other four passports, one after the other, and slowly and deliberately tears them along their spines before dumping them in the bin. I am too stunned to protest.

"It seems you have no passports. So you do not qualify as residents." He smiles for the first time. "Are there any other questions?"

I shake my head dumbly, pick up the torn passports from the bin, and make my way to the British Embassy, barely a fifteen minutes' walk away.

There is a huge queue there which snakes right round the building. Luckily I am allowed straight in as I only want to collect the Visa Application forms.

As I drive home, my mind is in turmoil and I dread having to break the news to Mother and to the rest of the family.

Their reactions are totally unexpected. "Good," Maji says, summing up the others' feelings, too. "With the whole community leaving, this is not going to be like home anymore."

After lunch I call in on Devji, who helps me fill in the forms and collate the necessary documents. Then I drive back to Kampala and spend the night with my cousin, Amrit, who has planned to join the queue outside the British Embassy early tomorrow morning.

Chapter 71
Day 41:
14th September
Shashi: The Ordinary Folk - 3
Army Hospitality

I think it is time I mentioned some more neighbours in my diary. If you walk from our house towards Kampala Road, the last but one house on the road is where Chandaben lives. She is a widow. Her son and his family emigrated to UK last year. He wanted Chandaben to join them, but she had resisted, having lived all her life in Jinja. All her friends are here and she was not keen to start a new life in a very different country. She is a very friendly lady who is there to help whenever any of the neighbours require a hand with cooking for guests, or looking after kids. Whatever it is, she is happy to lend a hand.

Next to her, the last house on the street has a plaque saying "Dr. Ganesh Jobunputra, M.B.B.S." He is the only doctor on our street, so everybody just calls him *Doctorsahib*. He lives with his wife, Poojaben, and their three children. They are very friendly, warm people. I have always wanted to use the phrase *God-fearing*. I think it is a particularly appropriate phrase to describe Doctorsahib and his family. Kind, God-fearing folk.

Papa and Ramesh were discussing what happened to them and I have recorded their experience as I can imagine it.

*   *   *

Ganesh went round the house carefully taking down all the family photos from the walls. He hesitated in front of the picture of Gandhi, which his father had brought from India nearly half a century ago. He then lifted it from its hinge and carefully removed the picture from its frame and placed it along with the family pictures in-between two pieces of cardboard to protect them. He wrapped the bundle in the previous day's *Argus*, tied it with a string and put it in the bottom of his case. He then packed his personal belongings on top of it and placed the suitcase in the hallway next to the other bags.

After that he walked slowly round the house like a surveyor, viewing it as if he had never seen it before. He saw the crumbling plaster in the corner of the bathroom and the chipped dents under the window in the girls' room.

He then went out into the yard. The sky above him was clear but dark rain clouds were gathering on the horizon. A small group of crows cawed loudly as they hopped sideways on the yard wall. The metal bucket was nearly full, filled in a drop at a time from the leaking tap. More cracks had appeared in the cement floor so that they looked like lightning branching out during a rainstorm. He stood there for a couple of minutes.

Tomorrow by this time we will be out of our home, heading for the airport so that a plane can whisk us away to a strange land, he thought. *We will be poor and homeless. I will not have my medical practice anymore and no job at all. No doubt this is what was ordained. God is testing us and we have to bear our karma with fortitude and with our belief unshaken.* Despite the uncertain future, he felt at peace with himself.

He walked slowly back to the living-room, where he sat down on the sofa and picked up the leather attaché case lying on it. He checked through the documents one more time: My medical qualification certificate? Yes. Five passports? Yes. Five plane tickets? Yes. Five British Visas? He opened each passport and ascertained yet again that each passport had a Visa stamped in it. He carefully put the passports and the tickets in the front pocket of the folder and zipped it up. He then opened the main compartment, removed wads of bank notes and counted them. One hundred and twenty thousand Ugandan Shillings.

Finally, he removed a bundle, the family jewels tied in scarf.

It was a large orange scarf with a prayer written in Sanskrit script all over it. He used to tell mother to use a jewellery box and not an ancient scarf for her jewels. And now he was using it. He smiled at the recollection.

He quickly checked that all the items were there before putting it all back. He sat staring blankly at the wall for a few minutes and then returned to the bedroom where Pooja was packing her belongings. When she concentrated upon a task, she pouted her lips and opened her eyes even wider.

"Nearly there?"

She nodded.

"It feels so ..." he searched for an appropriate word. "So unreal."

She continued folding a red silk sari. He went and stood by the window. Already it felt like a strange place. There was no one on the street. Even before the exodus started, it was never very busy in the afternoon. Four of the neighbours had gone within the last week. His was one of the few cars parked on the street, as people abandoned their vehicles at the airport when they left.

"Hope whoever moves in here looks after your basil," he said, without turning around. He always referred to it as *her basil* because she was the one who had planted it in the front courtyard and tended it with care. She even did a little worshipping ceremony there on certain religious festival days.

"Not likely," she snorted. "It is not a holy plant to them."

He noticed Chandaben from next-door coming up the path. He went to answer the door as he remembered that it was not left unlocked, as in the past.

"Dinner is ready." Chandaben informed him. "Will you come over when you are ready? I assume we'll have it soon after the sun goes down, what with you having to make an early start tomorrow. Need any help with packing?"

"No thanks. We're nearly done."

Just then there was the squeal of a car brake. A black Mercedes pulled up on the road just outside the house. He noticed the gleaming number plate JJA 555 and saw a worried look cloud Chandaben's eyes.

"Oh my God," she exclaimed. "Oh my God. Help us. It is Nikhil."

Nikhil Subedar got out of the car, slammed the door behind him and approached them. He was dressed smartly as ever, dark trousers and a white shirt with a bright blue tie. He was always slim but looked thinner than normal.

"I heard you are leaving soon. Just came to offer my help. Any problems, let me know." He used the word *problems*. His Gujarati was adequate but like all UK-returns his speech was peppered with English phrases.

"We're still waiting for our Visas," Ganesh said. He had rarely lied in his life and felt uncomfortable doing so, but there was a nagging feeling at the back of his mind, warning him against revealing his plans to Nikhil. However, he noticed Nikhil peering over his shoulder at the ready-packed suitcases in the hallway. He hastily added, "But we are ready to go as soon as we get the Visas."

Nikhil smiled and walked back to his car and opened the door. "Whenever. Feel free to contact me if you need me."

Ganesh and Chandaben watched the Mercedes zoom up to the end of the road before it turned left and disappeared from sight.

"What a calamity! What can we do now?" Chandaben looked deeply worried as they went indoors to break the news to Pooja.

Pooja sat down on the bed and held her head in her hands. "I can't face any more trouble. Good God, please help us."

"Let us be rational," Ganesh tried to reassure her even though he himself felt a deep sense of dread. "People are just superstitious. How can Nikhil just calling on us bring bad luck? He stopped here to offer his help as he was passing by."

"But it has happened three times," Chandaben reminded him. "He visited three families to offer his help and soon after that the military descended upon them."

"Coincidences happen. It does not prove anything."

"But three times? Not just once. Three times!" Pooja pointed out.

They all sat in silence mulling over the fact.

"You are right." Ganesh realised he was almost shouting excitedly as realisation dawned upon him. So he dropped his voice and continued. "You're so right when you say three times is too much of a coincidence. He doesn't bring bad luck. He brings the army."

"What can we do?" Pooja asked. "Asha is asleep and the boys have gone to say good-bye to their friends. Besides it'll be dark in about half an hour." Travelling after dark was too hazardous to contemplate.

"Come and stay at our place," Chandaben offered.

"May God bless you." Pooja hugged Chandaben. She went to the bedroom and picked up Asha, who barely stirred from her sleep. Next to her lay her beads, which Ramesh had given to her as her second birthday present six months ago and had informed her, "Some people call them *worry beads* in UK." And now she was inseparable from her '*wuddy beads*'.

"Wait," Ganesh sprang to his feet and rushed to the living-room and returned with the attaché case. He undid the orange scarf and, lest they forgot, stuffed Asha's beads in there with the rest of their jewels. He placed the scarf in the attaché case, and handed it to Chandaben, who placed it under her arm and covered it with the end of her sari.

"Let's go. You two wait next door while I get the boys."

As they stepped out of the house, they heard the screech of brakes. Three military trucks pulled up right outside the front door. "If they take me away, call Nikhil," he whispered as he pushed them ahead and stepped back on the threshold. He waved at the women as if they were visitors going home. Several soldiers hopped out of the back, and rushed to the front gate of the house. The women found their exit blocked.

An officer in dark glasses walked up to Ganesh in several large strides. "Are you Doctor Gane, um, Gane Jobupoo put, put." He stumbled upon the unfamiliar name and then read the name from the paper he clutched in his hand. "Gaanesh Joboonpura."

"Yes, I am Ganesh Jobunputra. I was just saying good-bye to some friends." Ganesh waved at the women and shouted, "Bye, ladies."

The officer considered the situation and then nodded at the soldiers. The men moved aside and let the two women with the little girl asleep in one of their arms walk past them.

Two soldiers grabbed Ganesh and frogmarched him to the army truck. They pushed him into the front seat next to the driver, who stared ahead as if he was not part of the group.

Some other men stormed into the house. A couple of them ferried the suitcases from the house and put them in the back of one of the trucks. He could see through the open doors and the windows that the men were carefully ransacking the house. A short while later, the officer came and sat down next to him in the truck and nodded at the driver. The truck started haltingly and then picked up speed.

"What have I done?" Ganesh asked the officer, his sunglasses reflecting the red evening sky. It was as if he had not heard Ganesh.

"I'm leaving the country anyway. And I have committed no crime." Ganesh tried again.

"Shut up."

Ganesh sat tight-lipped as they sped on the way towards the Army quarters outside the town on Kampala Road. It was just getting dark by then.

*　　　　　　　*　　　　　　　*

"I will do my best, Auntie," Nikhil assured Pooja. "Captain Kinyanga and I often have a game of snooker together. You see, we started when we were students and often met in East Africa

House in London. They had a full-size table in their basement there. I will speak to him but he will demand money. Oh yes and gold, too."

Pooja handed him a little jute shopping bag with an image of Goddess Lakshmi in purple ink on it, and a bundle tied with an orange scarf. "This is all we have."

Nikhil held the bag in his right hand and the orange bundle in his left hand at waist height, as if weighing them. "He is a greedy man," he said. "You can't raise any more money? Or any more jewels?"

"This is all we have. I swear by my husband's life that it is the truth. It is all our money. And all our jewellery." Pooja touched her heart.

*   *   *

Nikhil placed the jute bag on the table in front of the Captain. It was then that he noticed the image of Lakshmi printed on it. "That is Lakshmi - the goddess of wealth."

"How appropriate!" The Captain laughed as he shook hands with Nikhil. He lifted a bundle of notes out of the bag and flicked through the bank notes. "How much?"

"One hundred thousand."

"Not bad. Nothing else?" The Captain asked.

"There were a couple of small pieces of jewellery which I have kept. That's fine, yeah?"

"Yeah, gentlemen's agreement." He held out his hand and Nikhil clapped it.

"Fetch the prisoner," the Captain told the orderly standing by the door.

Ganesh lay naked on the wooden bunk with his knees drawn up against his body, as the cell felt damp and cold. In the dark he felt his bruised lip and swollen eye. He sat up as he heard footsteps outside the door. The door creaked open.

"Here," one of the guards said as he threw Ganesh's clothes at him. "The Captain wants to speak to you. Now."

Ganesh struggled into his clothes and hurried behind the soldier to the Captain's office. Nikhil was standing near a window, a few feet to the right of the Captain. "I have decided not to press charges against you. You can go now." The Captain's voice implied that he was doing Ganesh a favour. Nikhil nodded at him and gave him an encouraging smile.

"Thank you, Sir. Just one favour to ask. Could I please have our family pictures back? They only have sentimental value."

The Captain replied in a stern voice, "I have no pictures of yours. Family or otherwise."

"They were in one of the suitcases."

"Are you suggesting I took your cases?" The Captain shouted as he stood up.

"It's OK, Peter. He's just going." Nikhil said, stepping forward. He gently guided Ganesh out of the door.

Nikhil drove fast because there was hardly any traffic on the roads late at night. They exchanged only a few words on the way. As he braked sharply outside Ganesh's home a bundle shot forward from under Ganesh's seat. Ganesh recognised the orange scarf with letters in Sanskrit on it. He had placed his little daughter Asha's beads with the jewellery and tied up the scarf into a bundle only a few hours ago. He looked at Nikhil, who had obviously seen him stare at the package. Nikhil looked slightly embarrassed but did not say anything.

"Thank you." Ganesh told Nikhil as he stepped out of the car. "Thank you for all your help."

Early next morning, several friends and neighbours came round with wads of Ugandan shillings for Ganesh, to give to the soldiers at army checkpoints on the way to the Entebbe Airport. They also brought their spare suit-cases. Ganesh and his family packed a few more of their possessions in the cases and waved good-bye to their well-wishers.

Just after they departed, Asha remembered her beads and

demanded, "I want my *wuddy beads*."

Pooja promised, "We will buy you nice new ones in England."

"I want my wuddy beads," Asha wailed.

"Look. Look Asha, there is a big cow there," one of the boys tried to distract her.

She looked at the cow and wailed even louder, "I want my *wuddy beads*."

They managed to distract her for short periods but she always came back to her demand.

On the way to the airport, seventy miles away, they were stopped more times than they had expected and ran out of all their money.

At the last stop, just a couple of miles from the airport, Ganesh told the soldiers that he did not have any more money because he gave most of it to Captain Kinyanga. They looked at his bruised face and accepted his word. They did, however, rummage in their suitcases and took whatever they fancied. There was not much left. A young soldier, barely a teenager, took the last of the boys' clothes. Perhaps for his brothers, Ganesh thought, and offered him the now empty suitcases as well.

The young man said, "Are you sure?"

Ganesh thrust the bag in his arms. "Yes, I am sure."

"Oh, *asente sana*. Thank you, sir."

As he was picking up the case, Asha cried out, "My *wuddy beads*," pointing at a beaded wristband the soldier was wearing. The young man realised that Asha was after his bracelet and he removed it with a smile and handed it to her. "Here you are, little one. It is a good luck charm."

Asha beamed as she accepted it and corrected him, "They *wuddy beads*."

"What a nice young man." Ganesh told Pooja, as they arrived at the airport, with nothing but their documents. And Asha's new *wuddy beads*.

Chapter 72
Day 42:
15th September 1972
Velji: The Queue

We get to the Embassy at six, just before sunrise. Light shines through some of the large glass windows showing the movement of cleaners inside the building.

"Be back in a minute," I tell Amrit as I wander to the front of the line, which almost exclusively consists of men. Several of them nod at me or exchange greetings. An elderly man in a woollen hat, similar in age to me, stands with his shoulders hunched and holds a document wallet pressed under his tightly folded arms. "It will soon start warming up," he says, looking at the horizon where the early rays from the sun are just beginning to creep up the sky.

"Yes," I agree. "How long have you been waiting?"

"Only about ten minutes but I am glad I came early because, look!" He points at the queue, which has now extended to the end of the building and continues on down the side street.

When I get back, Amrit is rubbing his hands vigorously, as he talks to three young men standing just behind him in the queue. I inform them, "There are only thirty-eight people ahead of us."

The young men laugh. "Did you actually count them, Uncle?"

I smile. I do not tell them about my obsession with quantifying everything. I estimate how many bricks are needed for a particular job with what my friends call an uncanny accuracy. I count the number of steps when I go up a building and the shops on the main road as we drive through villages. Sometimes I calculate how many people there are in a hall at social functions by counting the rows and the average number of people in a row. Once I even tried to estimate how many stars are visible to the naked eye by counting the number in a sector. However, I abandoned the task when I realised that more stars became visible the longer I stared at the sky.

"I assume your forms are all completed," says one of the young men. He has long wavy hair, which reaches just below his collar. "I could check them for you, if you wish," he offers.

"No, son. There is no need. My friend double-checked them for me and he is a lawyer."

"Our forms are OK," Amrit says. "It's just that I'm not quite sure about what other information they will need or what questions they will ask."

"I wouldn't worry about it," replies the second young man, who is tall and chubby. "As long as you can recite the British National Anthem, you are OK. I assume you have learnt it Uncle, haven't you?"

I smile but Amrit's face clouds with worry. "I didn't realise you had to learn it."

"They are pulling your leg," I tell him.

"No, Uncle, that is one thing you have to know," the third young man says, pushing his horn-rimmed glasses further up the bridge of his nose. "But don't worry. It's easy. Here, we'll teach you. *We all live in a yellow submarine,*" he sings out in a pleasant lilting voice. His friends join in, "*Yellow submarine, yellow submarine.*"

"*In the town that I was born,*" join a few other voices from up and down the length of the queue.

Amrit laughs. "You youngsters of today have no respect for your elders. Shame on you."

When the singing dies down, I tell the young men solemnly. "My lawyer friend was involved in the Indian independence struggle and he taught me another British patriotic song. You may have heard it? It's called *Cruel Britannia*."

"You got it wrong, Uncle," *Chubby Cheeks* corrects me. "It's called *Rule Britannia*."

"Not the version that my friend taught me. It goes:
Cruel Britannia, Britannia made us slaves.
We should never ever let them do it again."

Chubby Cheeks laughs but then suddenly becomes serious. "You sing that and they will never let you into their country."

"Only teasing," I tell him. You youngsters were not even born when this version of the song might have meant anything to you. I know things are totally different now."

"My cousin telephoned me from UK a couple of days ago." *Wavy Hair* informs us. "His family were fed and housed when they arrived there and now they have been offered a council house in a place called Stoke-on-something. So the British are treating us really well."

I nod. "I couldn't agree with you more. They could have closed their doors in our face. A few years ago they announced that the British Protected Person's passport does not entitle you to settle in UK. But now that we have nowhere else to go, they are being kind, generous and humane."

"Many of us had applied to go and settle there anyway but would have had to wait for years if not for ever."

"It's all right for you young folk, but I didn't want to start somewhere new at my age," I announce shaking my head.

I notice that the sun has now risen and it is pleasantly warm in the golden light. "A new dawn," I say aloud. "In all our lives."

When the nice middle-aged man at the British Embassy

sees our torn passports and hears about what happened to our Uganda documents, he clucks his tongue sympathetically. He picks up the phone and speaks to someone. "I suggest you go to the New Zealand office. I have explained your situation to them and they will help you," he says, replacing the receiver.

Chapter 73
Day 42:
15th September
Devji: A Nice New Owner

People are fleeing in droves. The UK is the main destination followed by Canada and America. Folk you have known all your life are being scattered all over the world.

It is mid-afternoon now and just Shashi and I are in the house. The others have gone out to bid final farewell to their various friends.

I am going through my papers, trying to decide what to carry with me when we leave. The doorbell rings. It is followed by a gentle knock. I can hear Shashi going to answer it. I expect it is one of his friends. But then I hear a man's voice say, "Is your father in?"

And Shashi calls out, "Papa, there is a visitor for you."

I sigh. It must be another desperate person needing my help to fill in the documents. But, no, it is a tall, slim army Captain with his hat under his arm. "Good Afternoon," he says. He smiles and his tone is friendly.

"Good Afternoon," I reply.

"I am Captain Onyango. Sorry to bother you, Mr. Mitani, but I would like to ask a favour of you." He speaks good English. I can't help wondering how he knows who I am. "Would you terribly mind if I had a quick look around your house?"

He must have noticed a look of puzzlement on my face for he quickly adds, "I know it is a strange request. But, you see, I have been promised this house, and it would be useful if I could check it out in advance. You know, just to get an idea of what it is like inside."

I am so resigned to leaving behind not just our home, but everything that we own, in the near future, that the request sounds unusual, but not preposterous. Obviously he would want to see the house before he moves in.

I can see from Shashi's face that he is about to comment on this unusual situation, but before he says anything I address the Captain. "Certainly. Please, come in." And I show him around the house. Shashi accompanies us.

"A nice size living-room," the Captain comments. He walks in large measured steps to the windows and back to the door. He then produces a little black notebook from the front pocket of his khaki shirt and makes a note in it.

"Would you like a tape measure?" I offer.

"Oh, do you have one? It would be very useful. Thanks a lot."

Shashi fetches a tape measure from the cupboard in the hall. He holds the measure down at one end while the Captain pulls it to the opposite end of the room. The Captain then writes down the length and width of the room in his notebook. He screws his eyes up as he reads the measurement again.

"That's useful. Very useful." He looks around. "Very well furnished. I assume the furniture is staying. Mind if I sit down?"

He sits on the sofa and bounces up and down a couple of times. "Very comfortable."

He surveys the room again from the comfort of the sofa. "It seems you do not have a television set." He looks disappointed.

"It's in our smaller sitting room," Shashi informs him.

"You have another sitting room?" There is a broad smile on his face. "That's good! Very good."

So we lead him to our second living-room. He surveys the

room and is obviously very pleased.

"This is also fair-sized," he says with satisfaction. He notices the chess set on the side table. "Do you play chess?" he asks Shashi.

Shashi shrugs, "Sometimes."

"That's good. Very good. I have always wanted to learn it."

"Perhaps I better stay behind so that I can teach you," Shashi says.

The Captain scrutinises his face and realises he is only joking. He laughs. "That's funny. Very funny."

He takes the measurements of all the rooms in the house and enters the size of each room in his little notebook before placing it carefully in his pocket. "It's much bigger than it looks from outside. Five bedrooms! That's spacious. Very spacious."

He does not want to see the garden. I presume it is because he has surveyed the house from the outside anyway.

When the tour is over, he thanks Shashi for helping him to take the measurements. He then turns to me. "Have you decided where you are going?"

"We are hoping to go to the UK. But we are waiting for my sister's Visa to arrive."

"I went to UK for six months for training," he says. "Nice country. Good luck to you there."

At the front door, he shakes our hands before marching back to his car. He waves to us as he drives away. We watch the car go round the corner, and then we turn back into our house. Shashi shuts the door. He and I look at each other silently for a moment. I sense he wants to say something but he doesn't.

I go to my room to continue sorting the papers. I have

barely sat down when the doorbell rings again. Shashi gets to the door before I do. It is the Captain.

"Terribly sorry," he says. "I put this in my pocket and forgot to return it to you." He holds out the measuring tape.

He shakes our hands one more time and drives away.

"A nice guy," Shashi says.

I agree.

Chapter 74
Day 43:
16th September 1972
Shashi: Drawbacks with Life in the UK

The pattern of our life here has radically changed. Now that Kumar has left, Ramesh and Rehana Bhabhi have decided not to open the office. Papa has stopped going to work as well. But I am sure people will call at our house to seek advice on filling in forms or on legal matters.

In the afternoon, I hear a car screech to a stop outside the front door. The bell rings and I answer the door.

It is Laljibhai, dapper as always in his three-piece suit. He smiles at me. The young man who has come to drop him nods at me. He has a pinched face with a sallow complexion. He is awfully thin. I realise with a shock that it is Nikhil. He still looks cocky but has lost a lot of weight. His light blue shirt hangs loosely on him and his fawn trousers are secured with a crocodile leather belt over a thin waist. He has a large boil on the side of his neck.

He addresses Laljibhai, "I'll pick you up in an hour, Papa, is that all right?"

"An hour should be fine," Laljibhai says and enters the house.

Nikhil walks back to his black Mercedes and speeds off.

Laljibhai shakes hands with Papa and they head for the living-room. Papa turns to me and says, "If Ramesh is free, ask him to join us."

I gently knock on Ramesh and Rehana Bhabhi's door. There is no sound, so I turn back to go when I hear the door open. I give Ramesh the message and he tells Bhabhi that he won't be long and joins me.

"Nikhil came to drop Laljibhai," I tell Ramesh. "I had difficulty recognising him. He has lost so much weight."

"I know. I've noticed it, too. I just hope it's not the *'slimmer's disease'*."

"Is he trying to slim? Why?" It does not make sense to me, as he was never fat.

"It's called the *'slimmer's disease'* because the person infected with it loses weight."

I have never heard of it before.

"It's increasingly common amongst young Africans," Ramesh informs me. "I've had clients with it or their family members suffering from it."

"I suppose it takes time to recover from it."

"As far as I know there is no cure." Ramesh shakes his head. "It does not seem to be fatal in itself, but it seems to lower one's resistance to other diseases, especially pneumonia."

Just before he enters the living-room he adds, "However, I am not a doctor."

I go back to my room and read for a while. But my curiosity gets the better of me, so I creep to the living-room doorway. Papa notices me standing there, but does not signal me to leave, so I tiptoe in.

Ramesh and Papa are sitting next to each other on the sofa and Laljibhai sits facing them on an easy chair by the window. Sunlight falls on his head so that his brown bald pate shines. I quietly slip into the chair near the door - slightly apart from the others.

"As you can see, I have two priorities when I get to UK. Get Nikhil checked at a specialist clinic there and sort out the documents," Laljibhai says in his high-pitched, clipped tone.

"I'm afraid I cannot help any more with the legal side as

343

I'm not familiar with the British Company Law," Ramesh says apologetically. "You'll need to consult an expert when you get there."

"I already have one." Laljibhai replies. "It's just that I'm not sure about what happens about producing new documents. I've already sent the copies by post as you had suggested. But under the present circumstances one can't be sure if they will get there."

I gather he has business interests in UK, Canada and India.

"Take only the important originals with you," Papa suggests.

"I can't carry the contents of my whole filing cabinet," Laljibhai complains. "Also, they may fall into the hands of the Ugandan Government if the army finds them at one of their road blocks on the way to the airport." He starts fiddling with the gold chain that leads from his tiepin into the waistcoat pocket. "Besides the planes are flying full these days and so they are extra strict about the weight allowance." Then he looks up and says in a sour voice, "I just can't understand why all these people are clamouring to get to UK. They have no idea of what it's like there. They will have a better life in India."

"What's wrong with the UK?" Ramesh asks.

"You must know what's wrong with UK." Laljibhai has a flat in Mayfair and knows what it is like to live in England. He throws his head back and narrows his eyes in surprise for he obviously thinks that Ramesh, having spent a few years in London, ought to know the reason. He snaps almost impatiently at having to state the obvious, "*Domestics*. It's so difficult to find good *domestics* there."

Chapter 75
Day 45:
18th September 1972
Shashi: Migration

Jinja is already turning into a ghost town. Many doors are padlocked. Each day you wake up, you hear that a few more families have gone. People are afraid to announce their plans in advance because the army swoops down on the house if they hear about your imminent departure. The soldiers make their raids then because all the valuables are ready packed. It saves the army the trouble of searching the whole house for them.

From my class, Chitu, Anver, Madhu and Kanti have already gone to the UK. So have Malkit and Rafiq. And Kirti, Muneera and Jyoti. I hope I will be able to find them when I go there.

But some people are being scattered to far-flung corners of the world. Gulzar, Suru and Rajni have gone to Canada. Nilu went to Austria and Vibhu to Sweden.

Today I woke up before dawn, quickly showered, dressed and hurried out to say goodbye to Vinod next door before he left for New Zealand. They had told us because we are like family but no one else in the town knew they were going.

But I was nearly too late. They were already in their borrowed car. It was one of those seven-seat Peugeots. Vinod was in the back seat with Sunita. I reached in and he pressed my hand. His grandmother was in the middle row of seats. She was upset and crying, but she placed her open palm on my head and blessed me, *May God guard you and your family.* Then they drove off. I felt sad. I probably won't ever see them again.

I dragged my feet as I headed home. I passed Poppy on the way. She was sniffing around the fence but ran up to me, wagging her tail. She stood there panting, her mouth wide open with her tongue lolling on the side. I stroked her for a couple of minutes. She then rubbed herself against my legs and trotted away. I know that two weeks ago when Rajni's family went to Canada, they gave their house servant Otengo nearly five thousand shillings and made him promise that he would look after Poppy. She is well cared for but she obviously misses her family.

In the evening, De Souza Uncle telephoned from England. He said that they stayed in a camp in Sussex for the first few days, but then his cousin from Lancashire took them to his home. Lancashire! Textile mills and War of the Roses. That's all I know about it. Now I will associate it with our old neighbours and their pretty daughter Maria, and imagine them living there amongst the mills and with a rose garden of their own. I wonder in which part of England we will end up.

Now, I sit in my room, writing this diary. It is strange to think that I will be in a totally new place in a few days' time. We will know very few people in the community. A marked contrast to Jinja. The worst part is that I will never again see many of my friends and relations. Reincarnation in a new place if not in a new body.

Chapter 76
Day 45:
18th September
Velji: Newji-Land

"Where is this Newji-land?" Mother wants to know on the way to the airport. I pretend not to have heard her question. Besides I have to concentrate on driving.

"It is New Zealand, Dadima," Vinod corrects his grandmother. "Not Newji-land."

"That's what I said. Newji-land. Is it near England?" Mother persists.

"It is at the other end of the world from England," Vinod replies. I remember him telling me that they had to study about Australia and New Zealand in Geography. He now recalls some of the things he has learnt in school. "It's an island. Or really two islands."

"Oh God." Mother is worried. "I saw some islands in the Lake when we went to Tanzania by boat for Reena's wedding. They were tiny. Barely a mile across. There were just a few thatched cottages. Fishermen and their families lived in them. If this place Newji-Land is just two islands, will they have room for more people? And do they have proper houses and electricity? I don't think I will like it there. Why couldn't we have just gone back to India?"

Vinod tries to put her mind at rest. "They are big islands. And they have cities and all, Dadima."

Mother is still upset. "And how about food? Don't they eat mostly fish on an island? Under no circumstances am I going to eat fish."

"If I remember it right, they export a lot of food. Mostly, mutton and beef."

347

"What? Beef?" That distresses her even more. "Oh my God, what have I done to deserve this?" she wails.

"Don't worry Dadima, they will have a lot of vegetarian food, too," Vinod says, though he himself does not sound too sure about that.

I tell Vinod, "We will have to rely on you, son, to keep us informed. Isn't it strange? We are going to live in this place - maybe for the rest of our lives- and I don't know a thing about it. I meant to look at the book that the Embassy gave me but I could not find the time in the mad rush during the last few days. Is it big? Or is it small? But judging from the staff, who issued our Visas, I believe it is white people who live there. At least I know that they speak English, so for you children, your education will not suffer."

There is silence in the car. I slow the car down a little as a couple of monkeys run across the road. I muse aloud, "We had no choice in where we settle - it was a bit like a lucky dip."

Chapter 77
Day 46:
19th September 1972
Shashi: Progress Still too Slow

BBC News Bulletin:

The Government has announced that plans for airlifting British Asians to the UK by East African Airways, in collaboration with BOAC and British Caledonian Airways are finalised.

I heard on the news today that less than 200 refugees have been transported to UK. And half of the 90 days have just gone. If the process is not speeded up we will end up in a concentration camp.

I know I have lightly remarked in the past about my diary being found like that of Anne Frank. But it is no laughing matter now. I am worried - like everyone else.

Chapter 78
Day 46:
19th September
Shashi: A Knock on the Door

Kumar and Ramesh have been friends since they were little boys. They are both idealists and studied law not just because they wanted a good career, but also because they thought they could serve the community that way. After Amin's announcement, they did not just pack up and leave but continued opening the office. They had never been this busy at work. There was a steady stream of people with worried looks, clutching document wallets, and seeking help with filling in Visa applications.

The two friends probably would have stayed almost to the end of the ninety day deadline, had they not had the nasty experience with the army. Ramesh told me what happened and I have described the events below:

Kumar and Ramesh had stopped charging for their services - Ugandan money had no value to them now.

Yesterday, Tapu *Mochi*, the shoemaker, walked into Kumar's office after having waited in the foyer for a couple of hours for his turn. "I can just about write my name in English," he said sadly. "How am I going to manage in UK?"

Kumar tried to cheer him up. "Just have faith, Uncle. You will manage. Your children will help you at first and then you will pick up enough English to get by."

"My son has got Visas for Canada."

"And your daughters?"

"All three will come with me."

"So, they will help you."

"But one day they will marry and then belong to their in-laws' families." He ran his palm over his shiny, bald, head.

"Uncle, you will have to learn not just a new language but new customs, too. In the UK, girls often help their own parents as well as their in-laws."

"Really?"

"Yes, really. And also it is a well-organised society. The state will provide you with shelter and food until you are settled and start earning yourself."

"So it's not just a rumour."

As Kumar started filling in the forms, he discovered that Tapu had not brought all the necessary documents. He was not even sure about his wife's date of birth.

"Why don't you come back tomorrow with all the details, Uncle, and we will fill the forms then."

Tapu's face fell. "I have arranged to go to Kampala tomorrow with my cousin from Bugiri, so we could queue up together." Everyone had heard stories about the horrendous queues outside the British Embassy. People took their bedding with them and slept overnight outside the Embassy so as not to lose their place. It was advisable to queue with someone else so that you could save each other's place when you had to go to the toilet or just to walk around the place to stretch your legs.

Kumar looked at the clock on the wall. It was twenty past five. Tapu lived near the Bus Station in New Jinja, about half an hour's walk away. There just was not enough time.

"I will come and see you tonight after dinner at eight."

"Are you sure you don't mind coming out after dark?"

"It's OK, uncle. I will drive up there. It shouldn't take too long. Just make sure everyone in your family is there and that you have all the necessary documents."

Tapu stood talking to them as they locked the office. "Do you remember," he told them, "you boys brought a picture of some fancy boots when you came home from UK for holidays?"

"Yes, *Chelsea boots*. And you made pairs just like that for us

351

- only better, as you used the best leather one could get."

"Well, if I wasn't about to leave I would make a pair like that for each of you to show my gratitude."

"How about doing that when we see you in the UK?"

"It's a promise. I will make you *Chelsi - Belsi* boots or whatever they are called."

*   *   *

"When are we leaving, Kumar?" After dinner Manjula asked the same question she had asked practically every day since they had received their Visas for the UK just over a week ago.

"Why are you stalling, son?" His mother Jayaben supported her.

"There are still many people who need help with their papers. So, just a few more days, I promise."

"You have to think of our family, too," Manjula reminded him. "Nimisha comes first."

"If I thought even for a minute that it was unsafe here, we would leave on the next available flight."

"But we don't feel safe here."

"It's not that bad. Life is still continuing. I go to the office every day. You go to the market and buy vegetables. It's only at night time we don't venture out." As Kumar said that, he remembered his promise to Tapu. He decided not to mention it just then but waited until after dinner.

Manjula sat in the living-room breast-feeding little Nimisha and then took her to her bedroom, where she left her in the cot. She rejoined Kumar and Jayaben in the living-room. Jayaben was saying how two more families they knew had left that morning. People did not announce their departure anymore, so as not to alert the military of their plans.

After a while Kumar stood up and announced that he was going out. Manjula looked up at him, as he stood in the doorway, her large brown eyes clouded with worry. "Only a few minutes ago you were the one saying that it isn't safe out there after dark."

"I will be driving and be back in half an hour. Don't worry, I'll be alright."

He did not wait for her reply. She heard him pull the front door shut and the lock click.

*   *   *

They heard Nimisha crying when they were clearing up in the kitchen. Jayaben nodded at Manjula and went to the baby-room. The crying stopped.

As Manjula was drying her hands there was loud knocking on the front door. She rushed into the hallway and stood there quietly. The baby-room door was slightly ajar and she could see her mother-in-law sitting cross-legged on the floor, holding the baby in her arms and gently rocking while singing a lullaby.

Jayaben looked at her with a steady gaze and raised her eyebrows questioningly. Manjula shrugged her shoulders and shook her head. She put her forefinger on her mouth and they waited, each rooted to their spot, silent and apprehensive.

The knocking on the door grew louder and more insistent. Manjula hoped and prayed that the door would not give way. She hurried to the living-room.

The curtains were drawn but they lit up in the glow of the headlights of a vehicle just outside their house. The telephone was on a low table by the door. She crouched down by it, as she rang the police.

Whoever was at the door now thumped the door with an even greater vigour.

"Come on. Come on. Somebody. Please answer," she prayed. She had heard that the police did not answer calls anymore. As the banging on the door went up another notch she cut off her call to the police.

She did not know where Kumar was and so rang Ramesh, who detected the panic in her voice. "I am coming right over. Just don't open the door to anyone else. I assume the back veranda door is secured, too," he said before he hung up.

She knew that the door was locked but remembered that she had not secured it fully with bolts at top and bottom. As she rushed to the back, she heard the sound of glass breaking. And saw a dark hand reach in and unlock the door, with a loud click.

*   *   *

Ramesh knew it was madness to interfere but he could not sit back and do nothing.

He drove along Gabula Road but just before he reached the Fire Station, on the spur of the moment, swerved towards the Main Street and braked sharply outside the police station. He left the engine running and the front door ajar as he hopped out of the car and rushed into the police station.

Captain Onyanga stood talking to the policeman on duty behind the main counter. "Hello, Ramesh," he said with a warm smile. Ramesh had often dealt with him professionally. "What's the matter?"

He listened sympathetically but then said, "Listen, my friend. You know we cannot touch the military. They would shoot us."

"But we do not know for sure if it is the army. Supposing they are just bandits? Please, Patrick, come with me."

After a brief hesitation, Captain Onyanga asked one of the policeman to accompany him and they got into Ramesh's car.

*   *   *

The back door was pushed open violently. It struck the wall on the side with a loud thud and bits of plaster scattered on the floor. A short, skinny soldier burst in, pushed past Manjula and opened the front door. Three other soldiers entered the house. One of them was very large, wore baggy trousers and was obviously the man in charge. He marched up to Manjula and said, "We believe you are hiding enemies of President Amin."

"It's just our family here," Manjula said. Although her voice seemed to come from far away, she was surprised that it was so steady.

354

"We will check ourselves." He nodded at the others, who immediately spread out and rushed into different rooms.

As one of the soldiers went into their bedroom, Manjula heard Nimisha make a gurgling noise.

When the men had a look around, they came and stood in front of the Captain and shook their heads.

"Alright, wait outside. I'll check it myself," the Captain said.

He turned to Manjula and said, "You show me around."

Manjula led him to the living-room and the dining room. He glanced at them and nodded.

"This is our bedroom." She pushed open a door and stood aside for him to go in.

He looked in without entering the room.

"And this is my mother-in-law's room."

"Where is she?"

"Putting the baby to sleep in that other room."

Once again he just glanced in. She stopped in the hallway.

"And how about this one?"

"That is only the store-room for food."

"Open it."

The light switch was on the right of the door and she had to step in to switch on the light.

As she turned around, she found him standing right behind her, his bulk almost filling the doorway, silhouetted against the hall light. The room had sacks of rice and *toor daal* in one corner and jars of several other lentils on shelves along the side. He moved in further as if to inspect the sacks and suddenly lunged at her and grabbed her by the waist. "Shh," he said. "You don't want your baby to be disturbed now, do you?" His tone was calm but it had a threatening undercurrent in it. He pinned her against the wall with his right forearm against her shoulders. He raised his left hand and squeezed her breasts.

Just then they heard voices by the front door. He let go of her and pushed her away so violently, she fell on a rice sack.

He walked out to the front door. Ramesh was there with the

police officer.

"What is it?" The Captain addressed the policeman in an angry voice.

The policeman stuttered, "I...I...I am sorry, sir. I didn't know this was a military operation. I thought I will check in case bandits were involved."

"Well, there are no bandits here. So go away."

"I am sorry, terribly sorry for the mistake. So sorry." The police officer walked backwards apologising until he was out on to the road and then he turned around. His junior officer joined him and the two men walked away at a brisk pace.

Just then, Kumar returned from his visit to Tapu. Seeing a military vehicle outside the house, he parked his car on the road and limped hurriedly towards the front door.

"And who is that?" the officer asked Ramesh.

"This is his home."

"Then who in the hell are you?"

"Just a friend."

The Captain suddenly lost interest in the venture. He turned around and shouted in the house, for Manjula to hear, "I will be back tomorrow."

He walked up to the army vehicle and climbed into the seat next to the driver. The noisy motor of the lorry sounded loud in the otherwise quiet street.

Early next morning Kumar, Manjula, Kamlaben and the baby were on their way to Entebbe Airport. They were eager to catch the plane, which would take them as far away as possible from what had been their home all their life.

Chapter 79
Day 47:
20th September 1972
Devji: Decisions

Our Visas are ready to be collected from the British Embassy in Kampala. After queuing for a long time, we collect Visas for all except Lalita. She has still got an Indian passport. I explained to the Embassy staff that we are her only family, and that she has lived with us for many years now, and that she has no close family in India, etc. The officer was sympathetic, but said that she will have to wait as they need to issue Visas to the people with British passports first.

Ramesh drives us home. It is muggy when we get back to Jinja in mid-afternoon.

"I say, I am back," I shout in the direction of the kitchen before heading for the living-room. I wipe my face with a handkerchief as I collapse into my chair by the window.

Savita appears a couple of minutes later carrying a circular stainless steel tray, balanced on which is a glass and a large jug of water. She places it on the side table next to my seat, and pours out water in the glass before handing it to me. She stands near me while I gulp it down. Without a word I hold the glass out for her to refill. I drink the water more slowly this time and Savita tops it up again.

Just then Lalita arrives and the two of them sit down facing me, waiting for me to give them the news. I shake my head.

"No luck, yet. We haven't yet got Lalita's Visa. The British Embassy is understandably under great pressure at the moment. They are dealing with the British passport holders first and said they will be able to process the other applications soon. We will just have to wait."

"What about the rest of the family?" Lalita asks.

"We've all got ours."

Lalita sits forward and looks me straight in the eyes, "As I have said before, all of you should go now. I will join you when I receive my Visa."

"Do you seriously expect me to fly away to a distant land, leaving you here all on your own in the present uncertain climate? No way." I turn to Savita. "But you and the youngsters should go now."

"I won't leave without you." Savita says immediately. She rarely defies my decisions on important matters. But I have learnt from past experience that, when her face takes on this stubborn look and there is such finality in her voice, it is futile to argue. And that she just would not change her mind.

After a short discussion we agree that Ramesh, Rehana and Shashi should leave as soon as possible.

Lalita fetches the others to hear our decision. As I suspected Ramesh puts up an objection. "I need to stay," he says. "I can help if there are any other problems."

"It's not just yourself you have to think about," I point out. "There is Rehana and Shashi. So, please, do not argue. And now that we have heard of Kumar's and Ganesh's experiences we are worried about everyone's security. We would feel so much happier if we knew that you were safely away from here. And the sooner the better. Also you would then be in the UK to help us when we get there."

I finally persuade him to leave if Lalita has not received her Visas in three or four days' time.

Chapter 80
Day 49:
22nd September 1972
Reconciliation

Morning Radio News:

The Uganda Government has announced that it is not satisfied with the progress of Asians' exodus. To hurry up their exile the Government has issued notices to 8,000 Asians asking them to leave in 48 hours' time. Those who do not heed the notice will be severely dealt with.

(1) **Shashi:** Lecturing Adults
Time: 10 a.m.

Ramesh, Bhabhi and I are amongst the 8,000 to whom this forty-eight hour notice applies. Yesterday Papa tried to persuade Ramesh to leave with Rehana Bhabhi and me as soon as possible. But now we have no choice.

Once Ramesh decides his course of action, he moves fast. "I am just going to ring the airlines' offices and try and book us on tomorrow's flight," he announces and then turns to Bhabhi. "I know you want to say farewell to your parents and make another attempt at reconciliation with your father."

"We will come with you if it helps," Ba tells Bhabhi.

"I don't think it will, but we can try." Bhabhi replies. Then she turns to me. "As Ramesh may be on the phone for a while, Shashi, do me a favour. Please go and check if both my parents are in now."

I spring to my feet and leave the room without a word. As

I put on my shoes in the hallway I realise that I have been humming the Beatles' tune, '*Help*'.

I know that Bhabhi needs help. I try to put myself in her position. Zubeida Auntie secretly comes to visit her, but her father still refuses to have anything to do with her. I would be miserable, too, if one of my parents disowned me.

I am aware of the fact that I only have the experience of being a son and not a parent. It is like when I am late home after visiting my friends, *Ba* often sits at the dining table waiting for me. I tell her, "I am not a kid anymore. I will soon be seventeen. I don't want you worrying about me." Her standard reply is, "When you are a parent, you will understand."

Do I have to be a parent to also appreciate why people get so worked up about whom their son or daughter marries? I know that I am partly brainwashed by Ramesh telling me about the freedom enjoyed by young people in the West. Also, I have seen how Papa and *Ba* accepted Ramesh's decision when they realised how much Ramesh and Bhabhi love each other. Why can't Bhabhi's father do the same?

These thoughts go through my mind as I walk to Bhabhi's parents' house. When I ring the bell, Yusuf Uncle answers the door. Last time it was Zubeida Auntie who had let me in. I have never before spoken to Uncle and that gets me flustered. So I say, "Is Auntie in?"

He turns round and shouts, "There is someone for you." It pricks a bit for I am sure he has guessed who I am, so that when Auntie emerges from the living-room, I say, "Actually, I have a message for both of you."

Auntie hesitates, not knowing whether to ask me in, while Uncle stands firmly at the door. I have read in many novels how the person breaking important news asks others to sit down. So I say, "Can we sit down?"

"Oh please come in," they chorus. I know Auntie would have asked me in anyway. As for Uncle, his good manners triumph over his reluctance to welcome me.

I kick my shoes off in the hallway and follow them into the living-room. As soon as we are seated, I inform them. "We have been ordered to leave in forty eight hours. And we are going tomorrow."

They have known all along that, like everyone else, we will depart any day, but the news still shakes Auntie. She just utters, "Oh," and puts her hands in front of her mouth and looks miserable. I can see her eyes are beginning to glisten.

I take a deep breath and inform them, "Rehana Bhabhi wants to come and say good-bye."

Auntie looks at Uncle, who continues to stare at a spot above my head on the wall behind me. I try to imagine what is going through their minds at that instant. This is an important moment in their lives. I think of all those characters in the novels, who make one false decision and regret it for the rest of their lives. Like the guy called Henchard in a Hardy novel who auctioned off his wife after a row with her. Or Natasha in "War and Peace", who rashly tried to run away with Anatol, and thus lost Prince Andrei's love.

These thoughts coupled with a desire to help Bhabhi makes me feel reckless. So I tell them, "This may be your last chance. The decision you make now may haunt you for the rest of your lives. Adults are forever telling us that parents would do anything for their children's happiness. I am sure you would make any sacrifice to see Rehana Bhabhi happy. And reconciling with her is what will make her happy. So what's stopping you? I am sorry but I don't understand this honour business. She is married now, anyway. Tell me what's more important- your daughter's happiness or what some busybodies in the society say?" All this comes out in a rush, as I am afraid they will stop me any minute and throw me out. But they just listen in silence without interrupting me. They look stunned. Uncle seems to be glaring at me first but as I continue his gaze seems to soften. Auntie nods as if in agreement but she keeps turning to look at Uncle's face to see his reaction. A lot of what I said is not new - I have heard most of it from Ramesh or Papa - or read it in books.

I am aware that I am being rude, lecturing adults. So I apologise, "I am sorry to speak plainly. It may sound disrespectful. I know a boy has no right to talk to adults like this, but Rehana Bhabhi is such a warm and loving person that it saddens me to see her unhappy. And all for what? She has committed no crime. As they say in the song *'Mene Pyar kiya kutch chori na kiyi'* (I have loved, not committed a crime). A small gesture on your part would bring heaps of happiness to her." (*"Heaps of happiness"*? I can't believe I have come out with a corny phrase like that. How embarrassing!).

I expect to be thrown out by Uncle. He sits in silence for what seems like a long time but is only a minute or so before he clears his throat and says in a soft voice, "You have opened my eyes. They say one should listen to children, as they are not afraid to utter the truth."

I am about to object and say that I am already seventeen and not a child. But then I decide that it is childish to dwell on a minor point.

(2) **Devji:** Our Little Angel
Time: 11 a.m.

Ramesh puts the phone down and announces, "It's done. Tomorrow afternoon's BOAC flight to London."

Rehana now picks up the receiver to ring her parents. She stands there, with a worried look as she waits to speak to her parents. After a few minutes she puts the phone down. "No-one is answering the phone."

"Let us do the final packing for tomorrow and then try again." Ramesh suggests.

Just then we hear the front door open and Shashi calls out from the hall, "Bhabhi, you have visitors."

Rehana rushes to the front door, followed by us. There on the threshold stand Zubeidaben and Yusufbhai, who spreads his arms out wide and embraces Rehana, whose eyes brim with tears of joy. As he holds her, he sways a little and I am sure his eyes are moist.

He notices Ramesh standing behind Rehana. He frees his right arm and pulls Ramesh towards him and then embraces Rehana and Ramesh simultaneously. When he releases them, they bend down and touch first his feet and then Zubeidaben's feet. Both parents bless the young couple.

It is only then that Savita speaks, "Please do come in." From the tone of her voice it is obvious that she is on the verge of crying, too.

As we start moving towards the living-room, Shashi, who has stood there as a silent witness, announces, "I must go and say good-bye to some of my friends," and rushes off.

We all go and sit in the living-room.

Yusufbhai sits in the middle of the sofa, with Ramesh and Rehana on his either side. He holds their hands as he addresses us, "Shashi informed us that Rehana and Ramesh are leaving tomorrow. And I felt this was my last chance to make up with my *Beti* (daughter)." He puts his arm round her shoulder and she snuggles up against him. After a pause, he adds, "In fact, Shashi said a lot more." And tells us what Shashi had said or *preached* as he describes it.

"And we could not let you go away without reconciling with you," Zubeidaben says tearfully. Rehana gets up and sits next to her mother, and holds her hand. They are both crying. And I notice Savita and Lalita are also dabbing their eyes.

We talk about our future plans and how we should find each other if we end up in different parts of the UK - or maybe in different countries.

Just before they get up to leave, Zubeidaben picks up a cloth bag she has brought with her and has placed by her feet. She reaches in, takes out a jewellery box and hands it to Rehana. "These are meant for you. Now at last you can have them."

Yusuf and Zubeida both embrace Rehana.

I think of the difference between this and our visit to their house. I would of course never remind Yusuf of his parting words when we saw him last. But he himself brings it up.

"Last time I told you that an angel will have to descend from heaven to persuade me to change my mind. Well, it looks like your younger son is that angel." He laughs. We all do. A burden has lifted from our hearts.

Chapter 81
Day 49:
22nd September
Shashi: Choosing a Book

Last year we studied The Mayor of Casterbridge as a text for our English Literature course. One of the chapters starts with the sentence: *The day and the time came. But it was raining.* Or something like that. I remember Mr Banerjee commenting, "Typical Hardy. There's always a 'but' in his story. All doom and gloom. If something can possibly go wrong, Hardy will make sure it does. Gloom sounds like another word: 'glum'." I remember our homework was to write a paragraph creating a gloomy atmosphere and another one describing the mental conflict raging in the head of a real or imaginary glum person.

I asked if I could write about Raskolnikov. Now I realise I was only trying to impress Mr Banerjee. Showing off that I had read *Crime and Punishment*, a book he had once recommended to us. I may as well have said, *Look. Look, Mr. Banerjee. Aren't I a good boy? I've read a Russian classic that you happened to mention in passing.*

But I am digressing.

What I meant to say was that at last for us the day and time has arrived, and I hope that there are no buts. I hope Mr. Hardy is not writing the story of our lives. On second thoughts, he is probably helping with the script as Auntie still has not received her Visa, and so Papa and Ba are staying behind until she gets her documents sorted.

After several phone calls and a lot of arguing and pleading, Ramesh has managed to book us the air tickets. And we are leaving tomorrow for UK. At last.

So, I have packed a small case for my journey. We are not allowed to take anything other than our personal belongings.

"How about books?" I ask Ramesh.

He smiles, "I am sure they are not interested in your books. You could take them but you will have to carry your case. And we might be living in a camp to start with and there will be no storage space. When we are leaving so many of our personal possessions behind, why choose to take books? You can always buy them or borrow them from a library in the UK. They have excellent public libraries there. Just take one as a memento."

He is right. So, I am sitting in our own little library browsing through our books. Sort of saying good-bye to them. And trying to select just one.

Our library is the room at the back, next to the kitchen. The window overlooks a small paved compound, which leads into the garden. In the middle of the compound sits the basil plant, which after starting off as a sapling has now grown into a bush. I can see the red thread that Lalita Auntie has tied around its trunk as part of her religious ceremony when she worships it.

The library is not very big. It has just one small table and two chairs but every wall is covered with bookshelves from the floor to about six feet high. Mostly they are Papa's books. One of the walls is covered with boring law journals with their brown bindings. The shelves next to the window have mostly reference books. There is a huge selection on Hindu religion and philosophy - a big illustrated edition of Mahabharat, a Gita, collected works of Swami Vivekanand's commentary on religion and even a Bible. There is a huge tome by some ancient philosopher called Patanjali. I have been meaning to look at it but just have never got round to it. Perhaps I never will find out what this guy was famous for.

There is a whole shelf of books about health - *Ayurveda*, Culpeper's Complete Herbal; books about natural cures and old editions of an English journal called *Health Today*. I run my finger along their spines. I stop before I reach the end of the top row of books. For some reason a small selection of books not related to health are at the end of that shelf. There are a couple of volumes of The History of the Second World War by Winston Churchill, The Decline and Fall of the Roman Empire, a biography of Lenin, in Gujarati, with a black and white picture of him on the cover. He is smiling and has a small beard. He looks a bit like one of our History teachers, Mr. De Silva. Next to it is a booklet called *The Collected Letters to the Swiss workers from Lenin*. I flick through it quickly and it abounds with so many words which I do not understand. What for God's sake is a *revolutionary proletariat* or a *republican bourgeoisie*?

The other two shelves are lined with fiction in English and Gujarati. Now, many of those I have read. I pick up one of the volumes of *War and Peace*. I raise it up and down like one does with a dumbbell and decide against taking it. Too heavy. Besides I would not mind reading the English translation in UK to see if it reads better than the Gujarati one. I further hesitate over Gandhi's autobiography *Experiments with Truth*. The Gujarati and the English versions sit side by side.

In the end, I put a pile of books on the table and sit there trying to decide which book to pick. I look out of the window. Outside in the garden a couple of big yellow and red butterflies are fluttering by the basil bush. Several pigeons are stepping around gingerly, picking at the rice grains that Ba has scattered on the ground, as she regularly does. Today she has put out a lot more.

After much thought, I choose my book. As I emerge from the library, I pass Ramesh on his way to his room.

"Let us see what you have chosen," he says, and then looks at the precious book I am clutching in my hand.

"*Chhel and Chhabo*?" He laughs. "I don't believe it. *Chhel and Chhabo!*" It is a children's book about the adventures of Chhabo, a short rotund man and his thin tall friend, Chhel.

"Yes. *Chhel and Chhabo*," I say. But I do not laugh. It is the first book I read aloud to Ba and Papa. And I recall the occasion well. When I finished reading it, they both cheered and clapped. We were in the living-room at the time and the sun was streaming through the window. Ba wore a bright green sari. I remember the colour vividly because she used the edge of her sari to wipe tears from her face.

Chapter 82
Day 49:
22nd September
Shashi: Nylon and Silk

Today is my last day in Uganda. I sit at my desk and vividly remember an incident from about a year ago. Some guests from Kenya turned up unexpectedly. Papa showed them into the living-room and asked Ramesh to join them. It was Saturday, Okello's day off, and Ba was out visiting friends. So, I took a tray with glasses of water for the visitors, and sat down with them for a few minutes.

Soon afterwards, Ba came back and served tea and snacks to the guests, and I rushed out to see my friends. However, before I left I heard enough to gather that the guests had come to check Ramesh out for their niece.

Later that evening, Ramesh came to my room. "The guests were full of praise for you," he informed me. Guess what they told Papa. What a *dahyo dikro* (sensible son) you have." In teenager talk "*dahyo*" is also used for a goody goody.

"I only served them water," I said modestly, "But I hope you behaved yourself as they really came to check you out for their niece."

He put on his hangdog expression and shook his head. "No. They were so taken by you that they lost interest in me. They have a younger niece and they are instead trying to fix you up with her. In fact, I am having this conversation with you now because I have been entrusted with the task of finding out if you are ready for matrimony."

Of course I knew he was having me on. I threw a cushion at him, which he expertly caught with his left hand.

"Of course, I am kidding," he admitted. After a short

pause, he added, "But, you know, in the west many boys your age would already have a girlfriend."

If that happened here, the boy would be labelled as a loafer and, as for the girl, no respectable family would accept her as a daughter-in-law. So I asked, "How do girls' parents in UK react if they find out?"

Ramesh went on to explain the customs in UK. As there are no arranged marriages, people find their own partners. They check them out themselves from a very young age, from when they are still in their teens. So the teenagers there have a lot more freedom compared to us.

Ramesh then added, "It is natural for young teens to be interested in the opposite sex, so why suppress it?"

I recall that conversation now because of the feelings I am hiding, and feel the urge to be totally frank.

It is drummed into us from an early age that *good boys* do not chase girls. And everyone says what a *good boy* I am. If our society was free like in the West, I would have faced the truth by now. I have never confessed it to anyone, not even to my diary. And if I am going to be a writer, I have to be honest - brutally honest - with at least my Diary. So here we go.

Tomorrow when I leave, I will miss my friends, our neighbours and family friends. But above all I will miss Smita terribly. I have not confessed my interest in her to anybody. Who am I kidding? It is not just an 'interest' - it is love.

I see her on every school day as she is in my class. She sits on one of the front benches occupied by the girls. I sit right behind her and have to make an effort to keep my eyes off her. She occasionally turns round and we exchange smiles and occasionally talk to each other. I am sure she likes me, but we cannot seek each other out, or have lengthy conversations, for then people's tongues would wag.

Sometimes, we come across each other when we walk by the lakeside in the evenings. We stop to have a little chat but then move on. We also see each other at weddings and other social functions. During Navratri festival, hundreds of people whirl around in unison, doing the *garba* at the temple. I feast my eyes, watching her slender frame sway rhythmically to the vibrant music.

Once, she came to a disco party thrown by one of the UK-returns in the Amber Club. She wore a sleeveless blouse and I found her slender smooth arms ever so sexy. I danced with her for only a few minutes before she sat down with her brother. She dances sensuously, but then I find everything she does is sensuous. She did not dance with anyone else after me.

She is the most beautiful girl I have ever seen. Her skin is fair with a slight rosy tint, and she is slim and tall. Her large almond-shaped dark eyes light up when she talks. And when she laughs, she narrows her eyes and displays even teeth - like pomegranate seeds- except that her teeth are white. She normally ties her shiny black hair in two long pigtails, which reach down below her waist and swing across her back as she walks. I could kiss the ground she walks on. I long to hold her in my arms and kiss her, but I know it will never happen. I am flying tomorrow to UK and her family have just received Visas for Canada. Our paths are not likely to cross again, and she will never find out how I feel about her.

Ramesh has half-guessed my interest in Smita for he has teased me about her in the past. He has told me that her older sister Naina, who was in school a year ahead of him, was also beautiful. The boys had given her the nickname Nylon Naina.

"Nylon! Why Nylon?"

"Because the material Nylon was new in those days. It was

soft and smooth and considered a beautiful material."

If I were to compare Smita to a material I would call her Silky Smita. But I have not the courage to go and tell her.

I ask myself, why don't I write to her? I have packed my bag already. So, I have time to pen a few lines and deliver the note to her early in the morning before we leave.

I sit here with a blank sheet in front of me for a long time and cannot decide where to begin. In the end I just pour out my feelings. I compare her to the beautiful heaven and how looking at her brings back my faith in a creator - otherwise how is such exquisite beauty possible? I write high-flaunting sentences and use flowery prose, for that is what seems to express my feelings most accurately.

I then re-read what I have written.

What's the use? I ask myself. She will either laugh at me or, if she reciprocates my feelings, she will only be sad. And even worse, if the letter happens to fall into other hands, her reputation will be ruined. I have no desire to cause her any trouble. To protect her happiness, I decide not to reveal my feelings. I clutch the letter next to my heart for a couple of minutes, and then tear it up into tiny pieces. I feel miserable but I have no doubt that I have done the right thing.

And if in future I also destroy this page in my diary no one will ever know the love and yearning I feel for this angel.

I spend hours tossing and turning in bed before I fall asleep. In my dream she says she loves me too and then puts her arms round my neck, as she snuggles up to me. I hold her in a close embrace. But then I am woken up by Ramesh shaking me.

I have a quick shower and tell Ba that I do not want any breakfast.

"You have a long arduous journey ahead of you. You

must eat something before you leave." Ba feels happy when she has fed you. But there is no time.

"It's alright. I'll get a meal in the plane," I try to assure her and then bid farewell to her, Papa and Lalita Auntie. I get into the car where Ramesh and Bhabhi are waiting for me.

"Wait a minute," Lalita Auntie shouts as she hurries back into the house and emerges with an envelope.

"Someone pushed this letter under the door earlier this morning. It's addressed to you, so I left it on the dining table. But then you decided not to have breakfast."

I tear open the envelope as the car speeds towards the airport. There is a little card in it with a hand-drawn red rose and a simple message,

"Shashi, I will always remember you. Smita."

Chapter 83
Day 50:
23rd September 1972
Devji: Waiting for Visa

Uganda has been my home since I left college and now I am going to a different country for the twilight years of my life.

We are worried that Lalita with her Indian passport may have a problem getting British Visas. The British officer I spoke to said that she has a good case and she should get her Visa within a few days. We will have to wait just a little longer as the Embassy is still dealing with the British citizens. It is a relief to think that our family will remain together wherever we settle.

I know that many people talk about paying for our sins in the past lives. They say God decides and that He moves in a mysterious way. In that case, all I can say is thank God I am not a believer.

Chapter 84
Day 56:
29th September 1972
Devji: Treatment of an Ex-Minister

I noticed the following news item in The Times of London:

Captured Ex-Minister Paraded at Amin Party

A former Ugandan Cabinet Minister, wearing only khaki trousers and socks and with his hands trussed behind his back, was dramatically produced before diplomatic guests at a state reception in Entebbe last night. ... The impact of the spectacular production last night of the half-naked prisoner, (Mr Alex Ojera, who was Minister of Information and Tourism under President Obote,) was described picturesquely today in the Government's own account of the incident. This stated: "visitors were struck with awful surprise at the ghastly sight of a man whom they had known before as a respectable gentlemen."

Mr. Ojera, a former teacher, is indeed remembered here as one of the most fastidiously-groomed members of the ex-President Obote's government. Last night, with his tattered trousers held up by string, he appeared understandably humbled.

Chapter 85
Day 60:
3rd October 1972
Devji: News from England

The boys rang from London today.

They are obviously worried about us. Ramesh repeated several times that we should not delay our departure. "If Auntie does not get British Visa, then go to India. Or she can go there and join us later. Whatever. The important thing is that you all get out of Uganda soon as possible. It is just not safe. *We are very worried about you.*"

I tried to reassure Ramesh that things had not deteriorated since they left. Which is true. But it is still very worrying.

The line then became unclear but I gathered that Ramesh has a job and that they have found a place to live in.

Also, Shashi has already started going to a local school. This has taken a load off my mind.

We could not hear Shashi over the crackly line, so I urged him to write a letter.

Chapter 86
Day 66:
9th October 1972
Devji: A Letter from London

Dear Ba, Papa and Lalita Auntie,

I hope you do <u>not</u> receive this letter. By the time it arrives there, I hope that you would have left Jinja, and would be safe and sound in London. But in case you are still there, we want to let you know that we are all fine. You need not worry about us – not the way we worry about you.

The day after we arrived, Ramesh contacted David, his friend from University, who helped him find a job, and only four days later Ramesh started work. And Rehana Bhabhi has an interview next week.

We have rented a house in a London suburb called Kingsbury, and I have got a place in the local high school. Many Ugandans have settled around here, especially in Harrow. In my class, there are two girls from Kampala and a boy from Gulu. I intend to take my O Levels in December, just as I was going to do in Jinja. But I will have to wait until September to join an 'A Level' class.

Last night I went to a launderette to wash our clothes. I told Ramesh and Bhabhi that in future, it will be my contribution to the housework, as it is something I have been looking forward to doing for some time. They think I am joking, but I am not.

So you can see we are already settling down to our new life here. And we are looking forward to you joining us here as soon as you can.

Lots of Love,
Shashi

Chapter 87
Day 70:
13th October 1972
Devji: The British and Us

People are leaving as fast as they can. If prominent citizens like Manubhai Madhvani, an Asian, or the ex-minister Mr Ojera, a black Ugandan, are not safe, we feel very vulnerable. We will leave as soon as Lalita receives her British Visa.

Yet another chapter in our lives is about to begin. The ancient *Shastras* describe four stages in human life which, roughly translated in present day terms, are: childhood, student age, being a householder, which includes raising a family and being a responsible member of society, and finally *Sanyas*, when one gradually frees oneself from one's attachments in life.

An average person goes through all four stages in one place. However, in my case, and for a large number of Asians in Uganda, our lives will also have three main periods defined by widely separated geographical locations: India, Uganda and finally the UK.

Until Uganda gained its independence eleven years ago, I had only lived under the British Rule. First in India, and then in Uganda.

Of course, I opposed the colonial system. As a student in India, I went on Civil Disobedience marches demanding independence for India. I was already in Uganda when India finally became free.

The world changed rapidly in the next few years. In 1957, Macmillan made his famous *winds of change* speech.

Following that, the British negotiated a peaceful handing over of the power in many countries under its rule, including Uganda.

But despite my opposition to their colonialism, I am a great admirer of the British - their literature, their contribution to science and, above all, their political system. Mother of Parliament and all that. It has resulted in the ordinary citizen being given a considerable number of rights and individual freedoms. In practical terms, this has meant that there is very little corruption, bribery is not endemic and life for the man on the street is much better.

Whenever the topic of corruption comes up, I always tell my boys: "Sons, you have to do what is right, even though people are likely to ridicule you as a fool. Do not expect material reward. Or praise. You have to be strong and stick to what you believe in. The reward lies in knowing that you have not forsaken your principles."

I remind them about two different experiences I had: one in England and the other one in India.

Four years ago, Savita and I went to visit Ramesh in London. He had asked me to buy some cigarettes and a bottle of whisky on the plane to give as presents to his friends. At the airport, I obviously declared these items to the customs officer.

She said with a smile, "That's OK, sir. You are allowed them duty-free."

While waiting in the queue, I had read the customs declaration, so I pointed it out to the officer. "I understand they are only allowed for personal consumption. And I do not smoke or drink."

"So why did you buy them?"

"My son asked me to."

"Ah, it is all in the family. That's all right, sir," the officer, a bubbly woman, assured me. Instead of demanding a bribe, she was actually trying to find a loophole in the system so as to excuse me from paying the duty.

Ramesh tells me that I should have thanked the nice officer and happily moved on with a clear conscience. But I am afraid I could not do that.

"But my son does not smoke or drink either," I declared. "He is going to give them to his friends. So, how much duty should I pay?"

"Oh, you can always say that it's for personal consumption."

I know she was only trying to help, but I felt outraged. "I have always held the British Civil Servants in high esteem for their honesty and integrity. And you are telling me to lie." I know I should not have chided the poor woman, but at that instant, unbeknown to her, she was destroying my long-held respect for the British system.

She had a lot of patience. She smiled. "These are guidelines to stop smuggling, and I am convinced that you are not doing anything illegal. So I am using my discretion, and not charging you any duty."

This experience stands in sharp contrast to one that I had in India, where I thought that after many years of independence the situation would have improved.

A couple of years ago I was in Mumbai visiting family. I decided to treat my nephews and nieces to a Gujarati play.

It was an old, highly ornate theatre, with sculptures carved on the foyer walls and ceiling. Although I had bought expensive tickets, a couple of our seats had a restricted view due to pillars inside the theatre itself. I asked the usher if two people from our party could move to other unoccupied seats, which were in the same price range. But the usher flatly refused.

One of my nephews whispered in my ear, "Uncleji, he just wants a little bribe. Twenty or even ten rupees would do."

"No way." I was outraged. "The whole culture of bribery exists because people offer bribes. I can afford it but I am not going to be party to it."

So I went to complain to the manager. He was obviously in the scam, too, for he said that it was for the usher to decide. I came back fuming.

A few minutes later, the usher came back and this time told us that it was all right for us to move to other seats. The play was a farce and I am sure it was good, for there was a lot of laughter. But I hardly followed the plot as I was too puffed up with the thrill of this unexpected moral victory.

When we got home, I was still feeling high, and so decided to give a lecture on morality to my nephews and nieces. "We take the easy way out. By offering a bribe, one perpetuates the insidious custom. You have to be firm. You saw what happened. I stood my ground, and when the usher realised that I was not going to budge, he gave in." I looked around triumphantly at my audience.

"I have been honest all my life and guess what? So far I have found that it does not pay." I continued, still trying to contain the pleasure in my voice. "Today for the first time in my life I have enjoyed a victory. Now I know that evil does not always triumph."

The nephew, who had originally suggested that I should offer a bribe, spoke up timidly, "I am sorry Uncleji, but -"

"So you should be. Let this be a lesson to you."

He looked at me with guilt and fear in his dark eyes. "I meant to say I am sorry Uncleji, because I slipped a twenty rupee note to the usher."

I thought he must be joking. But then I realised that he was telling the truth. I looked around at my young audience, watching me anxiously to see my reaction. And as I saw the absurdity of the situation, I burst out laughing and the young ones felt that it was safe for them to show their mirth. Once again good did *not* triumph over evil, but it was funny.

Chapter 88
Day 70:
13th October
Devji: Looking Back at Recent Events

Amin still issues more decrees. And then contradicts them. Some people think that he acts like that because he is a buffoon. But I am convinced that he is evil, and also a scheming liar. I have a pile of old *Uganda Argus* from the last few weeks and I have just dug up another example of his dishonesty:

On 29th September President Mobutu of Zaire offered to improve the way Asians are being treated in Uganda. The headline in the 30th September *Argus* read, "PLEDGE BY GOVERNMENT: ASIANS IN UGANDA ARE SAFE. THEY WILL BE COMPENSATED FOR THEIR PROPERTIES"

A few days later on the 3rd October, after negotiations with President Mobutu, Amin agreed to postpone the deadline and to drop his threat to set up camps. He said he would also permit the Asians to transfer their assets.

But the day after President Mobutu went back to Zaire, Amin ordered a checking exercise for the citizenship of Asians, to be carried out by squads of police in order to speed-up their deportation.

Chapter 89
Day 75:
18th October 1972
Devji: Waiting

The town, which was mostly populated by Asians, is now nearly empty. I have noticed new African owners have moved into some of the houses, but most still have large padlocks on them. In the same way, some of the businesses have opened under new ownerships.

Yesterday, Ramesh's friend Kintu came round to ask if he could help in any way, which was very kind of him.

Later, as we just sat there talking about the future, he suddenly pointed at his shirt. "I bought this last week from *Jinja Suitable Store*. How much do you think I paid for it?"

It was obviously a good quality garment, but it was a strange question to ask of someone who is about to leave the country, and leave everything, including most of his shirts, behind.

I shrugged my shoulders and said, "I don't know. You tell me."

"I want you to guess," he persisted.

"Four hundred? Five hundred shillings?"

He laughed. "Fifteen shillings and fifty cents."

"You must be joking."

"No," he said. "I bought five of them for myself. All different labels. And each one was the same price. Fifteen shillings and fifty pence."

I must have looked puzzled, and he was even more amused. "I will give you a clue. I bought two more similar shirts - one for my brother, who is a big guy," he spread out his arms on either side to indicate a large girth. "The new shopkeeper charged seventeen shillings for it, and one for my little nephew cost thirteen shillings."

It suddenly dawned on me. "You mean he charged you by the size."

Kintu burst out laughing. "You have got it. When the original owners left, the shop was given to this man from North Uganda, simply because his brother-in-law is a Captain in the Jinja barracks. The day he opened the shop, someone came in looking for a shirt. And when asked how much it cost, he looked for the price tag, but couldn't find it. The only label had number sixteen on it. He decided that must be the price, and charged sixteen shillings for it. You can imagine. The word soon got round and we had to jostle to get into the shop. His shop has now no stock left."

As Kintu was about to leave, he stood by the door, shook my hand vigorously, and said, "We did not elect Amin, and we do not like his behaviour any more than you do. But no one dares to question him. I wish you good luck, and all I can say is I am terribly sorry for what is happening."

Chapter 90
Day 86:
29th October 1972
Devji: Phew!

The queue outside the British Embassy was not as long as it was in the first few weeks after the announcement. I did not have to sleep on the pavement the night before.

To be on the safe side, I arrived early - at seven in the morning - and joined a short queue. After President Amin's announcement, I had felt a gnawing worry (which I had tried not to show) that our family would end up totally destitute, struggling to survive in a foreign land. But since Ramesh, Rehana and Shashi have settled down in London, I have felt optimistic about the future. However, during the past few weeks, the question that has plagued my thoughts is what do we do if Lalita is not granted British Visas? Do we leave without her and let her go back to India? Or do we go with her to India, assuming we get Indian Visas? But that would mean being separated from our sons in England. And neither Savita nor I could cope with that.

So as I stood in the queue at the Embassy this morning, I fervently hoped - which is the same as praying for me - that there would be no more problems.

After just over an hour, I was called in and handed Lalita's passport with the Visa stamped in it.

The officer smiled at me. "Good luck," he said and shook my hand. "I hope in future everything goes well for you and your family in your new home."

I was overcome by having my faith in the human 'goodness' and justice restored. Despite their past colonial history, the British have acted honourably in this instance.

Then I walked on air straight to the travel office and booked three tickets on the next available flight, which is in three days' time.

Now as I drive home, I hardly notice the countryside. I suddenly realise that I have passed Lugazi and the huge sugarcane fields. I tell myself to concentrate on my driving, and as I enter the Mbira forest I pass a large military roadblock on the other side of the road. Two cars have been stopped, but the soldiers are only checking vehicles going towards Kampala and Entebbe. So I breathe a sigh of relief when I pass them without being stopped.

In three days' time, we will drive back along here on our way to the airport, and I will have plenty of cash ready to pay the soldiers at these roadblocks.

As I navigate round a bend, there is a sudden flash of yellow through the air in front of my car. It is a hornbill, and it lands in a tree on the other side of the road. If Savita and Lalita were with me, I would have stopped the car and pointed it out to them, as neither of them has ever seen a hornbill. A sudden realisation hits me then: maybe now they never will.

The Black Princess

Maggie Voysey Paun
Pages : 326
Edition : Paperback
ISBN : 978-81-9363-136-2
Subject : Biographical Fiction

About the Book

Who is Mrs Helena Bennett and how did she come to live alone in the remote Sussex countryside?

Her neighbours know her as an eccentric old woman who roams the forest with her beloved dog, is generous to the poor, and smokes a hookah. They call her 'The Black Princess', although she is not very dark-skinned nor of Royal birth.

It is spring 1853 when a chance visitor causes Helena to begin to recall her early life. Through her eyes the reader is transported to 1785 at the British Residency in Lucknow, India, a city renowned for its hybrid culture, the excesses of the ruling Nawab, and the avarice of some of the East India Company officers.

The Black Princess is based on a true story.

Maggie Voysey Paun has published stories about Indian children living in England and has written plays and adult novels which all have some connection with India. She has been married for many years to Rashmi and they have three sons and five grandchildren.

Her previous novel Sacrifices which is set in Africa, was published in 2016 by PublishNation and is also available as an e-book or in paperback from Amazon.com.